Muriel

A *Modern Fiction Studies* Book

Muriel Spark

TWENTY-FIRST-CENTURY PERSPECTIVES

Edited by David Herman

The Johns Hopkins University Press

Baltimore

The Johns Hopkins University Press
2715 North Charles Street
Baltimore, Maryland 21218-4363
www.press.jhu.edu

ISBN 10 0-8018-9553-7 (hardcover)
ISBN 10 0-8018-9554-5 (paperback)
ISBN 13 978-0-8018-9553-1 (hardcover)
ISBN 13 978-0-8018-9554-8 (paperback)

Library of Congress Control Number: 2009938663

A catalog record for this book is available from the British Library.

Chapters 1, 2, 4, 6, 8, 10 were originally published in the Fall 2008
issue of *Modern Fiction Studies.*

*Special discounts are available for bulk purchases of this book. For
more information, please contact Special Sales at 410-516-6936 or
specialsales@press.jhu.edu.*

The Johns Hopkins University Press uses environmentally friendly
book materials, including recycled text paper that is composed of
at least 30 percent post-consumer waste, whenever possible. All
of our book papers are acid-free, and our jackets and covers are
printed on paper with recycled content.

For more information about *MFS: Modern Fiction Studies,* please see:
www.press.jhu.edu/journals/modern_fiction_studies/

Contents

Preface

A special issue of *Modern Fiction Studies* devoted to Muriel Spark (54.3, Fall 2008) laid important groundwork for the present volume. Because of the addition of three new essays, a reorganization of the previously published essays, a reworked and expanded introduction, and a comprehensive index, *Muriel Spark: Twenty-First-Century Perspectives* affords a different—and, I hope, more cogent and cohesive—reading experience than did the special journal issue out of which the book grew.

As described more fully in my introduction, the volume is divided into three main parts, the first exploring Spark's contributions to Scottish and world literature, the second investigating how Spark's work relates to developments in late twentieth-century culture, and the third featuring detailed interpretations of texts by Spark. This organizational scheme should maximize the scholarly and pedagogical value of the book, since it enables readers to move naturally from material that focuses on Spark's background and influence as a writer, through chapters providing thick descriptions of her place in postwar culture, to chapters that offer interpretations of specific novels. At the same time, readers who wish to pinpoint discussions of particular novels, investigate Spark's use of a given fictional technique, or track recurrent themes will be able to do so by consulting the index that Adam Stier has compiled.

These features of the book underscore its main purpose: to provide students and faculty specialists alike with a one-stop resource gathering information about Spark's writing, its sources, and its legacies, while also offering current, theoretically informed but accessible interpretations of individual texts that can open up new ways of exploring and engaging with Spark's work. Target audiences thus consist of specialists in postwar British literature as well as instructors and students in upper-level undergraduate and graduate courses on twentieth-century British literature, the postwar British novel, and postmodern fiction, as well as single-author seminars devoted to Spark. The volume is likely to be of interest, also, to specialists in and students of recent women's writing[1]—what with Hope Howell Hodgkins' chapter on Spark's and Barbara Pym's work vis-à-vis that of their male contemporaries, and Lisa Harrison's and Bran Nicol's chapters on Spark's experiences as an author and treatment of the theme of authorship, respectively.

Many people and institutions helped make this book possible. A research fellowship from the American Council of Learned Societies, coupled with an external fellowship subsidy from Ohio State University, afforded me with the time needed to complete this project, and I gratefully acknowledge this support. For support of a different but equally crucial kind, I thank all the contributors, whose hard work, insightful scholarship, and patient collegiality made them an exemplary team to work with. I am also grateful to Suzanne Flinchbaugh for her enthusiastic initial response to this project and for her expert and unstinting assistance ever since; I thank her and others at the Johns Hopkins University Press, including copyeditor Michele Callaghan and designer Martha Sewall, for skillfully guiding the book through the publication process. Furthermore, I am grateful to the entire editorial staff at *Modern Fiction Studies* who worked on the earlier special issue out of which the present volume grew, including editor John Duvall, associate editor Robert Marzec, and editorial assistants Jason Buchanan, Michael Mauritzen, Rebecca Nicholson-Weir, and Martin Whitehead. I would like to single out Mike Mauritzen for his detail-oriented, proactive help with all aspects of the special issue. For his part, John Duvall approved the journal issue in the first place and provided additional financial support for the publication of this volume. I thank Adam Stier for his careful work on the index; Aileen Christianson, James English, and Alison Lumsden for their early advice about the project; and David McClay, Robin Smith, and especially Sally Harrower at the National Library of Scotland for their gracious assistance when I visited the Muriel Spark archive in November 2008. I am grateful both to the Library and to Penelope Jardine, the literary trustee of the Muriel Spark's estate, for permission to quote from materials I discovered at the archive. Thanks are also due to the external reviewer whose comments on my proposal for this volume helped me make it a better book.

Finally, I thank Susan Moss for treasured experiences—in the Scottish Highlands, on the Gulf Coast of Florida, in the deserts of Arizona, and near our sheltering apple tree in Ohio—in the context of which my work on this volume took shape.

Note

1. An undated fragment of a letter housed in the Muriel Spark Archive at the National Library of Scotland, however, reveals Spark's own reservations about the very concept or category of "women's writing." Commenting on the submission guidelines of a magazine

targeted at women, Spark writes: "What worries me, is the casual phrase 'of interest to a woman.' What is of interest to a woman? [. . .] most women's magazines assume a narrow range of interests in their readers" (Acc. 10989/118).

Muriel Spark

INTRODUCTION

David Herman

"A Salutary Scar": Muriel Spark's Desegregated Art in the Twenty-First Century

Intended in part to commemorate the death (on 13 April 2006) of Muriel Spark, one of the most important and innovative writers in English to come to maturity in the second half of the twentieth century, this volume also aims to take stock of Spark's enduring legacy—her status as an author whose writing practices have reshaped ways of understanding the scope and nature of fiction itself. The chapters assembled here explore, from multiple perspectives, the situation of Spark's work within the landscapes of postwar writing. What is more, the contributors collectively suggest the continuing relevance of Spark's oeuvre for the narrative traditions, representational projects, and broader cultural formations of the twenty-first century.

Spark was the author of twenty-two novels (seven of them published during the extraordinarily prolific period 1957–1963), more than a dozen short-story collections, several collections of poetry, a number of children's books, and multiple works of criticism, including volumes on William Wordsworth, Mary Wollstonecraft Shelley, and the Brontës.[1] She established early on the strikingly sui generis style that became the hallmark of her fiction—a style combining a self-reflexive focus on novelistic technique, including modes of metafictional play, with a probing investigation of the moral, psychological, and institutional dimensions of human conduct. Hence Spark in effect opted out of the two responses to modernism that David Lodge has called antimodernism and postmodernism. Antimodernist writers such as Kingsley Amis and Evelyn Waugh sought to continue the tradition that modernism reacted against, operating under the assumption that practices of realism "modified to take account of changes in human

I

knowledge and material circumstances" were still "viable and valuable" (Lodge 6). By contrast, postmodernist writers such as Samuel
Beckett and John Barth continued "the modernist critique of traditional
realism, but [tried] to go beyond or around or underneath modernism, which for all its formal experiment and complexity held out to
the reader the promise of meaning, if not of *a* meaning" (Lodge 12).
Spark, however, chose a third path. Her fiction embraces (or rather
extends and radicalizes) the modernist emphasis on technique while
also projecting complex social worlds—worlds in which, in texts ranging from *The Prime of Miss Jean Brodie* (1961) and *The Mandelbaum
Gate* (1965) to *The Driver's Seat* (1970), *The Hothouse by the East
River* (1973), and *The Only Problem* (1984), characters are impinged
on by powerful historical and political forces, their psychologies and
interactions shaped by entrenched educational and religious institutions, ideologies of gender, and more or less dominant assumptions
about the possibilities and limitations of human agency. Thus, as
Marina MacKay argues in her contribution to this volume, Spark is
"an amphibious figure"; in other words, her novels encompass tendencies displayed both by antimodernists advocating a midcentury
return to realism and by postmodernist practitioners who did not share
Spark's "capacious sociability, [her] meticulous curiosity about the
specificities of midcentury manners." Spark's amphibious narrative
practices set a precedent for later writers who have similarly worked
to wed sometimes mind-bending formal innovation with the nuanced
representation of sociohistorical circumstances, including not just
English-language authors such as A. S. Byatt and the Ian McEwan
of *Atonement*, for example, but writers from other traditions who
have likewise pursued this third way between antimodernism and
postmodernism, such as W. G. Sebald and Patrick Modiano.[2]

A number of commentators on Spark, as well as the author
herself, have provided context for understanding this dialectical
interplay between Spark's reflexive focus on narrative form and her
engagement with the historical contingencies of lived experience,
her dual commitment to innovation and representation. Spark found
a different balancing point for these two sets of concerns in different works, providing grounds for the strong claim that her writing
practices were in some sense dependent on the nonresolution of
this dialectical tension.[3] Reflexively foregrounding issues of form,
Spark's first novel, *The Comforters* (1957), focuses metaleptically on
a protagonist who gradually comes to realize that she is a character
in a novel.[4] In Alan Bold's characterization, this novel constitutes "an
experimental exploration of the formal nature of fictional truth" (34),
and in a 1963 interview with Frank Kermode, Spark herself referred
to the novel as "a novel about writing a novel, about writing a novel

sort of thing, you see" (qtd. in Bold 34). Situated near the other pole of the Sparkian dialectic—the pole of engagement with sociohistorical contexts and contingencies—is the novel that many commentators characterize as a kind of outlier or exception within Spark's oeuvre, *The Mandelbaum Gate*, which (as discussed by John Glavin in chapter 7 of this volume) is set in Jerusalem and includes details about the trial of Adolf Eichmann that took place there in 1961.[5] As Norman Page puts it, *The Mandelbaum Gate* "could almost have been written by George Eliot [. . .] if she had been writing in the 1970s instead of a hundred years earlier" (56).

Other texts in Spark's corpus, however, are more difficult to place (or place in their entirety) in relation to the twin concerns of formal innovation and responsible representation. For example, in *The Prime of Miss Jean Brodie* metafictional play trades off with analysis of group dynamics and the logic of fascism. Sandy Stranger and Jenny Gray string together the most glaring clichés of romance to compose "The Mountain Eyrie," an idealized narrative of Hugh Carruthers, Brodie's former lover; their account throws into question the status of the narrator's own discourse (to what extent is all narration an assemblage of clichés?). Yet the novel also probes how Sandy's bullying of Mary Macgregor is linked to her (Sandy's) fear of the disorder represented by the unemployed people she sees during the class field trip to St Giles Cathedral. More generally, through its portrayal of Mary the text suggests how scapegoating can serve, in the microcosm of the Brodie set and also the macrocosm of German and Italian fascism, as a mechanism for reinforcing group cohesion. Or take the 1970 novel *The Driver's Seat*, which Spark acknowledged to be her personal favorite among the novels ("The Same" 229). Here, as Norman Page remarks, the author may seem "to be following writers of the French *nouveau roman* such as Alain Robbe-Grillet, who conceived the role of fiction as the dispassionate description of the external world as a substitute for the traditional novel's concern with character" (73).[6] Yet the bizarre and macabre plot in which the protagonist concertedly brings about her own brutal murder also raises disturbingly far-reaching questions about the threat of sexual violence against women who seek to assert control over their own lives in the manner advocated in the feminist discourse that was contemporary with Spark's novel.[7]

Further, both Spark's 1971 address to the American Academy of Arts and Letters, "The Desegregation of Art," and *Curriculum Vitae*, the autobiographical volume that was published in 1993 and that covers the period from the beginning of Spark's life to her first real success as a writer in the later 1950s, throw additional light on this same tension between innovation and representation—reflexivity and reportage—in the author's oeuvre. In the autobiography, Spark frames her account in terms of a desire to set the record straight, a determination "to write nothing that cannot be supported by documentary evidence or by eyewitnesses" (11). Yet the sequence of rubrics used in the first chapter to organize Spark's presentation of her early memories ("Bread, Butter and Florrie Forde" [followed immediately by "Bread" and then "Butter"], "Tea," "Commodities," "Neighbours," "Myths and Images," "The Doorbell," and others) suggests in almost Borges-like fashion the multiplicity of ways in which situations, objects, and events can be ordered through categories or descriptive nomenclatures.[8] Spark thus highlights the arbitrariness of singling out any one system of categories as best suited for capturing the facts of the matter. Analogously, Spark recounts how after high school she enrolled in a college known for its practical and businesslike teaching methods and for its emphasis on scientific and technical instruction (102–3). It was here that Spark honed her skills in précis-writing and indulged her love of economical prose and her fascination with "good managerial type-speech"; it was from about this time, too, that Spark began to be convinced that "the essentials of literature were . . . outside of literature; they were elsewhere, out in the world" (103). But over the course of her apprenticeship as a writer Spark would also turn to literature itself to discover the essentials of literature—and even the essentials of the world. Hence her use of fictional plots to explore the more general strategies of emplotment by which human beings order events into narrative patterns so as to make sense of them.[9] *Curriculum Vitae* thus traces the formation of an author with dual values, interests, and priorities: the eager student of précis-writing in business settings whose first published novel was *The Comforters*, which Spark goes on to characterize as follows: "That novel was thought to be difficult, especially in those days—for it is true that one forms and 'educates' one's own public. Readers of novels were not yet used to the likes of me, and some will never be" (208).

In "The Desegregation of Art," from which the title of the present section is taken, Spark suggests a reason or motive for this double orientation of her fictional practice—her practice of writing under the assumption that the essentials of literature can be found both inside and outside literature itself. Significantly, the title of Spark's address—which was delivered in the United States in the same year that the Supreme Court ruled that forced busing of students may be mandated to achieve racial desegregation—enacts the logic of reintegration that also forms its topic. The title brings the subject of art into implicit relation with legal, educational, and more broadly social institutions bound up with attempts during the civil rights movement to overcome inequities based on racial identity. More explicitly, the address suggests that Spark's dual commitment to innovation and representation is rooted in what she takes to be the basic conditions for art, rather than in the vagaries of her personal experience or the idiosyncrasies of her own writing process. Spark begins by noting that "I have never from my earliest memories known any other life or way of seeing things but that of an artist, a changer of actuality into something else" (33). But the question foregrounded by the address concerns the calculus—or alchemy—that regulates such aesthetic transformations of the actual; at issue is what methods of transformation might make art a more integral part of everyday life, even as it maintains a necessarily critical stance toward the sphere of the everyday. Spark argues more specifically that the tradition of socially conscious art, and in particular literature based on "depicted suffering, whether in social life or in family life . . . isn't achieving its end or illuminating our lives any more" (34). Spark goes on to explain: "the art and literature of sentiment and emotion, however beautiful in itself, however striking in its depiction of actuality . . . cheats us into a sense of involvement with life and society, but in reality it is a segregated activity. In its place I advocate the arts of satire and of ridicule. And I see no other living art form for the future" (35).

One danger with literature that doesn't take ridicule as its guiding principle is that readers may well "feel that their moral responsibilities are sufficiently fulfilled by the emotions that they have been induced to feel";[10] another (related) danger is that "wherever there is a cult of the victim, such being human nature, there will be an obliging cult of twenty equivalent victimizers." Art, instead, should engage in a ruthless mocking of violence in any form, displaying "a less impulsive generosity, a less indignant representation of social injustice, and a more deliberate cunning, a more derisive undermining of what is wrong" (Spark, "Desegregation" 35). Whereas the spirit animating earnest protests is often short-lived, "the art of ridicule, if it is on the mark—and if it is not on the mark it is not art at all—can penetrate to the marrow. It can leave a salutary scar. It is unnerving. It can paralyze its object" (36).

Thus, what Spark calls for in her address, and what she exemplifies in her own fictional methods, is an art rich in Brechtian estrangement effects—effects that call attention to the constructedness of the fictional scenarios being portrayed in order to inhibit readerly immersion and promote instead a critical engagement with those situations and events. But the Sparkian art of ridicule also requires, beyond such illusion-breaking reflexivity, an active targeting of social practices and institutions that sanction any form of violence, in whose mocking, sardonic representation lies the raison d'être of art itself.[11] The *desegregation* of *art*: the phrase itself encapsulates both the scope of Spark's fictional project and the dialectical tension that drives it.

A Synopsis of the Volume

In a volume devoted to an author whose texts cut against the grain of master narratives about identity, gender, religion, culture, and history, it is especially fitting that the contributors would adopt a diversity of critical perspectives on Spark's texts and use a variety of analytic tools—historical/archival, psychoanalytic, queer-theoretical, narratological, and other—to take the measure of her achievement.[12] In their various ways, however, the chapters assembled here all suggest how Spark's work points the way toward desegregating fiction, by bringing it into a critical and, where warranted, mocking relation with the concepts, practices, and institutions of everyday life. Furthermore, the chapters discuss texts that were written over several decades of Spark's career, revealing, across the range of Spark's achievement, her longstanding concern with balancing the requirements of formal innovation against the imperatives of responsible representation.[13]

The two chapters included in Part I of the volume, "Spark as Scottish and World Author," sketch out Spark's situation in and contributions to both local and global literary traditions. These chapters provide context for understanding the forces that shaped Spark's corpus as well as the impact of that corpus on late twentieth-century (and now early twenty-first-century) literature and culture. First, in "'Fully to Savour Her Position': Muriel Spark and Scottish Identity," Gerard Carruthers outlines strategies for exploring Spark's relation to Scottish culture, in part by drawing on ideas from Spark's own novels to recharacterize culture itself as a multiplicitous convergence—an imaginary meeting point—of various texts and traditions. Next, Lisa Harrison, in "'The Magazine That Is Considered the Best in the World': Muriel Spark and the *New Yorker*," engages in a complementary investigation of how Spark's decades-long relationship with the *New Yorker* helped make her a world literary figure—especially when *The Prime of Miss Jean Brodie* appeared in its entirety in the 14 October 1961 issue of the magazine.

Carruthers begins by disputing the premises of an argument made by another Scottish novelist, Robin Jenkins—the argument, namely, that Spark is a kind of "cosmopolitan misfit" rather than a Scottish writer. Pointing to the "essentialist cultural nationalism" that underwrites this claim, Carruthers notes that Spark herself resisted such essentializing habits of mind, perhaps because of her own heterogeneous background and life trajectory as a half-Jewish, half-Protestant convert to Catholicism.[14] Here Carruthers points to the antiessentialism evident in Spark's 1963 story, "The Gentile Jewesses," generally thought to be a trial run at what became *The Mandelbaum Gate*: "the narrator refuses to be denied her Jewish heritage simply because of Talmudic law and defiantly embraces and gently mocks this law as a person who is possessed of enough imaginative empathy for her Jewish forebears for them and their origins to matter to her." For Spark, then, identity is not a built-in essence but a function of living in (actual and imagined) relation to people and places, texts and things; hence Spark's comment, which Carruthers quotes in his chapter, that "Edinburgh is the place that I, a constitutional exile, am essentially exiled from." True, Spark's oeuvre engages with aspects of the Scottish context; for example, both *The Comforters* and *The Ballad of Peckham Rye* use the then recently republished *Private Memoirs and Confessions of a Justified Sinner* by James Hogg (which were originally published in 1824) as a key intertext addressing the Calvinist world picture, which also plays a role in *The Prime of Miss Jean Brodie*. Yet because of Spark's scholarly studies of Mary Shelley and the Brontës she may have approached Hogg as a Romantic writer rather than a Scottish writer per se. As Carruthers puts it, "Spark certainly comes to have Hogg in her literary genes, but this is not some set of essentially national genes." After a discussion of *The Ballad of Peckham Rye* as a hybrid text in which Spark fuses (and also parodies) the "English" tendency toward domestic realism and an indigenous "Scottish" tradition of supernatural ballads, followed by a reading of *Brodie*'s similarly extended engagement with Scottish religious, cultural, and literary traditions, Carruthers concludes by arguing that in Spark's fiction "truth and transcendent identity can never be exactly located but are indicated through the imaginative aspirations both of Spark herself and her characters."

Meanwhile, Harrison uses Spark's relationship with the *New Yorker* to explore how the writer came to be seen not just as a Scottish author but also as a major contributor to world literature. As Harrison shows, Spark's connection with the magazine lasted throughout her writing career; her first appearance goes back to 1954, when one of the critical works that she co-edited with Derek Stanford received a brief review. Through her archival research on Spark's unpublished correspondence with the magazine's editors during her most prolific writing period, 1957–1967, Harrison throws light on the circumstances that led to the *New Yorker*'s publication of *Brodie* and the subsequent offer to Spark of a first-reading agreement, which, renewed annually through 1979, allowed the magazine the right of first refusal for all of the author's fiction and essays. As Harrison also shows, Spark's correspondence with the magazine's editors reveals Spark's activities and whereabouts during her extended stays in New York City during the years 1962–1967, affording new evidence for study of the effects of locale on (and its representation in) Spark's fiction. Going on to discuss Spark's later relationship with the magazine, Harrison indicates how the *New Yorker* not only shaped Spark's international reception but became the repository of autobiographical material that postdates *Curriculum Vitae*, some of it illuminating Spark's writing methods. More generally, Harrison's account of Spark's relationship with the *New Yorker* points up the need for a broader scholarly project: namely, reconceiving the modern Scottish literary canon by situating writers like Spark in an emergent world literary culture.[15]

Along these same lines, Part II of the volume is titled "Situating Spark in Postwar Culture." Although chapters 3 through 6, which make up this section, sometimes use particular works by Spark as case studies, they focus on how Spark's oeuvre relates to the broader contexts of postwar culture. Patricia Waugh examines how, after World War II, materialist philosophies morphed into a metaphysics of the material, and how Spark's texts respond both formally and thematically to this new worldview. Marina MacKay uses the idea of treason as a guiding thread in her wide-ranging discussion of Spark's oeuvre and its relation to contemporary developments in the cultural field. Bran Nicol relates Spark's texts to changing conceptions of authorship by examining Spark's self-reflexive treatment of authors in her fiction. Finally, Hope Howell Hodgkins, putting Spark's work into dialogue with the fictions of Barbara Pym, investigates how the two writers' concern with style links up with issues of gender in postwar contexts.

In "Muriel Spark and the Metaphysics of Modernity: Art, Secularization, and Psychosis," in a way that harks back to the dialectic between innovation and representation discussed earlier in this introduction, Waugh interprets Spark's defamiliarizing narrative experiments not as a retreat from but rather a strategy for engaging with broader intellectual and cultural developments. These developments include the consolidation of secularism and, with it, the rise of a radically materialist worldview. This worldview is grounded in "a kind of sociobiological and Hobbesian epistemology that reduces the human to an elaborate kind of machine open to purely causal explanation," and it is thus incapable of registering humans' experience of being-in-the-world or "ispeity," their "fundamental sense and experience of selfhood and being as well as their historical modes of expression." Rather than trying to (re)categorize Spark as a "Catholic writer," Waugh contends that one of Spark's overarching novelistic projects was to use the illusion-breaking potential of (meta)fiction to chronicle and interrogate what is entailed by the materialist world picture. To investigate that picture's power and reach, Spark relied on the ability of fictional narratives to unmake—or rather reflexively foreground the made-up-ness of—the worlds in which they simultaneously ask readers to participate imaginatively. Novels like *The Driver's Seat* and *The Hothouse by the East River* thus evoke strikingly vivid fictional worlds, while also using those worlds as thought-experiments exploring what it would be like to live out a radical materialism that leaves no place for ipseity. More precisely, these novels suggest that living in strict accordance with the materialist world picture would be tantamount to psychosis. Yet as noted earlier, Spark also rejected sentimentalism, or the deliberate elicitation of readerly empathy, as a counter-response to the mechanistic world picture. Drawing on multiple works by Spark to examine her strategies for dealing with this dilemma, Waugh's discussion demonstrates how Spark's innovative novelistic techniques, far from exemplifying a kind of metafictional introversion, instead foreground "the ethical consequences of expanding a reduced conceptualization of matter into a metaphysics of materialism and the kind of intelligence required to critique that process without falling prey to nostalgia or sentimentalism."

In "Muriel Spark and the Meaning of Treason," MacKay likewise connects Spark's fictional methods with larger cultural and historical concerns. MacKay argues that Spark's treatment of the theme of treason is "intractably real-worldly and historical, intimately connected to the political contexts in which she began her career as a novelist" while also providing "a different way of thinking about [Spark's] concerns with the textual, fantastical, and world-making force of the imagination that points toward an incipient postmodernity: treason, for Spark, is always aligned with forms of political and social creativity." MacKay grounds her analysis in a broader midtwentieth-century concern with the problem of treason—that is, "the individual's readiness to resist the claims that the nation-state makes on its citizens"—as World War II gave way to the Cold War. Here MacKay notes the relevance of another midcentury female author, Rebecca West, who wrote several studies of treason that were interested less in the specific traitorous acts involved than in what they suggest about the nature of the link between individuals and larger communities. Further, as in Spark's novels, West's studies explore the traitor's ability to construct and live within alternate realities—in parallel with the way Jean Brodie, for example, attempts to make her life extraordinary through fantasy. Likewise, MacKay finds in West's study of the 1945 trial for high treason of William Joyce a parallel to Sandy Stranger's experience as simultaneously an outsider and a member of the Brodie cult. MacKay also discusses Spark's participation during the war in Britain's campaign of black propaganda, or psychological warfare, in which radio programs purported to be authentic Nazi broadcasts were used to disseminate misinformation to the Germans. Spark's role in the production of these broadcasts provides context for understanding her use of metafiction in texts like *The Hothouse by the East River*, whose self-conscious narrative style foregrounds the malleability of what is taken to be historical truth. "In short," for MacKay, "what creative fiction-making and political treachery have in common in Spark's novels is their shared skepticism about orthodoxy, their resistance to consensual and monolithic understandings of what constitutes the real."

If MacKay explores how the authoring of fictions provides for Spark a model of the kind of creative power needed to counter dominant ideologies, Bran Nicol, in "Reading Spark in the Age of Suspicion," examines a different, deflationary aspect of Spark's treatment of authors and authorship. Using *The Comforters*, *The Driver's Seat*, and *Loitering with Intent* as his case studies, Nicol suggests that in Spark's texts the author, no longer a transcendent, Godlike being, has become "a deposed, humanized figure [. . .]; a small-scale, prurient, menacing entity, more like a stalker than a deity." Nicol disputes conceptions of authorship developed in previous studies of metafictions like Spark's; these conceptions, which are premised on an understanding of the imaginative writer as a highly self-conscious critic or theorist who builds into his or her fictional text a commentary on that very work, are "curiously at odds with the post-Barthesian disrespect for the author as transcendent figure which took hold during the same period in criticism." Also at odds with such rethinkings of the author are readings of Spark proposed by critics such as Malcolm Bradbury, who discerns in Spark's fictions an implicit analogy between the author-character relationship, on the one hand, and the relationship between God and the world, on the other. Reconsidering Spark's texts in light of more recent scholarship on the concept of the author, Nicol explores how in *Loitering with Intent* the author comes across as a petty criminal, "up to no good," while in *The Driver's Seat* the author is figured as a "shady, hidden, menacing presence," and more specifically as a stalker.[16] More generally, Nicol argues that Spark's works must be understood as part of what Nathalie Sarraute called the "age of suspicion" or "the cultural moment when the traditional realist forms of writing became regarded incredulously by both reader and writer, following the lessons they had absorbed about the complexity of human psychology from Freud and modernist writers like Proust, Kafka, and Joyce." Spark's metafictional method—in particular, her self-reflexive critique of authorial motivations and practices—thus reflects a broader postmodern decline in the power of metanarratives of authority.

The final chapter in Part II is Hope Howell Hodgkins' "Stylish Spinsters: Spark, Pym, and the Postwar Comedy of the Object." Hodgkins develops another strategy for studying Spark's desegregated art in its postwar contexts, showing how the Sparkian concern with style links up with issues of gender. More specifically, focusing on representations of spinsters in Spark's and Pym's work, she uses these "stylish spinsters" to explore links among (1) ideas of style embodied in the discourse of fashion; (2) Spark's and Pym's representations of fashion and style, particularly in connection with unmarried female characters; and (3) postwar conceptions of literary style, such as those associated with the Angry Young Men or Movement writers who included Spark's and Pym's male contemporaries. Hodgkins poses the question of why writers like Spark and Pym have not been viewed as "Movement novelists," despite their use of a comparably ironic and understated narrative style. After all, just as male writers like Alan Sillitoe, Philip Larkin, and Kingsley Amis "punctured, deflated, mocked, and refused to emulate [the] elaborate stylistics" that they associated with the earlier, modernist period, "these women writers too [. . .] developed a leveling aesthetic, the ostensibly shallow surface of a deep structure of protest." Spark and Pym focused especially on matters of dress, not only to celebrate individual female perception but also to satirize traditional literary ideals. But though the Movement writers and Spark and Pym thus used different strategies to accomplish parallel aims, the contrasting reception history of the male and female authors, and the failure of the Movement writers to recognize Spark (for example) as one of their own, points up the need for gender-oriented research on postwar literary history in general and on understandings of Spark's and Pym's work in particular. After tracing part of the genealogy of fashion and exploring the extent to which the distrust or repudiation of fashion involves "fears of change, of the temporal physical body, and of the welter of desires that drive human existence—all aspects of life that, again, often have been attributed to the female mind and world," Hodgkins turns to an investigation of the functions of the fashionable spinsters in Spark's *The Prime of Miss Jean Brodie* and *The Girls of Slender Means* (1963), on the one hand, and Pym's *Excellent Women* (1952), on the other. Whereas Spark uses Jean Brodie's stylistic flourishes to mock high-modernist artistic tenets, Pym details the brown dresses and coats of Mildred Lathbury in order to parody realism, recast here as "Realism with its grandeur erased." In *The Girls of Slender Means*, meanwhile, the stylish spinster Jane Martin can be read as a figure for Spark herself—"no pathetic single woman but a tough observing consciousness."

While the chapters included in Part II emphasize how Spark's texts are shaped by and also contribute to broader developments in postwar culture, those included in Part III, "Reading Spark," offer exemplary readings of specific works. The readings are exemplary not only in the sense that they are written by scholars engaged in best practices in the field of Spark studies; more than this, they exemplify how Spark's fictions can be productively explored from a variety of critical perspectives. In chapter 7, John Glavin revisits Spark's underdiscussed 1965 historical novel, *The Mandelbaum Gate*, and argues that this text, long assumed to be an atypical oddity in Spark's oeuvre, can instead be read as a kind of "gate" through which Spark passed while transitioning from her very earliest fictions to her more mature works. For his part Jonathan Kemp develops a reading of *The Driver's Seat* via ideas from Deleuze and Guattari's schizoanalytic framework, queer theory, semiotics, and (French) feminism, focusing in particular on the motivations and consequences of Spark's refusal to provide direct access to the interiority of her protagonist in the novel (chapter 8). Allan Pero draws on Lacanian psychoanalysis to propose new ways of thinking about the voice in Spark's fiction in general and in *Momento Mori* (her third novel, published in 1959) in particular (chapter 9). And in chapter 10, Lewis MacLeod synthesizes Michel Foucault's ideas with recent work in narrative theory to contest arguments by previous critics that two kinds of omniscience—omniscience as control versus omniscience as care—can be distinguished in Spark's texts.

In "*The Mandelbaum Gate*: Muriel Spark's Apocalyptic Gag," Glavin characterizes Spark's 1965 novel as the pivot on which her writing career turns—or, to use another metaphor, the gate leading from the novels written in her earliest style to those associated with her mature manner. Glavin argues that Spark inherited from Albert Schweitzer's *Quest for the Historical Jesus* (first published in 1906 but republished in 1954 after Schweitzer was awarded the 1952 Nobel Prize) an "anti-rapturous" model of apocalypse as *horizontal*, or spreading out across space in time, rather than *vertical*, or rising above time and space into eternity. According to Glavin, the apocalyptic vision that informs *The Mandelbaum Gate* is premised not on an expectation of the end of the world but instead "the disruption [. . .] of the way of the world. Not the end of time, but the end of the present." The novel suggests in turn that this subversive understanding of apocalypse—or of apocalypse as a kind of subversion—provides an alternative model for late-modern storytelling and more specifically a counter to the practices associated with the proto-postmodern antinovel. Foregrounding how apocalypse in the horizontal sense "can transform individual lives into something meaningful, effective, [and] exciting," Spark's sui generis fictional methods in the second half of *The Mandelbaum Gate* and then the rest of her career are best characterized, for Glavin, by way of the concept of the gag. Here, however, the term *gag* needs to be understood not only as a joke or funny story, but also as something that "silences, stifles, restrains." As Glavin puts it: "This is a key yoking when we recall that gag appears to move from the latter sense to the former as a term for the actor's ad-libbed interpolation within a scripted performance, no bad emblem for Spark's resistant disruption of modernism's script." Noting that the second half of the Spark's novel reads like an uninterrupted series of gags, Glavin finds here an anticipation of the other novels to come, in which "the apocalyptic will routinely stifle the plausible [and] the unpredictable will overrule the prosaic," underscoring fiction's fundamental capacity to invent.[17]

In their chapters, Jonathan Kemp and Allan Pero draw on a range of critical perspectives to examine two of Spark's more innovative and unsettling inventions—respectively, *The Driver's Seat* and *Momento Mori*. In " 'Her Lips Are Slightly Parted': The Ineffability of Erotic Sociality in Muriel Spark's *The Driver's Seat*," Kemp uses ideas from Deleuze and Guattari's schizoanalytic framework, queer theory, semiotics, and (French) feminism to explore Spark's refusal to provide direct access to the interiority of her protagonist. Kemp characterizes his interpretation of the novel as a "queer" reading "not because it argues for a homoerotic or same-sex desire at work within the text, but because it is pitched against the norm, buckling commonsense notions of the self by excavating all psychology; queer, that is, in that it offers no essence to the self, but rather posits the self as some form of discursive residue devoid of meaning or interpretable content." Spark's backgrounding of Lise's interiority can be linked with arguments that the sociopolitical order is in some sense contingent on the violent erasure of the self—an erasure thematized in the text by Lise's (self-initiated) murder at the end of the novel. Yet, in Spark's desegregated narrative art, what would assume the form of argument in political theory and philosophy takes on the guise of satire and ridicule, with the novel parodying both the girl-seeks-boy holiday romance and the whodunnit killer thriller. More than this, standing in an oblique or queer relation to commonsense notions of character psychology, *The Driver's Seat* both structurally and thematically ridicules conventional conceptions of the self and its place in the social order. In Kemp's words, the novel "disturbs our understanding of the modern subject by suggesting that we need to account for the queer interplay of pain and pleasure, death and the social, in order to have a fuller understanding of what is at stake in talking about the socio-political or ethical subject."

For his part, in " 'Look for One Thing and You Find Another': The Voice and Deduction in Muriel Spark's *Memento Mori*," Pero draws on

Lacanian psychoanalysis to propose new ways of thinking about the
voice in Spark's fiction in general and in her third novel in particular.
Foregrounding "the voice as a conceptual and theoretical difficulty
that requires a more inflected response," Pero begins by drawing a
distinction between speech as "the communication of words with the
instrument of the voice" and the voice itself, which can be construed
as "a symptom [in Lacan's sense] of what is left over from speech,
an uncanny object that speech cannot completely master." Hence,
in Pero's account, Spark's text figures the voice as an enigmatic
object of desire that drives the mystery of the plot, contributing to
the novel's parodic recycling of the genre of detective fiction. Further, Pero argues that rather than portraying the septuagenarian
characters as members of a community that responds in various
ways to the calls reminding people that they too must die, the text
represents "the telephonic voice . . . as the constitutive element of
surveillance that produces the communal identity of the characters."
In an extended (and witty!) close reading of the novel that also puts
Spark's text into dialogue with the ideas of Jacques Lacan, Slavoj
Žižek, Martin Heidegger, and Maurice Blanchot, while also drawing
parallels between *Momento Mori* and *The Driver's Seat*, Pero goes
on to suggest that the voice on the other end of the phone is "an
index of the gap in reality—desire itself—that is necessary for reality
to be constituted by us." The novel thus represents desire itself as
"a mystery governed by a deceptively simple premise: 'you look for
one thing, and you find' an other."

In "Matters of Care and Control: Surveillance, Omniscience, and
Narrative Power in *The Abbess of Crewe* and *Loitering with Intent*,"
Lewis MacLeod picks up the issue of surveillance touched on by Pero
but does so using different analytic tools and focusing on different
Spark novels as case studies. Specifically, MacLeod proposes to
synthesize ideas from recent work in narrative theory with Michel
Foucault's notion of the panopticon and the accounts of observation, power, and discipline to which Foucault's analysis has given
rise. A particularly important concept in this connection is that of
omniscience, which bridges procedures of surveillance and modes of
narration. Whereas previous critics have drawn a distinction between
two understandings of omniscience in Spark's texts—omniscience as
control versus omniscience as care—MacLeod seeks to contest this
division and instead draw parallels between Fleur Talbot's ostensibly care-driven, moral urge-to-omniscience in *Loitering with Intent*
and "the more obviously immoral (or perhaps amoral) urges" of Sir
Quentin in the same novel and of Alexandra in *The Abbess of Crewe*.
In *Abbess*, Alexandra's methods of observing the other nuns allow
her to construct for herself a position of power inside the convent.

Meanwhile, *Loitering with Intent* focuses on surveillance "in ways that are much more specifically interested in narrative procedure, in the ways narratives are produced and received." Here the nexus between narrative and surveillance is figured in the discussions between Fleur and Quentin about how details submitted by members of the Autobiographical Association should be organized, framed, and disseminated. Although some commentators on the novel have argued that Fleur's orientation to the autobiographical accounts is (in contrast with Quentin's) nonauthoritarian, MacLeod argues that "Fleur's project seems every bit as egocentric (if not as destructive) as everybody else's." Like Alexandra in *Abbess*, Fleur too seeks to take up an "'unchallengeable' perspective, a way of situating without ever being situated." MacLeod concludes his discussion by drawing on theories of fictional worlds to suggest how the demise of a singular Truth confers on characters like Alexandra and Fleur unprecedented world-creating powers, by means of which they control the intersections of nonfiction, fiction, and myth.

Finally, in an appendix to the volume, Allison Fisher (with the assistance of Shannon Thomas) has compiled a bibliography of recent criticism on Spark designed to supplement Martin McQuillan's very full listing (235-41) by incorporating several works that appeared before or around the same time as McQuillan's volume but were not included in his own list and adding references to studies of Spark that have been published since 2002.

Notes

1. See McQuillan, *Theorizing Muriel Spark* (230–35) for a comprehensive list of Spark's publications.

2. See Herman for a discussion of how Modiano's 1968 novel, *La Place de l'étoile*, by openly displaying its status as an assemblage of story-versions, engages in a "lateral reflexivity" that avoids hermetic self-enclosure (296).

3. Compare Alan Bold's remark: "As well as commenting on the emptiness of illusions, Spark regularly ridicules believers and exposes as fraudulent the realistic foundations of fiction. Yet she remains a woman with a religious creed and a genuine faith in art. There is, her novels show, a creative world of difference between false faiths and spiritual aspirations, between criminal plots and fictive ploys" (119).

4. Readers familiar with Marc Foster's 2006 film, *Stranger than Fiction*, starring Will Ferrell and Emma Thompson, will recognize the parallels between the movie and Spark's text.

5. Bryan Cheyette notes that the scenes involving Eichmann included Spark's verbatim transcriptions of the trial, which she had attended ("Writing" 109). In an interview conducted in October 1965 Spark herself characterized *The Mandelbaum Gate* as "a very important book for me, much more concrete and solidly rooted in a very detailed setting [than earlier works]" (qtd. in Page 55).

6. See also Spark, "The Same" (216), where Spark comments on her own affinity with the nouveau romanists.

7. For her part, Dorothea Walker interprets this aspect of the novel, too, as part of a metafictional design, suggesting that Lise's murder results from her attempt to make her own life assume the shape of a novelistic plot (84). See also note 9 below.

8. See Foucault's *The Order of Things* (xvi) where Foucault discusses how Borges's account of "The Analytical Language of John Wilkins" highlighted for him the context-bound nature of systems of classi-fication—that is, the way no such system maps transparently onto items in the world but rather derives from a particular vantage point reflected in the system itself. See also Carruthers's discussion of *Curriculum Vitae* in his chapter.

9. Consider in this light a remark included in the text that Spark used for the 16 April 1961 broadcast of the BBC's radio program "Bookstand": "For many years I was intensely occupied by Emily Brontë—almost haunted. What impressed me was the dramatic shape of her life. It's as if she had consciously laid out the plot of her life in a play called 'Emily Brontë.' She might have been invented by Ibsen—a parson's daughter with a terrifying soul" (Muriel Spark Archive, National Library of Scotland, Acc. 10989/169).

10. In an interview from 1970 quoted by Bold, Spark characterizes the promotion of readers' emotional engagement as a kind of authorial faux pas: "I think it's bad manners to inflict a lot of emotional in-volvement on the reader—much nicer to make them laugh and keep it short" (78).

11. This account of Spark's novelistic practices and their motivations stands in stark contrast to what Michiko Kakutani describes as the Sparkian "recipe" for writing fiction in her 1997 *New York Times* re-view of Spark's novel *Reality and Dreams* (quoted by Verongos and Cowell): "Take a self-enclosed community (of writers, schoolgirls, nuns, rich people, etc.) that is full of incestuous liaisons and fraternal intrigue; toss in a bombshell (like murder, suicide or betrayal) that will ricochet dangerously around this little world; and add some al-lusions to the supernatural to ground these melodramatics in an old-fashioned context of good and evil. Serve up with crisp, authoritative prose and present with 'a light and heartless hand.'"

12. See the essays assembled in Martin McQuillan's 2002 volume, *Theo-rizing Muriel Spark: Gender, Race, Deconstruction*, for interpretations of Spark oriented around the concerns listed in the subtitle of that volume.

13. Novels discussed by the contributors range from *The Comforters* (1957) to *Loitering with Intent* (1981). It may seem out of keeping with the scope and aims of the present volume that none of the chapters engages with Spark's subsequent six novels, particularly those published after the turn of the century—that is, *Aiding and Abetting* (2000) and *The Finishing School* (2004). However, the chief purpose of this book is to suggest strategies for reassessing, from a twenty-first-century perspective, the ongoing impact of Spark's contributions to literary and more broadly cultural domains, whatever the initial publication date of the contributions in question.

14. Hence Spark's comment in a letter to Alan Bold dated 22 April 1979: "I am certainly a writer of Scottish formation of course and think of myself as such. I think to describe myself as a 'Scottish Writer' might be ambiguous as one wouldn't know if 'Scottish' applied to the writer or the writing. Then there is the complicated question of whether people of mixed inheritance, like myself, can call themselves Scottish" (Muriel Spark Archive, National Library of Scotland, Acc. 10374/5). Compare also a remark Spark made some twenty years earlier, in response to an interviewer's question about whether she found her environment to be important to her: "Yes, it is. But sometimes not till a long time after I've left the place, and then the place comes back to me very vividly" (transcript of a telediphone recording from the Talks Department, *World of Books*, 18 March 1960; Muriel Spark Archive, National Library of Scotland, Acc. 10989/192).

15. Compare in this connection Cheyette's argument that "it is Spark's hybrid background—part English, part Scottish, part Protestant, part Jewish—which has enabled her to become an essentially diasporic writer. Always shifting in time, from the 1940s to the 1990s, her fiction encompasses Zimbabwe, Edinburgh, and Jerusalem and rotates, habitually, between London, New York, and Rome. No one time, place or culture has been allowed to delimit Spark's imagination" ("Writing" 96-97). See also Cheyette's *Muriel Spark*.

16. Apropos here is a remark that Spark made about *The Driver's Seat* in an interview from 1970: "I understand from people who have read it that it's frightening. I frightened myself by writing it, but I just had to go on. I gave myself a terrible fright with it. I had to go into hospital to finish it" ("Writers").

17. Compare Spark's assessment of her own achievement as a novelist, as stated in her 1996 interview with Alan Taylor: "I believe that I have liberated the novel in many ways, showing how anything whatsoever can be narrated, any experience set down, including sheer damn cheek. I think that I have opened doors and windows in the mind, and challenged fears—especially the most inhibiting fears about what a novel should be" (Spark, "Magical"; in Muriel Spark Archive, National Library of Scotland, Acc. 11621).

Works Cited

Bold, Alan. *Muriel Spark*. London: Methuen, 1986.

Cheyette, Bryan. *Muriel Spark: Writers and Their Work*. Tavistock, UK: Northcote, 2000.

———. "Writing against Conversion: Muriel Spark the Gentile Jewess." McQuillan 95–112.

Foucault, Michel. *The Order of Things*. 1970. London: Routledge, 2001.

Herman, David. "Lateral Reflexivity: Levels, Versions, and the Logic of Paraphrase." *Style* 34 (2000): 293–306.

Lodge, David. "Modernism, Antimodernism, Postmodernism." *Working with Structuralism*. London: Routledge, 1981. 3–16.

McQuillan, Martin, ed. *Theorizing Muriel Spark: Gender, Race, Deconstruction*. Basingstoke, UK: Palgrave, 2002.

Page, Norman. *Muriel Spark*. Basingstoke, UK: Macmillan, 1990.

Spark, Muriel. *Curriculum Vitae*. Boston: Houghton Mifflin, 1993.

———. "The Desegregation of Art." *Critical Essays on Muriel Spark*. Ed. Joseph Hynes. New York: Hall, 1992. 33–37.

———. "A Magical Mystery Tour in Tuscany." Interview with Alan Taylor. *The Scotsman*, 29 January 1996, 9–10.

———. "'The Same Informed Air': An Interview with Muriel Spark." Interview with Martin McQuillan. McQuillan 210–29.

———. "Writers of Today—Muriel Spark." Transcript of Interview with the BBC's Ian Gillham. Muriel Spark Archive, National Library of Scotland, Acc. 10989/195.

Verongos, Helen T., and Alan Cowell. "Obituary for Muriel Spark." *New York Times* 16 April 2006. <www.nytimes.com/2006/04/16/world/16spark.html?pagewanted=1&_r=1>

Walker, Dorothea. *Muriel Spark*. Boston: Twayne, 1988.

PART I SPARK AS SCOTTISH AND
WORLD AUTHOR

CHAPTER I

"FULLY TO SAVOUR HER

POSITION": MURIEL SPARK

AND SCOTTISH IDENTITY

Gerard Carruthers

In a moment of bad judgment, Robin Jenkins opined that it would be "very difficult to get any real Scottish person accepting [Muriel Spark] as a Scottish writer" (13). Jenkins is Spark's nearest contender for the title of Scotland's most senior novelist during the past fifty years, but he was not motivated by rivalry. Rather, Jenkins spoke as one entrapped by a predominant impulse in twentieth-century Scottish literature. Self-conscious of Scottish literature's supposedly inadequate criticism of its own national and international contexts through the nineteenth-century colonial period (both Scotland's alleged colonization by England and Scotland's enthusiastic collaboration in the wider British imperial project), early twentieth-century Scottish literature expended much inward energy reflecting historically on massive shortcomings both in itself and in Scottish society. The outcome of this new scrutiny included the promulgation of a vigorous nativism in expression—of which a Scots language revival was the most obvious exemplar—and a muscular corpus of Scottish fiction of historical and social critique, both of which were, at the time, creatively modern. It certainly could not be argued then (as it could be for the nineteenth century) that the nation indulged any longer in a frivolous, escapist, anachronistic, literary product designed to evade the contemporary realities of national behavior at home and abroad. However this might be, a negative countereffect of this understandable aspiration to engage with and, indeed, recreate Scottish national circumstance through literary expression has led to long lingering attitudes concerned in overwrought ways with realism and the priority of alighting on Scottish subject matter.[1] While the

21

construction of English literature (at least in university, college, and school courses) has tended to be historically rather unreflective and loose in its consideration of national parameters, the construction of Scottish literature (one of the most prominent cultural projects of twentieth-century Scotland) has tended toward an essentialist cultural nationalism that has continued to haunt it until very recently. As the twentieth century ended, Robin Jenkins sincerely voiced the opinion that Scotland's most successful writer of the previous one hundred years (no one else of her national origin in this time comes close to combining the critical and popular regard internationally that Spark garners) is a cosmopolitan misfit who does not, at least in the majority of her books, have an insistent enough agenda of being Scottish.[2]

Essentialism in identity is something that consistently, though often obliquely, concerns the fiction of Muriel Spark. Spark's own origins are problematically heterogeneous, as she herself indicates in her most revealing semi-autobiographical short story, "The Gentile Jewesses." Here we find the recurrent Sparkian motif of oxymoronic identity where the title alludes to the fact that the narrator is the third woman in a direct family line to be progeny of mixed Jewish and non-Jewish blood. What we have, then, is both recognition of the orthodox matrilineal means of Jewish succession and a brazen acknowledgment of the collapsing of this mechanism. This simultaneous invoking and ironicizing of tradition is a hallmark of Spark's fiction, indicating her view that stories, or history, ought to be replayed or even sometimes reworked rather than simply accepted as givens. Narratives for Spark are potentially both wonderful imaginative acts of transformation and, at other times, lazily and even nefariously designed. In this ambiguous nature of storytelling, Spark recognizes both the human aspiration toward transcendence over everyday materialist reality and the faulty, fallen human propensity toward selfishly motivated articulations. In "The Gentile Jewesses" the narrator refuses to be denied her Jewish heritage simply because of Talmudic law and defiantly embraces and gently mocks this law as a person who is possessed of enough imaginative empathy for her Jewish forbearers for them and their origins to matter to her. In this unwillingness by the narrator to be shut out by the tradition on this issue, we witness an important maneuver in Spark's Judeo-Christian anagogic practice, where the word is rendered precisely nonstatic and instead comes alive or, in a sense, is mischievously made awkward flesh.

The febrile imaginative capacity of the narrator in "The Gentile Jewesses" is such that she has consciously to remind herself of the distinction between the very little that she has actually witnessed in life and those big historical events she has merely heard about: "Was I present at the Red Sea crossing? No, it had happened before I was born. My head was full of stories, of Greeks and Trojans, Picts and Romans, Jacobites and Redcoats, but these were definitely outside of my lifetime" (312). Here Picts and Jacobites, both romantic lost or vanquished elements of "Scottish" history, are merely part of a wider pattern of struggling, antagonistic identity when set within the longer view of time that encompasses the stories of the Old Testament and ancient Mediterranean civilization—both cradle experiences in Western civilization. It is precisely because such instances of strife in identity are so rife, or normative even, that the narrator is licensed to be unperplexed by—and, indeed, exuberantly creative with—such fissures. As well as the coinage "gentile Jewesses," she has fun grafting together unrelated identities in response to the stereotypical expectations of her aunts who remark on her Scottish father's seemingly un-Jewish career as an engineer. In response, she asserts, "all Jews [are] engineers" (313). At this point Spark has very mischievously had her narrator transpose one of the most stereotypical occupations of the Scot onto her Scottish-Jewish father. A key Sparkian technique is here revealed. Lazy, or stereotypical, versions of the world license a certain amount of poetic justice, or payment in kind (which the narrator slyly visits on her aunts). This is a story, clearly, that to use an important Sparkian word, "rejoices"[3] in the actual plurality of the human world as we see again in the death of the narrator's beloved grandmother: "She was buried as a Jewess since she died in my father's house, and notices were put in the Jewish press. Simultaneously my great-aunts announced in the Watford papers that she fell asleep in Jesus" (314). Registered here is the fact that the truth is beyond any one human narrative, most especially any that attempts to be unequivocal. The narrator's grandmother is wonderfully evasive in her essence even as, and partly because of the fact that, set identities gather around her. At its conclusion, the story reaches consideration of the one unitary reality that is beyond the comprehension of humanity:

> My mother carries everywhere in her handbag a small locket containing a picture of Christ crowned with thorns. She keeps on one table a rather fine Buddha on a lotus leaf and on another a horrible replica of the Venus de Milo. One way and another all the gods are served in my mother's household although she holds only one belief and that is in the Almighty.
>
> My father, when questioned as to what he believes, will say, "I believe in the Blessed Almighty who made heaven and earth," and will say no more, returning to his racing papers which contain problems proper to innocent men. To them, it was no great shock when I turned Catho-

lic, since with Roman Catholics too, it all boils down to the Almighty in the end. (315)

Here we have a tender docketing of a welter of images and stories extending even to a horrible item not to the narrator's taste. All of these aspire to a larger truth that benighted humanity can never actually hope to encapsulate. On the other hand, the narrator's father is an innocent man, which carries the connotation of a certain purity shown in his resistance of concrete imagery with which to describe God. The one human universality among the attitudes of the narrator's parents though (and by extension, the attitudes of many different world faiths) is the belief in something transcendent. In the narrator's comment on her conversion to Catholicism (which, of course, mirrors Spark's own spiritual peregrination) she offers the offhand remark that with her adopted faith, "it all boils down to the Almighty in the end." Drawing on this clichéd metaphor, the narrator cheerfully concedes the ultimately threadbare nature of human imagery so that the ending represents another oxymoronic moment where the sublime is dealt with in throwaway language, but attested to nonetheless.

"The Gentile Jewesses" is arguably more revealing of Muriel Spark's truly personal thoughts on identity than her autobiography, *Curriculum Vitae* (1992), in which one might sometimes feel that Spark (characteristically) is playing games with and teasing the reader. Spark in her introduction explains that the premise of her surely mockingly flat-titled memoir is utilizing "nothing that cannot be supported by documentary evidence or by eye-witness. . . . Truth by itself is neutral and has its own dear beauty" (*Curriculum* 11). Is it conceivable that the writer of "The Gentile Jewesses" believes that "truth" is so readily, neutrally, and uniformly available as these words taken at face value seem to suggest? (Whether these words with their Brodiesque turn of phrase are to be taken seriously is another question.) *Curriculum Vitae* documents Spark's early life in Edinburgh in a way that points to its author's lack of belief in autobiography as a practice involving much meaningful precision in itself (something that should little surprise students of her fiction). Paradoxically, this is implied in the throwaway cataloguing rubrics such as "Commodities," "Neighbours," and even "The Doorbell" that organize parts of *Curriculum Vitae* and that suggest that Spark's habitual sense of parody is slyly in operation. For Spark the artist and thinker on humanity, the actualities of physical location (as "The Gentile Jewesses" so clearly suggests) are not in themselves the really important things. Rather, for Spark the relationship *between* things, how they are configured, constitutes the realm of importance and of possibility. To clarify, we might turn to a statement by Spark herself on her national origins:

I am certainly a writer of Scottish formation and of course think of myself as such. I think to describe myself as a "Scottish Writer" might be ambiguous as one wouldn't know if "Scottish" applied to the writer or the writing. Then there is the complicated question of whether people of mixed inheritance, like myself, can call themselves Scottish. Some Scots deny it. But Edinburgh where I was born and my father was born has definitely had an effect on my mind, my prose style and my ways of thought. (qtd. in Bold 26)

This is Spark's response to a question about her feelings of national origin by the Scottish critic Alan Bold. It is ludicrously symptomatic of the essentialism of the Scottish literary critical mind that it needs to be posed in the first place. Spark's commonsense answer to the question points to the not-to-be-gainsaid interactions that any person must, of necessity, have with the environment in which they exist. Edinburgh has an "effect" on her; it does not simply define her. Spark is quite clear about the tense relationship she has to the city of her birth: "Edinburgh is the place that I, a constitutional exile, am essentially exiled from. I spent the first 18 years of my life, during the Twenties and Thirties, there. It was Edinburgh that bred within me conditions of exiledom; and what have I been doing since then but moving from exile into exile? It has become a calling." As in "The Gentile Jewesses," we find here Spark's wryness with regard to personal identity as she invokes the notion of the exiled Jew. If Edinburgh is humorously here Jerusalem, it is also, in the same essay, "no mean city" ("Edinburgh-born" 180).[4] Litotes and other deferrals of absolute material reality are a pronounced part of Spark's stock in trade and we become aware of this again in another of her descriptions of Edinburgh: "The Castle Rock is something, rising up as it does from pre-history between the formal grace of the New Town and the noble network of the Old. To have a great primitive black crag rising up in the middle of populated streets of commerce, stately squares and winding closes, is like the statement of an unmitigated fact preceded by 'nevertheless'" (22). Even the imagery of this statement is not quite as clear as it might at first appear. Spark's relentless, chiastic wit here has the "black crag" as the "mitigating" element and the seemingly rational activity of the city as that which needs to be reordered. Spark does not trust that place is easily (or unimaginatively) apprehended.

At the same time, elusiveness and slippage in reality and identity are characteristics that have allowed Spark's fiction to be appropriated, to some extent, by the Scottish canon. The overworked trope of "crisis in identity" is often applied to either or both manifest subject matter and mode in works of Scottish literature. One cited cause of confused, bifurcated Scottish impulse is the intrusive influence of

English culture. More recently, however, it has become fashionable to see the Scottish trauma in consciousness as related to Calvinism. This has attractions for Scottish critics in that it allows an emphasis on a supposedly indigenous *mentalité*, now very capable of rehabilitation (when puritanical Calvinism, as a historically antiartistic element in Scottish culture, had been for the first part of the twentieth century largely beyond the pale). The growth of this critical tendency in the embryonic postmodern age has its origins with the republication of James Hogg's *Private Memoirs and Confessions of a Justified Sinner* (1824) in 1947 with an introduction penned by André Gide. Largely ignored for over a century Hogg's novel becomes, as Cairns Craig has astutely remarked, "a part, almost, of twentieth-century rather than nineteenth-century Scottish writing" (38). Craig has documented the way in which Scottish fiction after the republication of *Confessions of a Justified Sinner* rediscovered something of the old Calvinist outlook of Scotland in viewing the world as a fearful place (since in the logic of the Fall, Earth becomes an outcast place, even its pleasures offer potential traps for those insufficiently mindful of the essentially ruined status of the human environment). Among the very wide list of examples in fiction inspired by Hogg in the return to a Calvinist *Weltanschauung*, Craig cites Spark's first novel, *The Comforters* (1957). It is true that the character of Georgina Hogg (probably including the name itself) is inspired by Hogg's novel in regarding herself as being among the elite members of her faith. Georgina has a resemblance to Hogg's central character of Robert Wringhim, particularly, since, as the central character in the novel Caroline Rose wisely speculates, "she has no private life whatsoever" (186). Georgina, then, is indicated to have erased the space of considered conscience in her blind adherence to Canonical regulation. A strange typewriter repeating Caroline's thoughts also echoes the (demonic) multiplicity of voice that is found in James Hogg's novel. Yet, even as *The Comforters* can be said to form part of a Scottish canon during the second half of the twentieth century revitalized by Hogg's work, it is in some ways an obviously problematic choice. The title itself, of course, derives from the Book of Job and Spark's interest in the long Judeo-Christian problem of the existence of suffering. Georgina Hogg is a Catholic and so speaks of a condition that is universal and not merely to be attributed to the Calvinist outlook. It should also be noted that the odd states of unreality that *Confessions of a Justified Sinner* and *The Comforters* share are ultimately of a different status. Whereas the voices and visions that afflict Wringhim, either demonic or stemming from a psychological illness, cause him to commit suicide, there is no such apocalypse for the beset Caroline in Spark's novel. For one thing, Caroline's numinous typewriter has its basis in Spark's personal biography as a result of delusions she suffered through overwork and using dexedrine as a dieting aid while living in London. The Jungian therapy that the writer underwent not long after coming off the drug at the hands of the Catholic priest, Father Frank O'Malley, is remembered in Caroline Rose's ministering from the character Father Jerome. Jerome counsels her to accept the intrusive voices as not necessarily worrying, with the casual diagnosis, "these things can happen" (63).[5] *The Comforters*, then, in the final analysis is not a novel of Calvinist mistrust in the face of the (demonic) world, but of Catholic acceptance that the numinous might commingle with everyday reality.

It was long an oversight in Spark criticism that the influence, generally, of Hogg's *Confessions of a Justified Sinner* did not register. In *Muriel Spark: An Odd Capacity for Vision* (1984), edited by Alan Bold, a concerted effort by critics informed about Scottish literature, Trevor Royle and Allan Massie (and the guiding hand of Bold himself), put this to rights to some extent.[6] Prior to this, it is little short of extraordinary that excellent studies (all highly aware of Spark's various literary lineages) by Peter Kemp, Ruth Whittaker, and even Massie himself should be essentially oblivious to the importance of Hogg, most especially with regard to *The Ballad of Peckham Rye* (1960).[7] This is probably symptomatic of the fact that, in spite of 1947 marking a watershed for the rediscovery of Hogg, it was only really during the 1970s that academic Hogg studies flourished. Even the Scottish critics who show an awareness of *Confessions of a Justified Sinner* do so rather belatedly when we consider the utilization of this novel by Spark. It would be interesting to know when precisely Spark became interested in Hogg. One might surmise though, that the new vogue for Hogg initially inspired by Gide—a cosmopolitan, gay French intellectual—represented confirmation of the European kinship within Scottish culture so proudly noted by her character, Jean Brodie. It should also be emphasized that with her interest in Mary Shelley and the Brontës, Spark was likely to be interested in Hogg as a Romantic writer. In editing the Brontë letters, Spark must have been very struck by the remark of Branwell Brontë about Hogg, that "the writings of that man . . . laid a hold on my mind which succeeding years have consecrated into a most sacred feeling" (Spark, *Brontë* 51). Spark certainly comes to have Hogg in her literary genes, but this is not some set of essentially national genes.

Let us comment more widely than has been done before on the treatment of the "Scottish" materials informing *The Ballad of Peckham Rye*. With regard to Hogg, the character of Dougal Douglas is cleverly made into a doppelgänger, a phenomenon by which Robert Wringhim is plagued, through the simple expedient of having Dougal reverse his name to become Douglas Dougal so that he can nefariously enjoy employment at two rival firms. Another feature of Hogg's novel is the apparent collapse of time-sense for its central character, which here, of course, is managed by the sleight of hand simultaneity of Dougal's working arrangement. We find, then, a characteristic Spark technique of economically (or artfully) mimicking the supernatural. It is a favored approach of anthologizers of the Scottish short story to include supernatural work by Spark on the basis that her interest in such terrain marks out an inherently Scottish mindset.[8] As *The Ballad of Peckham Rye* shows, however, Spark's highly playful incorporation of supernatural effects is altogether more literary than "folk-based" (there exists a prominent idea that Scottish literature is, or ought to be, based much more on demotic oral traditions in contradistinction to English literature, which is taken to be much more literary per se).

We see Spark, of course, in *The Ballad of Peckham Rye*, make use precisely of the oral medium of the Scottish border ballad known for its featuring of dramatically bloody deeds and its portrayal of internecine strife (both family and cross-border travail). Dougal Douglas is a visitor of such division on the dreary, preswinging sixties London suburb into which Spark parachutes him. He also represents, to some extent, an English stereotype of the Scot come to life. He is diabolic (and so roughly equivalent to the supposed bleak or dour Scottish type, even as this is contradicted by his demonic, shape-changing propensities, which involve joyfully madcap mimicking routines). Dougal is diabolic as well, the Jock-on-the-make stereotype of which James Boswell is the best example. Dougal, a writer of biography among his many activities, is also something of a hypochondriac in his fear of contact with illness, is sexually licentious, and is a skilful mimic. All of these qualities are associated with Boswell, and Spark is surely consciously drawing on his character.[9] As a Scottish outsider and someone noticed for his humped back—in the 1960s interpreted as a handicap, rather than in folklore as the mark of the beast—Dougal easily stirs up prejudice. He is sent to traumatize metropolitan modernity with his very deliberated and very Scottish grotesqueness.

Spark's choice of mode in *The Ballad of Peckham Rye* (albeit that it is consonant with the development that her fiction had been undergoing since the start of her career) represents the novelist at her most unfashionable (one suspects willfully so).[10] Flying in the face of the kitchen-sink realism of English culture during the late 1950s and early 1960s, Spark chooses to find exactly the opposite of the grimy, suburban, domestic attractiveness that underwrites this mode. Peckham is a location where the imagination is in danger of collapse. Oxymoronic, multifaceted Dougal (with the hallmarks of the imagination therein) is a literary judgment on the place for its sins of ordinariness. We find a nice example of this as Dougal's employer, Mr. Druce, murders his lover, Merle Coverdale, after Dougal has also become her boyfriend so as to turn an adulterous affair into a ménage à trois. Here the folk rules operate, as these are to be found also in Hogg's *Confessions*. The devil cannot simply create evil out of nothing (since in the divine economy God is ultimately omnipotent). Rather, he must be allowed in through the keyhole of freely chosen human badness, but can then exacerbate the situation of moral turpitude to which he has gained admittance. It is a typically Sparkian twist that Druce and Coverdale, like so many characters in the novel, have settled into a very mundane, threadbare kind of sinfulness. We see the pair sharing dull suppers together and Druce very neatly folding his trousers prior to their passionless lovemaking with the implication that they have lost not only a keen sense of goodness, but of badness too. An instrument of the divine economy rather than merely of the dark side, Dougal is justified in his claims to be an exorcist and to have "the ability to drive devils out of people" (*Ballad* 102). Thus he helps along an all too literal poetic justice as Druce, agitated by Dougal, murders Merle by plunging a corkscrew into her neck. This death is at once horribly violent, after the manner of the ballads, and mockingly reductive given the suburban weapon of homicide.

Dissonantly comic in its collision of the worlds of seemingly workaday London suburb and the ballads, the novel also reflects the fact that such discordance is much more normal than the inhabitants of Peckham would care to acknowledge. We see this in the Crewe family (given a typically and rather snootily disdainful unromantic moniker from the English town centered on the locomotive industry), which is conjoined of actually disparate elements where the father, Arthur, has not sired his daughter and may not be the father of his son either. The member of this family who most attracts the diabolic attentions of Dougal is seventeen-year-old Dixie. Dougal befriends Dixie, who is working hard to save for her wedding to Humphrey Place. Dixie's efforts involve her not only being employed by one of the firms for which Dougal works, but taking on an evening job as a cinema usherette. She is, then, (albeit more mildly) possessed of the protean propensity manifested by Dougal, and she is also illegitimate so that the folk equation of bastardry and the mark of the devil might be brought to mind. In another Sparkian turn, however, her own mother Mavis observes that Dixie should be out indulging herself while in her youth rather than fretting as much as she does over her respectable future (in her loss of the present, Dixie has a resemblance to Robert Wringhim, who loses sense of the temporal sphere). Mavis, it seems, has had a reckless time while young, so that she conceives Dixie with an American GI. We see here a pattern that is sometimes found in Spark's fiction where those who stand for the life principle are not, on the face of it, conventionally moral people.[11] Dixie's desire for respectability, presumably in the face of her anxiety over her own origins, leads her into a petty-minded narrowness that Dougal implicitly encourages by representing to her his roguish disrespectability. Dougal is licensed, yet again, to interfere in Dixie's life because of her existing predisposition. For Humphry's entertainment, he does a skit prior to the wedding of the groom refusing his marriage vows, which is what Humphrey does at the first attempted nuptials. Later, because of freewill (as guaranteed by God; even if Dougal is a real demon he cannot simply take control of someone's destiny in perpetuity), Humphrey does indeed marry Dixie:

> Humphrey drove off with Dixie. She said, "I feel as if I've been twenty years married instead of two hours."
> He thought this a pity for a girl of eighteen. But it was a sunny day for November, and, as he drove swiftly past the Rye, he saw the children playing there and the women coming home from work with their shopping-bags, the Rye for an instant looking like a cloud of green and gold, the people seeming to ride upon it, as you might say there was another world than this. (142)

Dougal has gone but his influence lingers, and we see that he is almost as much an agent of God as of the Devil. In Spark's beloved border ballads, the color green is very often notice of the intrusion of an ambiguous supernatural/fairyland sphere and its presence here extends the offer of possible grace to Peckham. As with so many of Spark's endings, a note of lyrical tenderness provides a counterpoint to the preceding human folly, and the possibility of forgiveness is registered. It is up to Humphrey in his conjugal state and his newfound apprehensions how he will attempt to manage his life from now on.

The Ballad of Peckham Rye shows Spark managing a hybrid form, the contemporary English tendency toward domestic realism and the notion of the Scottish supernatural tradition. Both of these things, in fact, are parodied even as they are effectively utilized to provide Spark's polished literary artifact (which is very unballad-like). Those critics who wish to see the novel as purveying some essentially different Scottish cultural mentalité, knowingly dissecting the English world, do not take enough account of Spark's construction of a plane of critique in this novel (as elsewhere) that is about showing the dissonance and fissures in universal human nature through wielding (and, indeed, welding) those materials she has most conveniently to hand. It is not a question, particularly, of any kind of national cultural inherence or partisanship on the part of Spark. Spark as author here might be thought to be very much like Dougal, himself as an outsider, making elegant oxymoronic patterns she is in full control of but from which she stands in comprehensive ironic detachment.

As with Dougal Douglas, Jean Brodie, Spark's most exuberant character creation, is constructed amidst somewhat well trod Scottish materials. *The Prime of Miss Jean Brodie* takes education as a theme, prompted by the supposedly prodigious historic success of Scotland in this sphere. It is a nice coincidence that Spark's novel should appear in the same year as the work that has become the most celebrated study of Scottish intellectual history, George Davie's *The Democratic Intellect* (1961), which expounds the idea that Scottish generalism represented the historic Scottish socioeducational ethic, as opposed to a narrower educational specialism manifested in the English tradition. At times, Brodie seems to be very aware of this tradition of the "democratic intellect," as, for instance, when she readily becomes pupil herself in the attempt to learn Greek from her chosen pupils as they are initiated into this language on entering the senior school. Brodie's Latin explanation of the term "education" also recalls the historic emphasis in Scotland on a classical knowledge in which careful etymology (as a subset of the philosophy of Common Sense, which Davie sees epistemologically underpinning Scottish generalism) is prized over systematic, potentially florid, fluency. Brodie speaks exactly to the Scottish commonsense educational agenda as espoused by Davie:

> The word "education" comes from the root e from *ex*, out, and *duco*, I lead. It means a leading out. To me, education is a leading out of what is already there in the pupil's soul. To Miss Mackay it is a putting in of something that is not there, and that is not what I call education, I call it intrusion, from the Latin root prefix *in* meaning in and the stem *trudo*, I thrust. Miss Mackay's method is to thrust a lot of information into the pupil's head; mine is a leading out of knowledge, and that is true education as proved by the root meaning. (36)

Here we find Jean Brodie determined to appear as a traditionally authoritative Scottish teacher. As we learn more, however, we realize that Brodie's demeanor in this regard has perhaps to do with the fact that her own educational attainments (especially when compared with those of the hated, younger Miss Mackay) are modest and her position as a minimally qualified female teacher at Marcia Blaine school is an unusual consequence of the social and cultural flux of the interwar years. We might also note, however, that Brodie's "leading out" is a function not dissimilar from Dougal Douglas's exorcism of moral propensities. As ever with Spark, the identity we might think we are fairly certainly dealing with is never far from revealing itself to be something sometimes differently edged.

Brodie, in the passage above, is seen clinging to a realism or a literalism, but she also practices linguistic transformation (this is one of several ways in the novel where we again encounter quasi-supernatural shape changing). While objecting to her girls using the words "comic" (11) and "social" (62) as nouns when these should be adjectives, Brodie utilizes the word "prime" (56) to describe her abstract state of maturity and so performs the same act of trans-mutation. If we are attuned to the social and historical particulars of the novel, however, we realize that Brodie is not gratuitously willful, but fighting to mark out a space in which she can exist. *The Prime of Miss Jean Brodie* marks a trend in Spark's novels where she begins to offer a more sympathetic view of cultural particulars than in her often severely *contemptus mundi* mode in novels previously, such as *The Comforters* or *The Ballad of Peckham Rye*. The beginning of chapter 3 of *The Prime of Miss Jean Brodie* brilliantly contextualizes Brodie in the interwar years (marking yet again an *inter*-terrain of the kind in which Spark specializes). Given the decade in which the novel appears, we find a poignant reminder that the freedoms of thought, particularly female thought that began to ensue during the 1960s, were a revisiting of social trends that had been apparent in the 1930s and that, arguably, were later dampened down by the uni-fied homefront of World War II. We are shown women like Brodie at "Edinburgh grocers' shops arguing with the Manager at three in the afternoon on every subject from the authenticity of the Scriptures to the question of what the word 'guaranteed' on a jam-jar really meant." These are women (yet again in an oxymoronic identity) of "war-bereaved spinsterhood" (42), so that the catastrophic loss of manpower (literally, but also in terms of authority) allows them, it is implied, a fairly sudden albeit partial liberation. Brodie herself, we should be aware, would most likely have become a housewife instead of a schoolteacher had her lover not died during World War I. Given her opportunity, Brodie is determined grab it, simultaneously working hard to appear like a dominie and exercising fictions that neatly shore up her position. Thus, her dead lover, Hugh Carruthers, is narrated fictively by Brodie to her girls as a man of the country with a store of wise sayings so that he might be seen to be a stereotypical version of Robert Burns. If, indeed, Hugh ever existed, he is an excuse for Brodie's single state and her dedication to her girls. Later his story is invested with his dual talents for singing and art as a codified way for the teacher to indicate her entanglements with her colleagues,

Gordon Lowther and Teddy Lloyd, music and art masters, respectively. What we have, then, is Brodie occupying a fragile space where fiction is her safeguard against forces that would not easily concede to Brodie her chosen career or her love life.

Calvinism appears in *The Prime of Miss Jean Brodie* so as to become part of the theme of the mystery of identity, which looms large thematically. We see this especially in the apprehensions of Sandy Stranger, who, with her name and her mixed Scottish-English parentage, is an outsider to some extent. Sandy contemplates Calvinism:

> Fully to savour her position, Sandy would go and stand outside St Giles Cathedral or the Tolbooth, and contemplate these emblems of a dark and terrible salvation which made the fires of the damned seem very merry to the imagination by contrast, and much preferable. Nobody in her life, at home or school, had ever spoken of Calvinism except as a joke that had once been taken seriously. . . . All she was conscious of now was that some quality of life peculiar to Edinburgh and nowhere else had been going on unbeknown to her all the time, and however undesirable it might be, she felt deprived of it; however undesirable, she desired to know what it was, and to cease to be protected from it by enlightened people. (108)

For Sandy, Edinburgh is suffused with a unique quality, even though Calvinism has seemingly ceased to have much of an existence on the surface of life. In fact, it is Sandy's inexperience that leads her to believe that things are so very different in her home locale. She herself at this point is inhabiting the stereotype of the cold, dour Scottish metaphysical mind (worse, apparently, in its conceptions than the "fires of the damned"). Sandy wishes to encounter Calvinism, which very much like her imaginative forays into *Kidnapped* or *Jane Eyre* or her other fantasies of being a heroine of one kind or another, is all too vividly realized in her growing perception of Jean Brodie. Fundamentally craving excitement, she brings to life a historic text (something not without irony given Spark's own practice in this mode) and uses it as an explanation for Brodie's behavior.

Sandy savors the fact that she stands outside Calvinism, but she nonetheless activates the idea of this religion. We should be aware of the full passage, too often precipitously drawn on by critics of Spark, which contains Sandy's crucial identification of Jean Brodie: "She thinks she is Providence, thought Sandy, she thinks she is the God of Calvin, she sees the beginning and the end. And Sandy thought, too, the woman is an unconscious Lesbian. And many theories from the books of psychology categorized Miss Brodie, but failed to obliterate her image from the canvases of one-armed Teddy Lloyd" (120). In seeing Brodie as a "Lesbian," Sandy is collaborating in the oppression of Brodie by a society that would like to mold her into an entirely conventional female type or castigate her for her deviation from such a role. Sandy's theorizing, we are told by the narrator, is somewhat indiscriminate even as it "fails to obliterate her image" in the paintings of Teddy Lloyd, to whom Sandy becomes lover. What is suggested is that Sandy cannot explain by any means the mysterious nature of Brodie's attraction for Lloyd (or, indeed, for others, perhaps, including herself). The mature Sandy, from the locus of her convent, comes to see Brodie as someone whose "defective sense of self-criticism" (86) ought to mark out the terrain of a "justified sinner" as "quite an innocent" (127). Sandy "clutche[s] the bars of her grille," which might seem to indicate punishment for her information to Miss Mackay regarding Brodie's flirtation with fascism that leads to Brodie having to resign her post. However, Sandy, visited by Eunice, is quite rightly hard-headed, saying of Brodie's old complaints of the betrayal the teacher has inferred must have come from one her girls, "it is only possible to betray where loyalty is due" (127). Sandy's own motivations in the downfall of her teacher are, undoubtedly, selfish, but the harm that the teacher does in encouraging Joyce-Emily Hammond to foolishly go off and fight in the Spanish Civil War, and, perhaps even more seriously, her lack of charity in the case of Mary MacGregor (whom she mocks), are sins of which Brodie is certainly not "innocent." Sandy, in fact, gripping her grille might be read by the end of the novel's events as undergoing the religious process of unselfing, something that is not necessarily without personal anxiety. She is divesting herself of images and stories of which previously she has produced a surfeit.

We see Sandy undergo a more profound set of transformations in the novel than Brodie, who for all her contradictory posturing remains a rather static character trapped in her own somewhat pathetic space. Sandy's youthful imaginations reach a pitch with her obsessive apprehensions of Brodie. Paradoxically, it is Sandy who manifests the mark of demonic enslavement, which the apprehension of being one of the "unco' guid," or Calvinist elect, is supposed to lead to. In a received image that goes back at least as far as Christ driving the demon into a herd of swine in the Gospel of Luke (9:33), she is seen to have pig-like eyes. In another porcine comparison, Sandy extracts from Lloyd his Catholic "religion as a pith from a husk" (123). She inspires in Brodie the greatest confidence of any of her "set" (5), and self-fulfills the Calvinistic situation where Brodie is encouraged to feel in command of the situation around her "so that [her] surprise at the end might be the nastier" (109). Sandy—embarrassed early on that her English mother calls her "darling" (18), untypical of Edinburgh behavior even among the middle class—has longed for a Scottish identity and unbeknown to herself has taken one on: that of Calvinism. Later, in converting to Rome and becoming a nun, Sandy clearly shifts in her perception of Jean Brodie. Inspired by her teacher, she writes her treatise, "The Transfiguration of the Commonplace," so that Brodie now is seen as quasi-Catholic by bringing about something that adds up to a bigger or transubstantiated total through wielding mundane materials (the various stereotypes and hackneyed stories that she employs). We are told that Sandy's treatise is on psychology, but one might well assume, given the title, that its conclusions are more religious than psychological, asserting presumably the indefinable essence of the human person—that the perception of any other individual alone is never enabled nor entitled fully to view. It is with regard to such a reading that Sandy's desperately enclosed state as a nun makes sense. She is struggling to divest herself of worldly involvements since these necessarily mean making images and stories that can never show anything like the complete truth. It is not the case that the world is completely fallen and corrupt (so that, as in the scenario of *Confessions of a Justified Sinner*, moral actions are neither here nor there, and those supposedly predestined to salvation can sin with impunity), but that human discrimination in the moral weighting of actions can never be absolute. It is in this subtle but profound difference between an extreme Calvinism and orthodox Catholic belief that the warp and woof of *The Prime of Miss Jean Brodie* lies. The crude predetermined drama of the former and the endless story of the latter where the battle between good and evil is never done and is never entirely predictable (an often surprising conflict that is the mark of so much of Spark's fictional oeuvre) makes for the essential difference.

It is perhaps no coincidence that Muriel Spark's two most Scottish novels should be published in close proximity. In these she works richly through a vein of received images and ideas of her country as well as any contemporary Scottish writer. That she does not take notions of Scottish identity as essentially different in their human dynamics and artistic potential from anywhere else should come as no surprise given Spark's theocentric view of the world. Imaginatively, Scotland is a strong site of the dissonant and interpolated human reality that she conveys throughout her fictional oeuvre, where truth and transcendent identity can never be exactly located but are indicated through the imaginative aspirations both of Spark herself and her characters. Scottish material continues to surface in her work from time to time such as the *Peter Pan* scenario in *The Hothouse by the East River* (1973), where the work of J. M. Barrie, the father of the supposedly diseased kailyard (cabbage-patch) school, is craftily utilized to deconstruct the outwardly hard-headed reality of contemporary New York. By and large though "Scottish" elements feature in smaller, parodied ways, such as the treatment of moral awareness in *Symposium*, where far from reliable characters say of Scotland that there "all the families are odd" (87) and "people are more capable of perpetrating good or evil than anywhere else" (159). This mischievous reiteration of the historic stereotype of the metaphysical Scot is supplemented in another Scottish reiteration with the appearance of Lord Lucan in Scotland in *Aiding and Abetting* (2001), an inversion of the infliction of Dougal Douglas on England, so that the notorious real-life English aristocratic murderer is returned to an appropriate locus of dark (ballad) legend. Simply, or perhaps complicatedly, Scotland is a place conjugated by Spark with many other sites and cultures in her work, and Scotland should be grateful that she utilizes it and her art so universally.

Notes

1. It is interesting that even James Kelman, the Scottish writer of impeccably left-wing credentials and most fêted as an urban realist, has recently complained of the constraining Scottish ideological preference for "social realism" in fiction (qtd. in Jamie 19).

2. Jenkins's principal distaste for Spark seems to arise from the fact, according to him, that apart from *The Prime of Miss Jean Brodie*, "all her other novels [are] set in Venice, they're set in London particularly" (13).

3. Fleur Talbot, Spark's fictional narrator and novelist in *Loitering with Intent*, ends the novel "rejoicing" in the free rein given to her imaginative faculties (158).

4. As Spark is well aware, the label "no mean city" is more usually applied to the Scottish capital's great civic rival, Glasgow, after the notorious novel, written in 1935 by Alexander McArthur and H. Kingsley Long, memorialized this title.

5. Spark's encounter with Fr. O'Malley is recounted in *Curriculum Vitae* 204–5.

6. Allan Massie in "Calvinism and Catholicism in Muriel Spark" refers to Hogg's novel and its influence on Spark's *The Comforters* and *The Prime of Miss Jean Brodie* as a lesson in "false religion, seductive and destroying" (98). Trevor Royle in "Spark and Scotland" is the first critic to read Brodie's personality as informed by Hogg's Robert Wringhim as a "divided personality" (156–57).

7. Peter Kemp's *Muriel Spark*, Allan Massie's *Muriel Spark*, and Ruth Whittaker's *The Faith and Fiction of Muriel Spark* are all extensive critical works showing great sensitivity both to Spark's religious outlook and her fictional antecedents, but without awareness of Hogg's *Confessions*.

8. We see this in, for instance, *The Penguin Book of Scottish Short Stories*, edited by J. F. Hendry, which selects Spark's "The House of the Famous Poet" for its *outré* qualities and in Moira Burgess, *The Other Voice*, which selects "The Black Madonna" and Carl MacDougall's *The Devil and the Giro*, which selects the same. In the coincidence between the latter two cases, one can see the abundant supply of Spark short fiction being squeezed to suit this national literary agenda.

9. With regard to the lesser known attributes of Boswell as a mimic, see Pottle, *James Boswell: The Earlier Years 1740–1769*, pages 63, 93, and 180.

10. For my reading of Spark's developing usage of supernatural, including "supranatural," devices in her fiction see, "The Remarkable Fictions of Muriel Spark" in Gifford and McMillan's edited collection, *A History of Scottish Women's Writing* (514–25).

11. A good example of this type is to be found in "The Black Madonna" where Elizabeth, the sister of trendy, progressive Catholic Lou Parker, exists amidst a brood of illegitimate children, while Lou herself has her own child adopted because of the awkward appearance of her legitimate, but throwback, daughter. In this story the Virgin icon, to which the Parkers make petition after years of failure to produce children, has proved to be a dispenser of oxymoronic identity.

Works Cited

Bold, Alan. *Muriel Spark.* London: Methuen, 1986.

Burgess, Moira. *The Other Voice.* Edinburgh: Polygon, 1987.

Carruthers, Gerard. "The Remarkable Fictions of Muriel Spark." *A History of Scottish Women's Writing.* Ed. Douglas Gifford and Dorothy McMillan. Edinburgh: Edinburgh UP, 1997. 514–25.

Craig, Cairns. *The Modern Scottish Novel: Narrative and the National Imagination.* Edinburgh: Edinburgh UP, 1999.

Hendry, J. F., ed. *The Penguin Book of Scottish Short Stories.* New York: Penguin, 1970.

Jamie, Kathleen. "The Voice of the Oppressed." *Scotland on Sunday* 19 Feb 1999: 19.

Jenkins, Robin. "A Truthful Scot." By Inga Agustdottir. *In Scotland* Autumn 1999: 12–22.

Kemp, Peter. *Muriel Spark.* London: Elek, 1974.

MacDougall, Carl, ed. *The Devil and the Giro.* Edinburgh: Canongate, 1989.

Massie, Allan. "Calvinism and Catholicism in Muriel Spark." *Muriel Spark: An Odd Capacity for Vision*. Ed. Alan Bold. London: Vision, 1984. 94–107.

———. *Muriel Spark*. Edinburgh: Ramsay Head, 1979.

Pottle, Frederick A. *James Boswell: The Earlier Years 1740–1769*. London: Heinemann, 1966.

Royle, Trevor. "Spark and Scotland." *Muriel Spark: An Odd Capacity for Vision*. Ed. Alan Bold. London: Vision, 1984. 147–66.

Spark, Muriel. *The Ballad of Peckham Rye*. London: Penguin, 1963.

———, ed. *The Brontë Letters*. London: Nevill, 1954.

———. "The Black Madonna." *The Collected Stories*. London: Penguin, 1994. 38–57.

———. *The Comforters*. New York: Penguin, 1963.

———. *Curriculum Vitae*. London: Constable, 1992.

———. "Edinburgh-born." *New Statesman* 10 August 1962: 180.

———. "The Gentile Jewesses." *The Collected Stories*. London: Penguin, 1994. 308–15.

———. *Loitering with Intent*. London: Triad, 1982.

———. *The Prime of Miss Jean Brodie*. New York: Penguin, 1965.

———. *Symposium*. London: Constable, 1990.

Whittaker, Ruth. *The Faith and Fiction of Muriel Spark*. London: Macmillan, 1982.

CHAPTER 2

"THE MAGAZINE THAT IS CONSIDERED THE BEST IN THE WORLD": MURIEL SPARK AND THE *NEW YORKER*

Lisa Harrison

> I would really like to get something in *The New Yorker* before I die. I do so admire that particular, polished, rich, brilliant style.
>
> —Sylvia Plath, *17 January 1956*

Muriel Spark's relationship with the *New Yorker* began officially in 1957, cultivated by fiction editor Rachel MacKenzie; Spark's first short story "The Ormolu Clock" was published in the magazine three years later. By 1961, the *New Yorker* devoted a full issue to *The Prime of Miss Jean Brodie*—publishing the novel in its entirety. Spark would ultimately publish numerous short stories, poems, and excerpts of novels—as well as reviews and autobiographical pieces—in the magazine over the next five decades.

This essay develops new contexts for understanding Spark's works, as well as Scottish fiction more generally, by examining Spark's relationship with the *New Yorker*. As Scotland becomes an international and cosmopolitan space through the twentieth and twenty-first centuries, situating Scottish writing in its world context becomes increasingly important. Spark herself defied conventional cataloging, but the tenor of Spark criticism tends to favor aspects of thematic approach (Catholicism, for example) or view her work in light of national application (the so-called Scottish novels). Yet Spark's incisive eye and sharp satire found purchase in a multitude of genres, and her contribution to metafictional play and narrative ironies falls outwith such easily fenced, conventional criticisms.

The paucity of Spark's own autobiographical output post–*Curriculum Vitae* makes it all the more important to glean information about the international reception of her work and about other aspects of her life and career through her decades-long affiliation with the *New Yorker*. The relationship lasted throughout her writing career; her first appearance dates from 1954, via a small mention in the *New Yorker*'s "Books: Briefly Noted" review section that lists a critical work she co-edited with Derek Stanford (Wilson 132–33). Examining an overlooked portion of Spark's biography during her New York years (1962–1967) allows a more complete picture of the contexts in which she lived and worked, and understanding the extent of her connection with the magazine draws critical attention to Spark's legacy and influence in modern fiction by giving readers an *entré* to Spark's most prolific writing period, 1957–1967. In short, both the unpublished correspondence with the magazine's editors and pieces by Spark published in the magazine itself afford a new corpus; this material reveals aspects of Spark and her oeuvre that widen the range of contexts in which her writing—and by extension, Scottish postwar writing—can be understood.

Writing in her 1992 autobiography *Curriculum Vitae*, Spark examines her relationship with the American literary magazine:

> In March [1957], *The New Yorker* wrote that they had admired my story "The Portobello Road" which had appeared in Macmillan's *Winter's Tales*. They wondered "if you won't let us consider some of your stories for publication." This started my long and rewarding association with the magazine that is still considered the best in the world. Twice they have given up the whole of the week's issue to publish one of my novels in its entirety. (211)

Her response has the wryly direct tone also used to recount the startling death of her characters; it is also tantalizingly coy. The *New Yorker* did publish two entire novels: *The Prime of Miss Jean Brodie* in the 14 October 1961 issue, and *The Driver's Seat* in the 16 May 1970 issue, but it also substantially serialized *The Mandelbaum Gate* over four issues in 1965 and portions of her autobiography in the magazine's "Personal History" section in 1989–1992. Indeed, Spark's comment about the magazine belies a rather striking fact: she appears in no less than seventeen issues over the course of the 1960s, and primary material by Spark graces nearly forty issues of the *New Yorker* total, beginning in 1960 and ending in 2003.

Spark's Early Connection and Correspondence with the *New Yorker*

Harold Ross established the *New Yorker* in February 1925 and served as the magazine's first editor. David Remnick describes Ross as "a Western newspaperman who came to Manhattan with an idea. . . . He had notions of wit and clarity, about being 'human,' as opposed to corporate, about appealing to those with a 'metropolitan interest,' as opposed to that mythical lady in Dubuque" ("Introduction" 7). In his own words, Ross explained the aim of the magazine, "It will not be what is commonly called highbrow or radical. . . . It will be what is commonly called sophisticated, in that it will assume a reasonable degree of enlightenment on the part of its readers. It will hate bunk" (qtd. in Remnick, "Introduction" 7).

By the mid-1950s, the magazine had achieved significant cultural totemizing for American literary excellence as "the repository for increasingly high standards of English prose, conscience, and civility" (Yagoda 24). However, given the effects of postwar fallout, postmodernist literary innovation, the rise of Cold War paranoia, deep technological suspicion, and atomic anxiety, the literary scene of the time was volatile and interrogative, as attested by the appearance of George Orwell's *Nineteen Eighty-Four* (1949), Ralph Ellison's *Invisible Man* (1952), and Ray Bradbury's *Fahrenheit 451* (1953). During the 1950s, the *New Yorker* was also enmeshed in change. A new general editor replaced Harold Ross after his death in 1951: William Shawn, a one-time *New Yorker* staff writer and idea man, "remarkably efficient and dogged about unearthing facts" (Yagoda 244). The 1950s change in editorship may not have ushered in a complete change in context, but it brought about a decisive change in tone:

> Ross and Shawn differed in almost every conceivable aspect, which was a problem in the early years of their association . . . no one expected [Shawn] to make any changes, and he didn't, with one exception . . . "Shawn," [writes Katherine White] "feels that if we use serious poetry, we ought to get the best there is." . . . In a 1954 article heralding the possible beginning of a "poetic golden age" in America, Donald Hall singled out *The New Yorker* as the popular magazine that had been the most receptive to the new generation of poets. (Yagoda 255–57)

The focus on "serious poetry," coupled with such juggernauts of American and international fiction as Truman Capote, Vladimir Nabokov, Philip Roth, and J. D. Salinger, revealed a singularly fertile context at the magazine for the sharpness of Spark's incisive prose. "A new generation of innovative, funny, edgy writers—not comedians but writers—was coming up in the fifties and early sixties, all of whom would have been delighted to be published in *The New Yorker*, and a few of whom who did" (Yagoda 274).

Muriel Spark's first mention in the magazine in 1954 is short but significant. In the "Books: Briefly Noted" section, Edmund Wilson, while writing only five sentences to review the Shelley book, nonetheless praises Spark and Stanford for "an oblique but extraordinarily intimate glimpse at the most pathetic of the pioneer bluestockings" (Wilson 133).

The *New Yorker*'s "Books" section generally began with a larger, more detailed article reviewing a particular author's newly published work, followed by truncated, short columned reviews, ending with a "Briefly Noted" section for Fiction, General Interest works, and the like. The first three mentions of Muriel Spark in the magazine follow exactly these in reverse, and the trajectory of increased attention reveals Spark's rise in estimation by the magazine. The second mention (for her first novel *The Comforters*) was in a longer column review. The third mention springboards her novels directly into the featured author's spot in a larger multipage spread. The article was entitled "The Burning Bush" and focused on her 1959 novel *Memento Mori*. The review is worth quoting significantly, for it glowingly praises and recognizes Spark's significantly talented voice:

> [Her] third novel, *Memento Mori* . . . [is] a dazzling performance . . . Mrs. Spark has got her fondness for the outlandish device firmly under control. Indeed, she uses it here, not for itself, but like the burning bush, to set up a superawareness. Her material demands a fearless approach, for it is nothing less than a celebration of death. Death, Mrs. Spark implies, is a god-devil and the basic paradox of human life. Without its benign propulsiveness, what would make us scurry and push and strive? We would have an eternity to go about our tasks, and consequently—barring a fundamental revision of human nature—do nothing at all. At the same time, death nibbles steadily away at us, which, of course, is what has kept the religions of the world in business. This is a hefty message, and Mrs. Spark offers it, lest it frighten us away, in the most palatable way. She coats it in comedy. The result is a funny and stirring piece of work. It is also flawless. (Balliett 127)

By the time this review was written (1959), the *New Yorker* had already contacted Spark about the prospect of publishing her fiction. Spark's "The Portobello Road" (1956) had caught the eye of fiction editor Rachel MacKenzie, who promptly wrote to Spark, encouraging her to submit to the magazine. "Dear Miss Spark," MacKenzie writes in 1957, "Some weeks ago [UK publisher] Hamish Hamilton spoke to us of his enthusiasm for 'The Portobello Road' and since then a number of us at *The New Yorker* have read it. We admire it, too, and wonder if you won't let us consider some of your stories for publication" (*New Yorker Records*: 28 March 1957).[1] The *New Yorker*'s publishing guidelines specifically exclude work published elsewhere, according to Rachel MacKenzie's return letter, dated 22 April 1957. Her response explains why "The Portobello Road," despite its glowing reception by the magazine, was not accepted for publication. The correspondence with Rachel MacKenzie and Muriel Spark during this formative year is quick and receptive for both parties, who pen responses immediately after receipt of the other's letter. By the end of April 1957, Spark sent the magazine the unpublished "Come Along, Marjorie." The story, however, was not accepted; the reasoning discussed by MacKenzie in the 29 May 1957 return letter has little to do with the story's aesthetics or efficacy and rather more to do with the magazine's glut of stories with the same subject matter.

By August of 1957, unhampered by a further rejection for her poem "Bluebell among the Sables," Spark sends "The Go-Away Bird." MacKenzie's response, even while it rejects the piece, is notable for its encouragement of material and the suggestion that Spark continue to submit, as she assured Spark "of [the magazine's] interest in whatever you write, whether we can use it or not. One day I feel sure that we shall" (*New Yorker Records*: 28 August 1957). Heady stuff from the magazine noted for the brevity of its rejections; according to *New Yorker* author, Brendan Gill, in 1997's *Here at the* New Yorker, the form rejection letter remained only two sentences long: "We regret that we are unable to use the enclosed material. Thank you for giving us the opportunity to consider it" (84).

The cultivation of Spark as a *New Yorker* writer by MacKenzie would have been especially encouraging to Spark in 1958, even with the rejection of "Bang-Bang You're Dead."

> I want to go on in a much louder voice to tell you that we all read the story with real interest—Mr Shawn, the editor-in-chief, included—and we all feel that it reflects originality and a talent with great promise for us. I was particularly impressed with the scenes between Sybil and the Westons. I hope you can be patient with us enough to continue sending in stories whenever you have a new one. . . . I continue to feel confident that you are a writer we shall publish with pride one of these days" (*New Yorker Records*: 3 July 1958).

"One of these days" came on 30 October 1959, with Spark's first accepted short fiction, "The Ormolu Clock." This first accepted piece debuted in the 17 September 1960 issue, and marked a significant shift in the relationship between Spark and the magazine, as they entered into discussions about proofs, editing, checks, and even advances. MacKenzie explains, "I go into this in detail because my hope is so strong that you will become a regular contributor" (*New Yorker Records*: 30 October 1959).

1960 continues as encouraging but ultimately rejection-filled year for Spark. The relationship with her editor at the magazine is at least positive and reciprocal. MacKenzie, understanding that a rejected author does not an enthusiastic submitter make, writes hopefully: "I'll get the sad chore of sending back 'The Father's Daughters' over [with] . . . so that 1961 won't have that blot on it. It goes back with my sorrow. . . . If I were you, I'd find it hard to be patient with us, and I've no doubt you do. One of my New Year's wishes is that you won't give us up. (I'm making just a few this year, and concentrating on them)" (*New Yorker Records*: 30 December 1960).

Whatever alchemy she imbued into those resolutions worked. 1961 marked a massive year for Muriel Spark and the *New Yorker*. Everything shifted into high gear by summer: in August Spark's agents sent the magazine *The Prime of Miss Jean Brodie*. The response was immediate and effusive. MacKenzie instantly telegrammed Spark's agents:

THE PRIME OF MISS JEAN BRODIE IS MARVELOUS AND WE WANT IT IF MRS SPARK WILL CONSIDER SOME MODEST CUTTING. WE WILL SEND GALLEYS FOR HER APPROVAL, OF COURSE. THE PAYMENT WILL BE SOMETHING OVER $6000. THERE IS A PROBLEM WITH TIME. WE DO NOT USE MATERIAL THAT HAS BEEN PUBLISHED AND WILL HAVE TO RUN THIS BEFORE ENGLISH PUBLICATION, WHICH YOU SAY IS OCTOBER. IS IT POSSIBLE TO POSTPONE THAT DATE TO NOVEMBER? IN ANY CASE, WILL YOU CABLE US COLLECT THE EXACT PUBLICATION DATE, ALONG WITH MRS. SPARK'S ANSWER? I LOVE THIS BOOK. RACHEL MACKENZIE (*New Yorker Records*: 31 August 1961)

Spark was delighted, and her agents in London entered into urgent negotiations to push back the British publication of *Brodie*, suggested for the end of October or early November at the latest (*New Yorker Records*: 1 September 1961).[2] Her novel was published in its entirety in the 14 October 1961 issue, commanding over half its 224 pages. Full publication of a single work in one issue had previously only been bestowed on John Hersey for the historical 1947 printing of *Hiroshima*, which was published in book form only after the attendant public reaction from the magazine's imprint. The international response to the magazine's editorial choice in publishing *Brodie* in this way is also swift. London's *Observer*, for instance, recognizes not only the success of the book, but also the significance of the publishing medium:

> This week's *New Yorker* contains to all intents and purposes the whole of Muriel Spark's new novel, "The Prime of Miss Jean Bridie" [sic]. It is a signal recognition of a rising reputation. The paper devoted a whole issue some years ago to John Hersey's *Hiroshima*. On two other occasions the greater part of two novellae by J.D. Salinger. But this is the first time it has done the same for a novel—by an Englishwoman [sic]. ("Cover to Cover" 9)

1961 was a banner year for Spark and the *New Yorker*. The magazine's current editor David Remnick, in the list of important *New Yorker* dates that attends *The Collected New Yorker*, devotes his description of what was published in 1961 entirely to Spark's work. "'The Prime of Miss Jean Brodie,' Muriel Spark's tale of an Edinburgh schoolmistress, is published in the October 14th issue. It becomes a book and then a hit play on Broadway and in London. An Oscar-winning film follows" ("A *New Yorker* Time Line" *11*).

1961 was not to be solely about one acceptance of one piece of fiction. In September 1961, in the wake of *Brodie*'s imminent publication, the magazine offered Spark a first-reading agreement. As MacKenzie explained to Spark in her 12 September 1961 letter, "We have [first-reading agreements] with a number of very good writers. . . . The value of a first-reading agreement to us is that it gives us the first look at a writer's work. The value to the writer is financial—a 25% premium on everything that is bought, and, in addition, a cost-of-living adjustment . . . running about 35%" (*New Yorker Records*). This annual contract allowed the *New Yorker* first refusal on all of Spark's "fiction, humor, reminiscence and casual essays" (*New Yorker Records*: 10 December 1963). As MacKenzie intimates, the agreement is an annual one, and the agreement is renewed every year through at least 1979.

The success of *Brodie* is well documented, but the international movements of Spark during this time are not. As her correspondence with the magazine indicates, on the heels of the momentous *Brodie* issue, her publishers organized a two-week promotional trip to New York beginning in January 1962.[3] She stayed in the infamous Algonquin Hotel, lunching with MacKenzie and editor-in-chief William Shawn and returning to London with another short fiction piece, "The Gentile

Jewesses," accepted by the magazine (*New Yorker Records*: 19–30 January 1962). After *Brodie*'s success, Spark made more frequent visits to New York, remaining for months at a time, even holding an office at the magazine for a short time in 1962 and 1964, and switching editors during her 1962 stay.[4] After her first two-week trip in early 1962, she stayed in New York for a few months every year from 1962 through 1967 before leaving, finally, for Italy in 1967.

The physical location of Muriel Spark in New York during this fecund period of literary development (1962–1967) is an area understudied in Spark criticism; her novels of the time are addressed in ways that do not take into account her geographical location. For example, critic Bryan Cheyette, even though he mentions the importance of geography within Spark's fiction, fails to examine the immediacy of Spark's own location: "But as soon as one compares her later and earlier works it becomes clear that *The Prime of Miss Jean Brodie*, along with *The Girls of Slender Means* (1963) and *The Mandelbaum Gate* (1965), have achieved a level of literary sophistication that does eclipse much of what has gone before. Unlike her previous books, Spark now takes absolutely seriously the question of locale and historical context" (52).

But to what extent did New York influence or succor Spark? As a locative influence on her fiction, there are several key examples where New York may be cited as referent. *The Mandelbaum Gate,* her first novel to be set outside of Britain, was written during Spark's New York tenure and subsequently serialized in the magazine, securing American publication later in 1965 by Knopf (Auden 244). The self-contained *Mandelbaum Gate* sections, submitted and published in the magazine, dovetail neatly with the *New Yorker*'s editorial design, suggesting, at least on the surface, that the novel had one metaphorical eye on her contractual obligations under the first-reading agreement as well as the magazine's penchant for editorial brevity.[5] Manhattan served very specifically as the purgatory-cum-Neverland setting of 1975's novel *The Hothouse by the East River*, her only work of fiction to do so. The crux of *Hothouse* takes the New York locale as an interrogation of both setting and death—for New York is the place and locus imagined by the novel's restless soul, Paul: "'After the war,' Paul is saying, 'Elsa and I are going to settle in America'" (123).

Spark gives readers tantalizing clues to what she means by locating the restless death-presence of Paul Hazlett in Manhattan. Manhattan becomes a figurative space, a type of teeming afterlife where death and life are entirely interchangeable; the dead do not realize they are dead, but more importantly, neither do the living: "New York, home of the vivisectors of the mind, and of the mentally vivisected still to be reassembled, of those who live intact, habitually wondering about their states of sanity, and home of those whose minds have been dead, bearing the scars of resurrection: New York heaves . . . agitating about her ears" (11). The living and the dead come together on the island, continually interacting with few blips in the status quo. This fictive play by Spark—life and death, reality and fantasy, real and imaginary—suggests that the space of New York, especially Manhattan, is utilized as the key setting for Spark's examination, written ten years after her stay there.

> Come back to Manhattan the mental clinic, cries his heart, where we analyze and dope the savageries of existence. Come back, it's very centrally heated here, there are shops on the ground floor, you can get anything here that you can get over there and better, money's no object. Why go back all that way where your soul has to fend for itself in secret while you conform with the others in the open? Come back to New York the sedative chamber where you don't think at all and you can act as crazy as you like and talk your head off all day, all night. (*Hothouse* 75–76)

Even in Italy the working relationship with the *New Yorker* does not wane, though Spark's visits do. Correspondence from editor Robert Henderson is professional but easy, with friendly reminders that New York misses her; Spark seems to genuinely consider at least another visit after 1967, but severe illness in that year stops her from returning. The magazine, however, continued to publish Spark's articles, fiction, or poetry from Italy nearly every year through 2003, with a mild hiatus in the mid-1970s.

Interestingly, the correspondence between Spark and the *New Yorker* reveals further connections above that of a published fiction writer and essayist; the magazine, after direct request from Spark, issues the author a press ticket in 1968, with editor William Shawn specifically enthusiastic about future articles benefitting from Spark's sharp eye and specific slant on Italian goings-on during the late sixties. The press ticket is issued, and while the suggested "Letter from Rome" never appears in the magazine, the press ticket allowed Spark ingress into certain out-of-the-way places that would normally be closed to her without such accreditation. While in Rome, she spent the remainder of the 1960s and 1970s writing prolifically, amongst a whirlwind social network of expatriates, artists, countesses, and cardinals. "And none of that social life will go to waste," writes William Weaver, "It'll all appear in her novels. In fact, I'm not sure I'd like to be one of those cardinals."[6] Spark arrived in Rome at the tail end of the Hollywood-on-the-Tiber era, made famous by Fellini's movie, *La Dolce Vita*. "I went because I thought it was exciting," she says.

"There were *very* amusing people, mostly expatriates and Italians, sometimes nobility. They're very amusing to watch and to write about and to be with. Rome was really the height of my social life" (qtd. in Schiff 37). Perhaps the effect of the press-ticket and the effect of Spark's social life on her novels cannot be quantified, but that the magazine was responsible for this ease of movement attests to its importance for understanding Spark's life and career.

Contextualizing Spark's Oeuvre via the Correspondence

The *New Yorker* correspondence between Muriel Spark and her editors at the magazine, while giving firsthand insight into day-to-day editorial practice and encouragement of Spark's early writing career, remains revelatory for the most prolific of Spark's writing years, showing that the magazine had a much larger impact on Spark than previously understood. This opens up new contexts for studying Spark and encourages a fuller articulation of her movements in New York and Italy. The correspondence, especially regarding *Brodie*'s publication, also sheds light on the process by which her writing is disseminated through international publication.

The first point of understanding must remain: the *New Yorker* courted her. Spark did not actively pursue publication in the magazine like so many writers of the era. By the late 1950s, the magazine (through Rachel MacKenzie) recognized in Spark a singular talent, enough to not only want to cultivate her as a contributor, but to actively do so. Critic Philip Weiss suggests that while the magazine perhaps "did great things for Spark . . . it also required of her an apprenticeship she didn't really need, and then when it had created her reputation, published mostly minor work" (Weiss). However, the editorial suggestions for Spark's early work must have been heartening to her, even when specific works were rejected. MacKenzie and Henderson (and much later, Charles "Chip" McGrath and, to a lesser extent, the magazine's poetry editor, Howard Moss) recognized Spark's voice, balance, and eviscerating wit, and their correspondence shows that they did not expect to change it or urge Spark do anything to make a piece "fit"—the universal exhortation was to request, always, that Spark continue to submit work.

Secondly, the magazine was the very first venue in which *The Prime of Miss Jean Brodie* was published, and while the consequences of this site for publication bear further study, it is safe to say that *Brodie* launched Spark's career and that the magazine was at least partially responsible for enhancing her international reputation through the publication of the work. Although Spark did have publication secured through a British publisher, the frenzy of telegrams and transatlantic cables regarding *Brodie* in the archive highlights that the prospect of having Spark's work published, in advance, in the *New Yorker* was sufficient incentive for the publisher to delay releasing the novel, despite marketing budgets and holiday sale plans. Would the book have done as well if the *New Yorker* had not published it? The immediate compliance by Spark's publisher to the magazine's schedule remains a testament to the *New Yorker*'s international clout.

The publication of *Brodie* (or, more specifically, the payment received for publication) meant that a number of practical difficulties were mitigated for Spark: the continued acceptance of works, specifically the post-*Brodie* pieces like "The Gentile Jewesses," in addition to the sweetener of the first-reading premium paid by the magazine, meant that for Spark, a writer making a living through writing, choices of work would become easier, as the payments received via the *New Yorker* allowed her to quit reviewing books.

Thirdly, the success of *Brodie* generated the first-reading agreement with Spark and the *New Yorker* that lasted well into the late 1970s. Contractually, Spark was bound to the magazine, which then had first-refusal on all her fiction and casual essays; this arrangement was approved by Spark every year for nearly twenty years. Whether the agreement suggests the reason for Spark's preference for the short fiction form, again, perhaps cannot be determined, yet the reasons most often cited by the editors for their rejection of a piece by Spark had to do more with space than with content—increasingly so in the 1970s. But by the same token, Spark submitted work that was obviously unacceptable because of length, sent merely to fulfill the contractual obligation: for example, the 1971 submission of novel *Not to Disturb* (*New Yorker Records*: 30 May 1971 and 14 June 1971). While the short form was preferred by the magazine, Spark did not suffer the magazine's parameters to influence her unduly.

Finally, all the fiction and essays run in the *New Yorker* were the first publications of those works. Below I provide tables listing the works published in the magazine; these tables suggest that, taken as a whole, a significant portion of Spark's oeuvre debuted in the *New Yorker*, revealing the magazine's sustained belief in Spark's talent, and highlighting the *New Yorker* as a considerably impressive repository for Spark material.

The *New Yorker* also shaped Spark's international reception and illuminated her emergence as a Scottish writer working in a global context. (As Barnaby and Hubbard point out, the 1960s saw the publications of the first foreign editions of Spark's work.) Much of the criticism about Spark focuses on her conversion to Catholicism;

specifically within the Scottish academic setting, Spark criticism seems to focus on her Scottish novels such as *The Prime of Miss Jean Brodie* or how her work exemplifies particularly Scottish attributes. Douglas Gifford exhorts that "[s]he has received extensive critical treatment, but perhaps not enough examination of the way her fiction implies a serious criticism of Scottish insularity and psychological complexity, in the frequent Scottish characters and characteristics of her novels. Even when set well beyond Scotland, her fiction shows a Scottish preoccupation with the grotesque and surreal" (861). However, Spark's act of self-exile from Scotland begs the question: how does her achievement of international acclaim through the *New Yorker* publications relate to her reception within the Scottish literary canon? Speaking with Frank Kermode in 1963, she admitted, "It was Edinburgh that bred within me the conditions of exiledom; and what have I been doing since then but moving from exile to exile? It has ceased to be a fate, it has become a calling" (63). If her calling brought her far away from Scotland itself, of what significance is her cosmopolitanism, her citizenship of the world? Her decades-long relationship with the very cosmopolitan *New Yorker* specifically refutes a potential insularity. *Pace* Gifford, can students and critics of Spark understand her status within the canon of Scottish authors if her international reputation is minimized in favor of other, more properly "Scottish" subjects? Simply put, Spark's sustained relationship with the magazine suggests ways of reconceiving the Scottish canon itself by revealing a body of material that directly speaks to a burgeoning Scottish cosmopolitanism.

Spark's Later Connection with and Contributions to the *New Yorker*

As the following tables indicate, during the period in which she made contributions to the *New Yorker*, beginning in 1960 with "The Ormolu Clock" and ending in 2003 with her poem "That Bad Cold," Spark published 14 poems, 12 of her 41 short stories, the better part of three novels, and significant portions of her autobiography in the magazine.[7]

Eagle-eyed Sparkophiles will of course notice not only what is in the *New Yorker*, but also what is not; for example, some of her best short stories—"The Portobello Road," "The Seraph and the Zambesi," and "The Go-Away Bird" notably—are not published in the magazine. Yet the rejections that Spark received were more typically refusals-with-encouragement, based on practical considerations such as space coupled with the editor's understanding of Spark's vision for a given work. Henderson's correspondence from 1963 is exemplary:

Table I Muriel Spark: Fiction published in the *New Yorker*

Title	Issue
"The Ormolu Clock"	17 September 1960
The Prime of Miss Jean Brodie	14 October 1961
"The Gentile Jewesses"	22 June 1963
The Mandelbaum Gate ("Freddy's Walk")	15 May 1965
The Mandelbaum Gate ("Barbara Vaughn's Identity")	10 July 1965
The Mandelbaum Gate ("A Delightful English Atmosphere")	24 July 1965
The Mandelbaum Gate ("Abdul's Orange Groves")	7 August 1965
"The House of the Famous Poet"	2 April 1966
"Exotic Departures"	28 January 1967
"Alice Long's Dachshunds"	1 April 1967
The Driver's Seat	16 May 1970
"The First Year of My Life"	2 June 1975
"The Fortune Teller"	17 January 1983
"The Executor"	14 March 1983
"Another Pair of Hands"	15 May 1985
"The Dragon"	12 August 1985
"The Hanging Judge"	2 May 1994
"A Hundred and Eleven Years Without a Chauffeur"	5 June 2000

I have bad news for you, which in a sense is not bad news at all. The reason we have decided against taking the section of the MANDELBAUM GATE is that it is too inseparable from the book. The book is, obviously, going to be wonderful, and we are already full of curiosity about what will happen next—which, as a couple of editors pointed out, is exactly right for a novel and wrong for this section as a separate story. Please let us see the rest of the sections as they come along. The fact that this one didn't work out is no sign whatever that the next one won't. (*New Yorker Records*: 20 May 1963)

A letter from 1972 reveals a similar rationale:

Table 2 Muriel Spark: Poetry published in the *New Yorker*

Title	Issue
"On the Lack of Sleep"	7 December 1963
"The Card Party"*	28 December 1963
"Canaan"*	16 April 1966
"The She Wolf"	4 February 1967
"Edinburgh Villanelle"*	26 August 1967
"The Messengers"*	16 September 1967
"Created and Abandoned"*	12 November 1979
"Conversation Piece"*	23 November 1981
"That Lonely Shoe Lying on the Road"*	20 September 1993
"The Dark Music of the Rue Du Cherche-Midi"*	21 February 1994
"Mungo Bays the Moon"*	25 November 1996
"The Empty Space"*	4 February 2002
"Holidays"*	16 December 2002
"That Bad Cold"*	10 March 2003

*Asterisks indicate which poems were published first in the *New Yorker* (see also Spark's *All the Poems*).

Table 3 Muriel Spark: Other articles published in the *New Yorker*

Title	Issue
"The Brontës as Teachers"	22 January 1966
"Bread, Butter, and Florrie Ford"	11 September 1989
"The School on the Links"	25 March 1991
"Visiting the Laureate"	26 August 1991
"Venture into Africa"	2 March 1992
"My Watch, a True Story (The Secret Life of Jewelry)"	2 June 1997
"My Madeleine"	25 December 2000

Your HOTHOUSE has gone back to [your agent], to the general regret, here. I found it fascinating—in your best vein, or in one of your best veins, certainly. The trouble is the old business of space—we can't give fiction that much, nowadays—and I'm awfully sorry. I'm sure the book will be a great success when it appears. Meanwhile, please send us more. And if they're book-length, and we still resist such things, at least several of us will have a rewarding time. (*New Yorker Records*: 16 June 1972)

And Henderson voices similar sentiments in 1975:

The problem is a familiar one—length—and the fact that, astigmatic as we may be, we couldn't find excerpts that would stand by themselves as single stories. This, of course, is a compliment to the beautifully knit organization of [*The Takeover*]. I admired the story, which, with your work, goes without saying, whatever the editorial limitations here may be—and for those I'm very sorry. Thank you, and we always hope for something more from you. (*New Yorker Records*: 19 November 1975)

As Henderson's correspondence reveals, of the ultimately rejected works sent to the *New Yorker*, the most common explanation was lack of room in the magazine. This perhaps might be diplomatic hypocrisy given the amount of space granted to *Brodie*, but the editors certainly encouraged more work even in their refusals, and the results of Spark's submissions over the years reveal that a significant percentage of her submitted work continued to be accepted by the magazine.

Given Spark's physical presence in New York and her continued relationship with the magazine during the decades it continued to publish her fiction and poetry, of increased critical importance are the later *New Yorker* articles and reviews about Spark that cultivated and sustained her international success. When read together with the correspondence material in the *New Yorker* archives, this work provides a fuller picture of Spark's international milieu. In keeping with my earlier remarks about Spark's cosmopolitanism, drawing new attention to the later articles in the *New Yorker* helps illuminate how Scottish writers like Spark were articulated within an international sphere. Barnaby and Hubbard, discussing the international reception of Scottish writing in the postwar period, specifically highlight Spark's reception: "Her work has appeared in twenty-nine languages and has enjoyed uninterrupted commercial and international success. . . . None of her contemporaries achieved a comparable international profile" (33). The "uninterruptedness" of Spark's international success is neatly echoed by the sustained continuation of *New Yorker* publication.

The *New Yorker* itself also remains an unparalleled fixture in Spark criticism as the repository for a number of articles by and about Spark that are uncollected elsewhere. Articles such as "My Watch, a True Story (the Secret Life of Jewelry)" (2 June 1997 issue) and "My Madeleine" (25 December 2000 issue) reveal tantalizing, post–*Curriculum Vitae* glimpses of a writer connected intimately with specific objects and situations that bear importantly on her own writing process.

"My Watch, a True Story (The Secret Life of Jewelry)," written in 1997, begins with Sparkian narrative irony. As a writer of fictions whose knowledge transgresses temporal boundaries, she utters, incredibly, "I will never know the full story." The titular watch was a secondhand purchase of self-approbation and self-congratulation on Spark's part; *Memento Mori* had just been published, and she "had determined that every time [she] had published a book [she] would buy [her]self a jewel to mark the occasion, for otherwise the money would disappear into the house-keeping funds." In this glimpse of home life (Muriel Spark, house-keeping?) she has readers caught; a slight mystery of movement, a hint of secrecy is all that Spark readers need to be ensnared into her continuing narrative. Like many of her fictional characters, here, in this treatment of a simple watch, even Spark's immediate life bears hints of the ineffability of fate, perhaps a "nasty trick" on which so many of her characters slip (48).

The article itself is relatively short compared with the 120 plus pages that *The Prime of Miss Jean Brodie* occupied in 1961. True to the title, Spark presents a simple piece of jewelry of unknown origins, but the secret life of her secondhand Cartier watch is captivating. Spark narrates her efforts to determine the loss: "Without seeing it, Cartier themselves were cautious, but opined a sum that I thought head spinning. . . . We thought of our jeweller, distraught, not a very rich man, not really. Not up to the Cartier level. And not young. I hoped he had eaten something" (49). Here Spark deploys the sly wit exhibited by her fictional narrators to characterize circumstances in her own life, revealing the interconnection between the author's narrative techniques and her deeper vision of the world.

Spark's oblique engagement with such small details of her life adds to the existing stock of biographical knowledge, but also suggests ways in which the biography of the author is relevant to the artist's oeuvre. Significantly in Spark's case, the placement of her attentions, the continuation of themes also present in her novels, and, especially, her engagement within internationality and cosmopolitanism via her autobiographical accounts, creates a multivalent context by which her narratives might be more fully understood—a type of meta-annotation that provides additional context for understanding her key fictional tropes and themes. As Margaret Elphinstone discusses, details of this kind were "always received with great interest because her work was so widely known, but also because Spark had always cultivated an extremely private life." Autobiographically based articles such as the ones collected in the *New Yorker* round out the information provided in *Curriculum Vitae*, while also drawing attention to how any account of a life is motivated by overarching narrational goals. If such articles highlight, as Elphinstone suggests, "the tension between authoritative narrator assembling evidence of the past in the present moment of writing and the present self linked intimately and subjectively to her past self through memory," then surely Spark's articles here remain significant in revelation, for the narrator is Spark herself, and the evidence she grants readers is her own experience (207). Spark's later writings for the *New Yorker* reveal that such tensions occur not only in her fiction and short stories, but also in accounts of her own actions. She treats both her fictional characters' and her own experiences with wit, attention, and, especially, an exploratory spirit.

December 2000's "My Madeleine" again presents a compelling picture of Spark's writing process, taking inspiration from, as she puts it, the equivalent of Proust's madeleine, that small fine indulgence that unlocks the memory. "My madeleine," she confesses, "is an empty notebook. . . . As soon as I see one (and I acquire many and many), I desire to fill it in. Whenever I am stuck for a subject or something to write I go to my stock of notebooks and select a new one" (105). This talisman of inspiration leads her, in 1951, to write her first award-winning short story, then called "The Seraph, the Zambesi, and the Fanfarlo," for the London *Observer*'s short story contest.

> I went out and bought a new notebook and then sat looking at the empty pages. My lovely school notebook, all ready to be written in, filled my mind. I started writing a story on my favourite subjects, which at the time were angelology (the fascinating study of the orders of angels), and the French poet Baudelaire. To make the story unusual, I placed it in Africa, on the River Zambesi, where I had lived for some years. (105)

The article explores what happened on the day Spark wrote her 1951 story and reminds readers about the tenuous beginnings of a writing career. More generally, autobiographical articles such as these insert Spark's work into frameworks for inquiry informed by an increased attention to (auto)biographical details and their bearing on the imagi-

native, as well as practical, activities of writers. Kate Douglas references Phillippe Lejuene's discussion of the "Autobiographical Pact"
when she asserts that autobiography in this fashion "transgresses
other genres . . . and [makes] the textual assertion that the author,
narrator, and protagonist are the same. In making this self-reference,
the author enters into an agreement with readers that they will be
reading about an actual person . . . [whose] disclosures, interpretations, and records of experiences are thought to provide capital for
readers to decipher their own life experiences" (807).

Spark's one-page article from 2000 appears in a year-end issue of the *New Yorker*, titled "The Fiction Issue," which features
contributions from such literary luminaries as John le Carre, Julian
Barnes, George Saunders, and Annie Proulx on the general topic of
influence. In these collected essays, prominent fiction writers openly
discuss what influences them, their writing, or their writing process.
By focusing on her own experiences in this way, Spark situates herself and her writing within new contexts for interpretation, not only
revealing her working methods but also constructing a distinct kind
of authorial persona.

Spark also comments on personal experiences directly related
to the writing process in interview material published in the magazine. Considering her continuous, long-standing relationship with the
magazine by 1993, it is perhaps not surprising that she converses
quite candidly with staff writer Stephen Schiff in his aptly titled article, "Muriel Spark Between the Lines." At one point, Schiff notes
that "Muriel Spark has written some of the best sentences in English.
For instance: 'He looked as if he would murder me and he did.' It's
a nasty piece of work, that sentence".

Taken together with *Curriculum Vitae*, as well as shorter pieces
such as "My Madeleine," Schiff's article reveals aspects of the writing
process, affording small trajectories into Spark's world that nonetheless give views into the author's habits, techniques, and dominant
concerns. As Schiff puts it, "[i]n a sense, everything about Muriel
Spark has to be read in between the lines. Nothing about her is
straightforward. Her demeanor is at once mandarin and schoolgirl-
ish, her accent half Edinburgh and half Queen's English, and her
conversation veers between space cadet fuzz to a satirical precision
that makes one grateful not to be its target" (36). Spark tells Schiff
about her parting of ways with Derek Stanford, revealing the costs
and consequences of her success as a writer:

> Some of my friends were absolutely wonderful, but some
> were just so jealous and nasty and wrote books and ar-
> ticles about me, and ringing me up with all sorts of barbed,
> double-tongued things, and intrigues. I had a terrible time.

You know, people would ring up to say, "Can you come out tonight?" And I'd say, "No, I'm writing." And they'd say, "Oh, yes, you're too grand now." And I'd say, "Yes, I've always been too grand—now go away." (qtd. in Schiff 37)

The article also contains an elusive glimpse into Spark's time at the *New Yorker* ("Instead [of remaining in England], in 1962 she decamped to New York and moved in the literary circles that emanated from this magazine" [37]) and very quickly moves on to her emigration to Italy. Thus Schiff's interview picks up where *Curriculum Vitae* leaves off—with the publication of Spark's novel and her cure from depression and breakdown. The author speaks about her own experiences in Italy, refuting a number of rumors and misconceptions about her life and filling in events that occurred later than her autobiography's time-frame (38–39).

Perhaps most important about the Schiff piece is its focus on Spark's writing process; in the last four pages, Spark explains a number of catalysts for creation, vividly and specifically:

> "I don't correct or rewrite," she says, "because I do all the correcting before I begin, getting it in my mind. And then when I pounce, I pounce. I can invent very easily. It really seems to come through my hand." She waggles her arm in the air, as if it were being buffeted by winds, then lunges into a pile of papers on her desk. "Everything's a great mess here. I never have tidiness," she says, in a tone more disapproving of tidiness than herself. She scoops up a pack of index cards. "These are notes," she says, "Something occurs to me or I see an incident or I hear a phrase. I make a note of that. Then I've got a bundle of notes before I begin my work, and I can go through them and read them, and it really starts me off on something. After that, the experiences simply come. One becomes a magnet for the experiences one is looking for. . . . But there comes the minute when I don't write any more notes. When I start to write, all I have are my character lists." Character lists? "Oh yes," she says. "I need a sheet for every character: what they say, what they wear, who knows what, who knows whom, and what they do—all cross-referenced. I have a page for everything that wriggles—human beings, dogs, ice cream. Then I can fit it all together. (42)

Like the fleshing out of one of her more iconic creations, such formative (auto)biographical material in the *New Yorker* articles might itself be thought of as a kind of character sheet for understanding the author-character Spark.

Future Directions for Spark Criticism

For students of Spark's work, the *New Yorker* is the repository of a vast number of reviews, interviews, and primary material. As a sustained engagement with the connections between Muriel Spark and the *New Yorker* shows, here was a magazine that recognized her talent very early on in 1957 and cultivated a relationship with Dame Muriel in order to broadcast Spark's vision throughout that career. As new contexts for Scottish literature and for Spark are refashioned, the magazine will continue to inform Spark studies after her death. Her autobiographical turn in the 1990s has not engendered as much critical reception as her fiction and poetry, but her biographical context has opened up productive avenues for research (for example, Spark in a Catholic context, or in the Scottish national and cultural context). Likewise, as critical awareness of Spark's creative trajectory, publishing history, and literary significance grows, the history of her long engagement with the *New Yorker* can only assume an ever more important place in understanding Dame Muriel Spark's contributions, not just to Scottish literature but to world culture.

Notes

This research was supported by a Research Grant from the Carnegie Trust for the Universities of Scotland.

1. These records include unpublished correspondence with Muriel Spark from *New Yorker* editors Rachel MacKenzie and Robert Henderson, with additional magazine and agent contract material, quoted here with kind permission of Condé Nast Publications.

2. A letter from one of her agents remains very professional throughout, but the general excitement about developments at the *New Yorker* comes out in a handwritten postscript: "How many instalments—or all in one go?!"

3. Writes MacKenzie: "It is Spark Week here, and we're in a celebrating mood" (*New Yorker Records*: 10 October 1961). She says directly to Spark:

    > I wish I could send you a tape of the reaction I've had to that story, because there is such an excited pleasure in the voice saying how they love it. What particularly pleases me is that it comes from people with a wide range of tastes. This shouldn't surprise, of course, and it doesn't really; when a piece has the excellence Miss Brodie has, almost everyone does recognize it and respond. (*New Yorker Records*: 18 October 1961)

4. The correspondence unfortunately does not explain the break with MacKenzie or why fellow fiction editor Robert Henderson replaced her, but the editorial relationship with Henderson lasted through the late 1970s. In general, Henderson's demeanor seemed, based on my perusal of the Spark/Henderson correspondence, to remain slightly more formal, focusing more on the works themselves. Philip Weiss suggests "that the relationship with MacKenzie was much too emotional for cool Muriel. For instance, when she heard of Spark's father's death, MacKenzie telegrammed her, "MURIEL DARLING. . . ." (Weiss).

5. The first section of *The Mandelbaum Gate*, "Freddy's Walk," was accepted for publication in October 1962; further sections were submitted through 1963–1965, with publication of the four accepted sections occurring in May–July 1965.

6. In addition to publishing works emanating from Spark's time in Italy, the magazine's 1993 "Muriel Spark: Between the Lines" discussion with Spark remains a rare first-person account of her time in Rome and Tuscany, exploring the effect of the social life she enjoyed during these years.

7. The information contained in these tables was compiled via the "search" function in *The Complete New Yorker* DVD-ROM set.

Works Cited

Auden, W. H. "Books." *New Yorker* 23 Oct. 1965: 226–48.

Balliett, Whitney. "Books." *New Yorker* 13 June 1959: 126–32.

Barnaby, Paul, and Tom Hubbard. "The International Reception and Literary Impact of Scottish Literature of the Period since 1918." *The Edinburgh History of Scottish Literature:* Vol. 3. *Modern Transformations: New Identities (from 1918)*. Ed. Ian Brown et al. Edinburgh: Edinburgh UP, 2007. 31–41.

Cheyette, Bryan. "Transfiguration: Edinburgh, London, Jerusalem." *Muriel Spark.* Tavistocke, UK: Northcote, 2000. 52–70.

The Complete New Yorker. DVD-ROM. New York: Random, 2005.

"Cover to Cover." *Observer.* 15 October 1961. 9.

Douglas, Kate. "'Blurbing' Biographical: Authorship and Authority." *Biography* 24 (2001): 806–26.

Elphinstone, Margaret. "The Human and Textual Condition: Muriel Spark's Narratives." *Edinburgh History of Scottish Literature:* Vol. 3. *Modern Transformations: New Identities (from 1918)*. Ed. Ian Brown, et al. Edinburgh: Edinburgh UP, 2007. 207–13.

Gifford, Douglas, et al. "Scottish Fiction Since 1945: I. Continuity, Despair and Change." *Scottish Literature: in English and Scots*. Edinburgh: Edinburgh UP, 2002. 834–98.

Gill, Brendan. *Here at the* New Yorker. New York: Da Capo, 1997.

Kermode, Frank. "The House of Fiction: Interviews with Seven English Novelists." *Partisan Review* 30 (1963): 61–82.

New Yorker Records. III. Editorial Correspondence, 3.3: Fiction Correspondence, 1952–1980. Astor, Lenox, and Tilden Foundations. The New York Public Library Manuscripts and Archives Division, New York.

Plath, Sylvia. *Letters Home: Correspondence 1950–1963*. Ed. Aurelia Schober Plath. London: Faber, 1999.

Remnick, David. "Introduction." *Highlights from* The Complete New Yorker. New York: New Yorker, 2005. 6–8.

———. "A *New Yorker* Time Line 1925–2005." *Highlights from* The Complete New Yorker. New York: New Yorker, 2005: 8–13.

Schiff, Stephen. "Muriel Spark Between the Lines." *New Yorker* 24 May 1993: 36–43.

Spark, Muriel. *All The Poems*. Manchester: Carcanet, 2004.

———. *Curriculum Vitae*. London: Penguin, 1992.

———. *The Hothouse by the East River*. London: Granada, 1982.

———. "My Madeleine." *New Yorker* 25 December 2000 and 1 January 2001: 105.

———. "My Watch, a True Story (The Secret Life of Jewelry)." *New Yorker* 2 June 1997: 48–49.

Weiss, Philip. "How *The New Yorker* Made Muriel Spark's Reputation." 17 April 2006. 17 December 2007. <http://www.philipweiss.org/mondoweiss/2006/04/ how_the_new_yor.html>.

Wilson, Edmund. "Books." *New Yorker* 3 April 1954: 119–36.

Yagoda, Ben. *About Town: The* New Yorker *and the World It Made*. London: Duckworth, 2000.

PART II SITUATING SPARK IN
POSTWAR CULTURE

CHAPTER 3

MURIEL SPARK AND THE

METAPHYSICS OF MODERNITY:

ART, SECULARIZATION, AND

PSYCHOSIS

Patricia Waugh

"How She Trails Her Faithful and Lithe Cloud of Unknowing": Keeping Spark's Metaphysics Warm

On 13 April 2006, Muriel Spark trailed her faithful and lithe cloud of unknowing out of this world.[1] Even in life though, she seemed always to be just out of reach, like the enigmatic smile of an ever-vanishing Cheshire cat. Now no more than the words that are her characters, she continues to disturb and still to haunt and taunt the contemporary world of letters: casting a shadow that never seems quite to fall in expected places, that won't fit tidily into convenient typologies and academic categories, and that seems to mock each and every exertion of critical containment. Indeed, part of her pedagogic intent was to show how the reading and writing of fiction might provide important lessons in how best to resist reduction and containment: how, in short, to read for plots. But the broader perspective taken here is that she is a writer who not only addresses incisively and re-vealingly the *material* conditions of late modernity but also lays bare its *metaphysical* roots and fundamental assumptions. She addresses not only our social roles and performances but also the very condi-tions of our *ipseity*: the ontological underpinning of our fundamental sense and experience of selfhood and being as well as their historical modes of expression. In doing so, she lays bare, uncannily, a sense of the way in which our contemporary metaphysics of materialism underpins not only a loss of embeddedness in the world but also an emptying out of the feeling of presence and self-presence. Her metafictional explorations of the relations between art and delusion, creativity and psychosis, also open up deeper questions about the existential and ontological sources of our world-making activities. For in this most economical of writers, the metaphysical matters, but matter is also metaphysical: her social imaginary is sharpened and pixellated through the economy of her ontologically disturbing metaphysical wit.

Recent criticism has focused on theorizing, historicizing, or claiming Muriel Spark for various identity politics or ethnic, national, religious, and cultural groupings. The critical project of opening up Spark's work to more diverse cultural and critical perspectives is an important one: criticism is not an activity of worshipping at a shrine or curating a museum of antiquities. However, there is always a danger in any critical approach, including those that are broadly "cultural materialist," of displacing or marginalizing what fails to fit the confirmatory bias of the perspective adopted. Art is itself, for Spark, a crucial vehicle for the correction of confirmatory bias, or the tendency not to let one's preconceptions be dislodged or modified, even in the face of contravening evidence. Her novels, protective of her "cloud of unknowing," are instructive in how we should read the *world*, as well as the book, with a critical but open intelligence that resists the consolations of premature closure. This *intelligence* (a crucial word for Spark) might also include the recognition that it is not necessary to kill off the "Catholic" Spark in order to liberate the postmodern or post-postmodern varieties and that, without some grasp of the intellectual sources of her Catholic belief, key aspects of her critique of the metaphysics of modernity may remain clouded by a different kind of unknowing.

I suggest that if we think of Spark not so much as a Catholic writer (for she herself found this conjugation problematic), but as a writer who chronicles and interrogates the historical process of *secularization*, then we may see more readily that there is not a stark and exclusive choice to be made between her metaphysical and her social and historical engagements. The Thomist tradition of thought that attracted Spark looks back to a pre-Reformation, pre-secularizing moment before the dualisms of modernity, the separation of mind and body, of reason and affect. The most that Spark has ever claimed for her Catholicism in direct relation to her writing is that it gave her a norm from which she was able to depart: a norm far removed from and therefore capable of disturbing those more invisible norms of the modern worldview. In this essay I will argue, more specifically, that her faith gave her an alternative perspective on the relations between reason and feeling, body and mind, that are at the heart of Western dualisms and the histories of Western secularization. But as a writer, it is most of all through language and form and narrative expectation that Spark disturbs norms. In the very opening line of *The Hothouse by the East River* (1975), the novel whose last words began this essay, a shoe salesman remarks to Elsa that the shoes "fit like a glove" (5). The dead because habitual and assimilated simile of "fitting like a glove" is re-fitted as something that fits only absurdly when applied to a foot and the fit of a shoe. In drawing attention to its own language, the text draws attention to the way in which the universe also slides into ready-made and habitual forms of thought. In disturbing those patterns, Spark helps us see the world anew; and if we see the things of world anew, then, as Viktor Shklovsky so famously remarked, we might *feel* again their *thinginess*. Stepping into Muriel Spark's shoes is like pulling gloves onto our feet: in her novels, clothing *never* quite fits the human body.

To understand any writer involves engaging with and under-standing the traditions, influences, and contexts of thought that have helped to shape her; we must try to see the relation of her fictional worlds to the world outside the fictional frame and become aware in the process of how our own assumptions are also grounded in a worldview. With a writer such as Muriel Spark, who is undeniably an intellectual, but whose learning and intellectual engagement are honed and distilled and wrought into a style spare in allusion, lean and poetically concise, this hermeneutic challenge is always going to be difficult. The specific historical and intellectual sources of Spark's metaphysical beliefs are hardly laid bare either in the interviews or in the biographical *Curriculum Vitae* (1992); instead, they lie deep in the novels. But what *is* very evident throughout her writing is that it is still possible in the late twentieth and early twenty-first centu-ries for a writer to address ontological questions without sacrificing or relegating the social and historical; to be a playful and inclusive ironist as well as a politically engaged commentator. This is probably harder for us to appreciate in a century whose thought has been dominated by varieties of the antimetaphysical: first, positivism and, more recently, the return of an expansionist style of naturalism. Yet, the latter, in its determination to reduce the physical world and *all* human experience to scientific *causal* explanation, might actually be regarded as a revived *metaphysics of materialism*, giving new and expanded explanatory power to the stark mechanistic philosophies of the seventeenth century. It is this mechanistic and, so to speak, metaphysically materialist worldview that Spark critiques through her complex modes of narrative irony.

"Not Really a Presence . . . The Lack of an Absence, That's What It Is": Being Present and Feeling Absent in *The Driver's Seat* (1970) and *The Hothouse by the East River* (1973)

Increasingly in her novels, and perhaps most emphatically in her novels of the late 1960s and early 1970s, Muriel Spark brought into being a fictional universe built on a *reductio ad absurdum* of mechanistic or radically materialist principles, a universe resting on a kind of sociobiological and Hobbesian epistemology that reduces the human to an elaborate kind of machine open to purely causal explanation.[2] Her exact contemporary, Iris Murdoch, claimed that human beings are creatures who create pictures of themselves and then, often unknowingly, climb into the picture. Murdoch and Spark, along with some of their contemporaries, such as J. G. Ballard, Ann Quinn, Doris Lessing, Alain Robbe-Grillet, Christine Brooke-Rose, and Nathalie Sarraute, were writers who tried to retrieve and stand outside of the frame of the picture. The work of these writers uses the characteristic modes of modernity, and in particular its mechanistic disengagement from the world, to estrange or disengage from that very disengagement. This method allows for the laying bare of a metaphysical infrastructure that is normally so taken-for-granted that it (and its effects) remains largely unnoticed and unobserved. The reader's experience of the world that is built through the frame of such fictional methods is a disturbing and uncanny one: familiar and yet displaced; almost realist, but not quite; seemingly postmodern, but not. Something central seems missing, something whose recovery might constitute, as Lise puts it in *The Driver's Seat*, "Not really a presence . . . The lack of an absence, that's what it is" (71).

Ipseity, the feeling of self-presence, of being a subjective center, comfortably held in and part of the world, is so assumed that it goes unnoticed unless or until it is no longer there. What is missing for Lise—and for Spark in the metaphysical underpinnings of modernity—is this comfortable sense of self-presence, of being held in and part of a world. Lise is there but without being present, and the world is there but has no presence. Such a world takes on the strange and disturbing sense of what psychiatrists sometimes refer to as the *Stimmung*, the feeling or mood of eeriness experienced by psychotic and, in particular, schizophrenic sufferers. Although there is no direct evidence available (as far as I know) that Spark read Marguerite Sechehaye's *Autobiography of a Schizophrenic Girl*, it was first published in the 1950s and was then reissued in a new edition in 1968, when Spark began to produce her three most distinctively spare novels, *The Driver's Seat*, *The Hothouse by the East River*, and

Not to Disturb—novels that seem curiously and uncannily close to the mood or *Stimmung* described by psychotic patients, particularly vividly in Sechehaye's autobiography. This account of schizophrenia as experienced from the inside made more of an impact on the *Autobiography*'s reissue in 1968, because of the existence, by the 1960s, of a more phenomenologically oriented (if small) psychiatric movement interested in mental illness from a broadly existentialist perspective influenced by R. D. Laing's *The Divided Self* (1960). The book was one of the first and fullest accounts, from a first person point of view, of the history and experience of schizophrenia. Whether or not Spark had read this text, its account of psychosis is a helpful starting point in trying to approach Spark's techniques of characterization in relation to her broader intellectual aims. Her novels, in various ways, circle peculiarly around absence, an awareness of a lack of fullness, an orientation toward a beyond. This experience of absence is also the most compelling aspect of *Autobiography of a Schizophrenic Girl*. Renee, the subject of the autobiography, describes the prodromal phase of her schizophrenic breakdown which begins in early adolescence with an arrested moment, accompanied by a "disturbing sense of unreality," where she passes the school and hears the familiar sound of children singing not in her own language, French, but rather in German. As she listens to the voices, the buildings suddenly become unrecognizable, and the children singing in the playground are illuminated, as if prisoners trapped in a barracks, locked in smooth stone, locked away from the world as if in another reality, while the world resolves into a dazzling vastness, lit by a yellow sun. The aura that accompanies this vision, she writes, "was the first appearance of those elements which were always present in later sensations of unreality: illimitable vastness, brilliant light, and the gloss and smoothness of material things" (Secherhaye 19). Renee feels as though she has *lost touch* with the real.

A consumer in a materialist world of gloss and smoothness and plate glass windows, a multilingual traveller through the spaces of high modernist design—international airports, apartments, shopping malls, and hotels—Lise in *The Driver's Seat* likewise constantly checks that she has not *lost touch*. Compulsively and obsessively, she handles and touches her parcels and packages and purchases, as if to reassure herself that she exists. As she prepares to move on to another location on her dark and deathly sentimental journey, she ritualistically places each item in her suitcase, handbag, zipper bag, and then one by one removes, checks, and finally replaces them as she arrives at her destination. She lingers to run her fingers over the wooden skis in the department store as she makes her way through the electrical appliances, nodding toys, and paraphernalia of modern living. In the very first line of the novel, her frantic tearing off the dress when she learns that "the material doesn't stain" conveys at once her yearning to get out of artifice and into something "very natural"—something that stains and does not reflect a smooth and polished and perfect surface. Later in the day, she looks through the window of the empty and abandoned café with its chairs and tables stacked on the black and white marble squares of the floor, and she seems to be staring at and on a world that is like the "strange museum" of a de Chirico painting. This moment, as she gazes through yet another window, is the only poignant and humanly emotionally charged one in the novel, a kind of affectively loaded moment of *anagnorisis*. It is the only moment when Lise recognizes *in the world* something that expresses and seems to stand in (as an objective correlative) for all of her own derealized and unfelt "lonely grief."

The experience of the world of *The Driver's Seat* is like stepping into the frame of de Chirico's *Enigma* paintings and trying to live in their represented worlds: the endlessly framed *mise en abimes*, the juxtaposition of modern and ancient worlds, the chequered marble, strange statues, shadows and looming clocks thrusting starkly and geometrically out of minimalist backgrounds. Lise is similarly contained by and yet always repelled outside of the frames of various spaces and interiors: her functional apartment with its swaying pines willed into concentricity, the airport lounge, the department store, the hotel room where she places her suitcase next to the chromium bedside lamp: "She switches on the central light which is encased in a mottled glass globe; the light flicks on, then immediately flickers out as if, having served a long succession of clients without complaint, Lise is suddenly too much for it" (45). Although she escapes the sterile and geometric modernism of her northern habitat and heads southward for more exotic climates, Lise's experience is of ever-more containment. Indeed the deep poetic structure of equivalence in the novel is a rhythm of *containment*—plots, interiors, bodies, clothing and uniforms, veils, bags, cars, traffic jams, aeroplanes, hotel rooms, cubicles, television monitors, department stores, stackable and collapsible furniture, suitcases, rice packets, packages, slogans, sound-bites encapsulation, the whorling shell of the snail of the final interrogation, and then the police cell—and *expulsion*—shouts, tears, steam, streams, laughter, giggles, screams, riots, stampedes, orgasms, violence, murder, and the final quality of finality. These are the rhythms of a vast and complex combustion engine. In the *Autobiography of a Schizophrenic Girl*, Renee goes on to describe a deepening sense of alienation, where "voices were metallic," and where from time to time, "a word detached itself from the rest. It repeated itself over and over in my head, absurd as though cut off by a knife" (22). The "paperknife" that Lise purchases is similarly fetishized in the overdetermined world of Lise's plot (and defetishized in the metafictional "paper" frame of the book). A bejewelled simulacrum of a scimitar, it is the selected weapon for the planned ceremony of her sacrificial murder in the more pastoral space of the Pavilion grounds, the main parkland of the city.

For Lise has planned her death as a very modern tragic performance—boy meets girl—of the ancient and ritualized expulsion of the *pharmakon*: the sacred and defiled outcast, the outsider and marginal, whose ritualistic murder and violent expulsion (here like pressure released from a canister of laughing gas), served cathartically to restore and preserve the order of Law—*catharsis* being etymologically linked to *expulsion* and to the figure of the pharmakon. But the Aristotelian concept of justice and order, conveyed through the vehicle of empathetic pity and spectatorial fear, is here replaced by the blank screen of authority gleaming off the buttons and epaulettes of the policemen who finally stand over Lise's corpse waiting to escort the unwilling slayer to his cell. Ancient catharsis gives way to contemporary "letting off steam" in the modern carnival of mechanical efficiency. Lise's quest and her narrative become the vehicle for an unsentimental journey where, as she takes the driver's seat (in a rewriting of Yorick's mounting of his carriage and his narrative in Laurence Sterne's *A Sentimental Journey*) every expression of emotion sought as a form of resistance to the Hobbesian robot, the man-machine, reduces to the biomechanical processes of drivers and combustion. This materialist reduction is facilitated by the vocabularies of the contemporary therapist: the vocabularies of desire, repression, sublimation, and the Freudian "drives."

This vocabulary was also pervasive in the 1960s in the understanding of aesthetic creativity as a kind of sublimation of the drives, Freud's own version of "letting off steam" through the displacement of libidinal or thanetic drives into the highly wrought economy of the work of art. For if there was one authorial construct that perhaps subsumed all others and proved most problematic, and most crucial, for women writers in the sixties, it was what Al Alvarez would later refer to as "the myth of the artist." Alvarez defined this as a "general belief—by the public as well as the artists—that the work and the life are not only inextricable but also virtually indistinguishable" (196). The myth took sustenance from the enormous influence of Freud's theory of creativity (art as a sublimation of the drives and a displacement of neurotic or psychotic pressures), particularly in the United States, in the 1950s and early 1960s. It was also nourished by Edmund Wilson's influential essay, "Philoctetes: The Wound and the Bow" in his 1941 book *The Wound and the Bow*; this essay had explicitly married the Greek tale of the wounded artist to the Freudian account of the grounding of art in madness, pain, and suffering. The midcentury antipsychiatry movement influenced by Laing was responsible for popularizing this line of thought. In the same vein, Sylvia Plath had notoriously represented herself in her poems as a tragic heroine writing a fictional and gothic plot that closes round her (much like Lise) to become a burial urn. Muse to her own autopoetic voice, the Plath of the late poems also presents a suicidal drive motivated by a desire to hone the body entirely into a condition of disembodiment, into the cold perfection of words. In Plath's penultimate poem, "Edge," the body of the woman is eradicated altogether as, wearing the "smile of accomplishment / The illusion of a Greek necessity" (85), she is perfected ekphrastically in marble, but actually of course in the Grecian urn, the burial urn, the well-wrought urn, which is the poem itself. The world becomes the stage set of the poem and of the act of writing and the perfection of plot the ultimate mode of self-murder. Lise is strangled by her plot before she is murdered by the paperknife of her assailant Richard.

Renee also describes her experience of the world becoming a place of the dead and of herself as a corpse in a world of zombies and robots, mannequins, and "lost souls" (37), a world where looming "things" "began to take on life" (40). She refers repeatedly to the uncanny sense that the world has become a stage set, peopled by automata: "each object was cut off by a knife, detached in its emptiness, in the boundlessness, spaced off from other things. Without any relationship with the environment, just by being itself, it began to come to life" (57). In order to escape this world, a world of stasis and emptiness that is now "unworlded" and that she curiously refers to as "Enlightenment," she begins to build an alternative world, a place of escape from containment, an alternative plot that will give her back vitality and purpose, allow her to scent the breeze again and part her lips expectantly as she enters the sublime perfection of an aesthetically ordered world of words. It is hard to imagine an account of psychosis that could more closely approximate the "feel" of the world of Spark's novel.

But in her very first novel, *The Comforters*, published in 1957, Spark had presented another alienated character *caught between worlds* who increasingly experiences her thoughts as objects in the world. Caroline Rose begins the novel feeling alienated from her old Bohemian "set," yet unable to feel any sense of belonging with the Catholics of St Philumena's where she has taken up her retreat. Increasingly, she speaks to herself in the third person, also employing a technique of mimicry, using an internal mocking voice, to fend off the intrusiveness of grotesque characters such as Georgina Hogg, a technique that, we are informed, extended her "customary habit of self-observation" (47). But the defensive strategies soon become part of the problem as Caroline begins to feel that she is no longer centered in herself but externally located somewhere outside and that "the mocker is taking over" (36). Losing her sense of temporal order and succession (a common symptom in schizophrenia and a necessity for the design and interpretation of plots), Caroline begins to hear her thoughts coming from outside, played back to her in the third person, before she has experienced them internally. In *Reading for the Plot,* Peter Brooks, further developing Frank Kermode's account of plot in *The Sense of an Ending,* suggests that narratives are always proleptic, in that they always seem to imagine in advance their own act of transmission or their moment of being read, even though this moment of reading is always belated, a moment that is posthumous and exists in the afterlife of narration. Plots are always forward-moving, intentional and oriented toward goals, and the sense of a beginning is always structured through the sense of an ending: "We might say that we are able to read present moments—in literature and, by extension, in life—as endowed with narrative meaning only because we read them in anticipation of the structuring power of those endings that will retrospectively give them the order and significance of plot" (94). In this sense, narrative is a kind of obituary, and the more we are required to meditate on the plot, the more we seem directed toward meditation on human ends as well as endings.

Caroline Rose of *The Comforters* is a character who is haunted by an awareness of this peculiar condition of anticipation of retrospection, aware that her life is shaped by a compulsion toward ends and endings that seem to be writing her present. What she sets out to discover is whether she is in a plot of her own making—a structure generated by the proleptic impulse of her own mind—or whether she is caught in someone else's. Radically disembedded from the world and in the transitional state of "conversion," Caroline has lost all sense of where she stands. For without that sense of phenomenological grounding that comes from the temporal flow, from sensing herself as a continuity arising out of a past and gathered toward a future that also gathers up that past, she becomes adrift in time and experiences her own thoughts as though they have already been recorded and exist out in the world, in the pages of a book.

Spark deliberately removes from her fictional worlds—and especially in the poetic and minimalist novels written in the decade between the mid-1960s and mid-1970s—those tacit and invisible threads that serve to bind selves to their historical worlds and that weave the texture of the realist novel, with its psychological depth, temporal and spatial anchorage, and close and multi-perspectival observations of behavior. Instead, Spark presses to its limit that characteristic dualist mode of modernity as an experience of the world and a relationship to it as a "world-picture," in Heidegger's phrase: the feeling that one is somehow screened from the world, outside the frame of it, merely looking on, or that the frame of the picture, if one manages to crawl inside or under the net, is in turn experienced as inside another picture where other observers look on watching, and so on, *ad infinitum*. Scientific naturalism assumes that consciousness is placed in a world that is already there, but consciousness is implicated in the building of that world and, when it is disturbed, the process of building is no longer unconscious and assumed, but disturbingly and consciously willed and deliberative. The world so built exists in a perpetual condition of "as if," a staged artifice that has to be persistently and continuously willed into existence for those who inhabit its frame ("as if" is probably Spark's most reiterated phrase: I counted eight uses of it in just one chapter of *The Driver's Seat*). This world is a world imagined *as if* scientific naturalism goes all the way down and swallows up consciousness: a version of Warhol's "I want to be a machine." Being "oneself" is conceived as breaking or bursting out of a container or breaking the "rules" or the plot and *standing even further outside*, in an ever-increasing condition of hyperreflexivity, a loss of the tacit and of the emotionally intelligent dimensions of being human.

Louis A. Sass has used the phrase "operant hyperreflexivity" to describe the disturbance of thinking and feeling characteristic of schizophrenia. This mode of intellectualized hyperawareness converts the body into an object for contemplation rather than a place in which to dwell, and the ensuing disconnection requires that the world be brought into being from nothing, built painstakingly out of words and ideas, in effect, like the fictional worlds of a novelist. What is assumed as "background" in the normal world of experience does not exist until it is explicitly encoded as part of the world. The tension of maintaining this kind of precarious hold on the world eventually gives way to a final stage where a delusory world is substituted almost entirely for the historical one and where the psychotic subject experiences him or herself as both the generator of this new world and as subject to its powerful and invisible forces. It is thus not surprising that many of Spark's "delusives" and borderline psychotics are artists of a kind. For example, Paul claims to have called up the characters of *Hothouse* himself, recalled them from the grave with his jealousy and emotion. But his wife Elsa has taken on a life of her own, refusing any longer to be contained by him (though he has committed her to a mental asylum in the past) or to live outside of the knowledge of their purgatorial and Dantesque condition, her awareness that they are not alive but they did not die. She waits patiently for the reunion of flesh and spirit. More generally, because the line between delusion and art, madness and creativity is such a fine one, Spark's work emphasizes that in the modern world the responsible artist must operate with a mode of *critical* reflexivity, an "intelligence" curiously akin to but distanced from the sickness of operant hyperreflexivity—a sickness that responsible art must also address as an expression of the deeper structures of modernity. For there can be no return to some ideal and pastoralized space of premodern reconciliation; we are in the world of history and we must use the tools of that world to challenge its more damaging preconceptions.

Sartre's starting point, in his study of emotion, was the assumption that "the emotional consciousness is primarily consciousness of the world" (Sartre 36). Emotion is out there in the world as a quality of things; it is how the world appears to us, our sense of the real, and not simply what we feel in the body. *The Driver's Seat* opens with Lise on a shopping trip to purchase clothes for her vacation. Eyeing with disbelief the garish riot of color in the ensemble that she has put together, the assistant in the dress shop replies to her insistent, "absolutely right for me. Very natural colours," with a placating, "Oh, it's how you feel in things yourself, Madam, isn't it?" (11). The bizarre carnival of her dress, the costume for her Saturnalian rites and essential to her plot, also conveys the disturbance of her mind; the sales assistant knows it, as do the many other characters who instinctively recoil with fear from her presence. For feelings, even when unremarked and unfelt and apparently absent, still continue to do their job of building worlds. But in many of Spark's worlds, feelings are no longer the inhabited medium of an attitude, constituting a comfortable background out of which the world and its objects arise. In this world of disturbed affects, objects loom with strange signifi-cance and the prereflective sense of existing as a self-presence is so tenuous that selfhood and presence have to be continuously willed—as if the self were indeed a character being imagined into existence by an external force, a controlling author outside. Experiencing herself as no more than a bodily container or machine that emits, from time to time, a combustive shower of laughter or tears, Lise's precarious hold on the world is symbolized, as suggested, in her mechanically willed, laborious, and obsessive-compulsive sorting and arranging of packages within her zipper bag. But the deeper implication of the novel is that in this world of scientific naturalism, this is all that Lise is too: a zipper bag, a bag of organs, parts, and circuits. She is like Bill, with his scheduled daily orgasm and his bursting bags of rice (when he doesn't get it) and his inane New Age philosophy of you are what you eat, or the shopper who "bursts out of her cubicle" in the Ladies

Room of the department store, or Mrs. Fiedke who gets trapped in a similar cubicle, or the herds of buffalo who charge across the T.V. screen like the street rioters across the roads, or, finally, Lise's own body at the end, trussed and packaged, already prepared for the assembly line of the mortuary.

In *The Hothouse by the East River*, published three years after *The Driver's Seat*, Spark refers explicitly to schizophrenia and delusion. The reference comes in a scene where Paul, already recoiling from Elsa's habit of staring out at the East River, from where she appears to receive the mysterious light causing her shadow to fall in the wrong direction, reels back in terror at her insistence that she has seen Helmut Kiel, the German spy with whom they were both erotically involved in 1944, and who was killed at the end of the war: "His heart thumps for help. 'Help me! Help me!' Cries his heart, battering the sides of the coffin. 'The schizophrenic has imposed her will. Her delusion, her figment, her nothing-there, has come to pass'" (15). But Paul and Elsa were also killed at the end of the war while both working in British military intelligence in a compound deep in the English countryside. If the human as steam engine and the carnivalesque bursting of containers is the controlling conceit of *The Driver's Seat*, that of *Hothouse* is *intelligence*. On the one hand, the word occurs in its seemingly ordinary uses many times in the novel. "Mother is no fool," says Pierre. "Mother is intelligent. More than one can possibly calculate, she's intelligent, it gives one a jolt sometimes" (37); and later Pierre remarks, "'What does it matter? Spies don't matter . . . There isn't any war and peace any more, no good and evil, no communism, no capitalism, no fascism. There's only one area of conflict left and that's between absurdity and intelligence'" (63). But on the other hand, it should also be noted that 1944 was the date of the first use of the ballistic missiles, the V-2s, referred to in the novel as "robot bombs" and dropping silently out of the skies to kill Paul and Elsa just as they are planning to begin a new life in New York after the war. The V-2s were the first cybernetic "intelligent" weapons working on the principles of self-organization and feedback loops, arriving silently, unannounced, dropping suddenly from clear skies. Their sinister mode of operation prompted George Orwell to pronounce that "only the mentally dead are capable of sitting down and writing novels while this nightmare is going on" (Orwell 72).

Outside its military uses, cybernetics would more generally exert an enormous pressure for change on machinic or behaviorist models of human activity, and introduce the idea of humans as not simply machines, but *intelligent machines*. Indeed, this concept is the connection in the novel between the manner of Elsa and Paul's death in 1944 and the manner of their living death in present-day

New York. From 1840, scientists had begun to conceive of the body as a kind of steam engine: a thermodynamic machine distributing flows of energy and wastes, maintaining equilibrium homeostatically, and in need of maintenance, ergonomic attention, dietary regimes, and regulation of flows. One hundred years later, statistical thermodynamics was merging with information theory to produce the first phase of the mathematization of biology in which the chemical or electro-chemical machine becomes fully an informational flow. In 1945 the first electrical circuits for a digital computer were developed by von Neumann, and in 1946 the Macy conferences began to plot the connections between the human nervous system, computers, and cybernetic models of information flow. In 1948, Wiener published *Cybernetics: Or Control and Communication in the Animal and the Machine*; this book was the outcome of military research on gunnery processes, conceived as circuits where machine and human are equivalent components, feedback systems engineered to produce maximally efficient transmissions of information. Humans are understood to be intelligent machines, and feedback systems and homeostasis render intention redundant. Here metaphors gave way to models and very quickly the machinic and information *model* of the human would begin to be perceived *as* the human, and bodily life as a kind of stored digital program. The following decades would see the birth of cognitive science as an umbrella discipline and the displacement of the third person behaviorist account of human activity with another, more scientifically grounded, third person account of human behavior through the study of the brain. As the brain began to be understood as a kind of computer, psychosis came to be seen as a failure of information flow, a breakdown of the homeostatic circuit, or an overload of the system, and a kind of "cyber-psychiatry" followed. As Pierre, Elsa and Paul's son, looks around at his lover, Peregrine's, apartment, at the adapters and sockets and Byzantine electrical circuits feeding heaters and lights and razors and irons and coffee pots and electric cork-openers, he thinks how remarkable it is that "Peregrine's fuse has not blown," but that it must happen soon: "my mother and father, and the rest of us will blow a fuse and the current will stop flowing, thank God" (30).

For if Paul and Elsa are the living dead, purgatorial spirits seeking atonement and haunted by the sins of their past, they are surrounded by a city of zombies—also the cybernetic name for a robot or "intelligent machine" that functions in quasi-human ways but is bereft of qualia or the ability to experience the world as a subject. All around them are bodies without souls, cancelled selves, slaves to money and hyper-sensationalism, neuronal circuits plugged into global circuits. The decade before Spark's novel appeared had seen a number of popular songs and films on the zombie theme, such as George A. Romero's *Night of the Living Dead* (1968), which explicitly made the connection between consumer culture, the exploitation of humans as alienated labor, and the idea of the zombie as a kind of emptied-out husk. In Jacques Tourneur's 1943 film, *I Walked with a Zombie*, there is a husband also called Paul whose wife is a cataleptic schizophrenic, but who is also suspected to be a zombie. But in Spark it may be Paul himself who is suffering from a delusion in the form of the condition known as Capgras syndrome, in which the sufferer believes that an impostor or double has been substituted for his or her partner or spouse. "'She's not real, Annie,' says Paul to his psychoanalyst. 'Didn't I tell you?'" (107).

But as she waits patiently for the end, knowing their purgatorial condition, Elsa has, in the meantime, also distracted herself with the consolations of money, materially hunkered down, tight and secure, on her valuable real estate; solid territory precipitated out of years of dealing in the spectral worlds of global high finance. She distracts herself playing games with her therapist—one of the three key figures who, along with the artist and the manager, play an important role in Spark's novels of this period, and who are also are seen by the philosopher Alistair MacIntyre as symbolic of the peculiar form of contemporary instrumental thinking. Elsa enjoys also misleading her husband's psychoanalyst, Annie, whose new method "does not involve the personality of the subject" and is "strictly bio-psychological," locating the problem in specific organs and treating the organ. Thus, she is treating "schizophrenia of the pancreas," "euphoria of the liver," a "manic-depressive kidney" and a "libidinal spleen," among other conditions (130). For Elsa requires distraction: in this fictional space and time, this *Aevum,* or "time of the Angels," she will always continue to sit in her New York apartment, bathed surreally in the afterglow of money, the red glow of the Pepsi-Cola column, and the intermittent flickering of the Pan Am sign from across the quivering dark blue water of the East River. She will continue to smile enigmatically and to laugh (merrily, fearfully, maniacally), like her sister protagonists in each of these most spare and economical novels of the late sixties and early seventies, Spark's own favorite texts within her oeuvre. Outside Elsa's window, but still in the world of the book and the "mental clinic" of New York, the crowds continue to sicken in the heat, "with riots in their hearts and heads" and riots on the streets and pavements. As the noise of a million air-conditioners whirs and purrs across the urban undergrowth, fuses threaten to blow in the great electric circuit of the city, and in all the micro-electric circuits of the brains of the city's myriad dwellers. "How long cries Paul in his heart, will these people, this city, haunt me" (88).

In estranging her readers from such existentially lived modes of estrangement, Spark increasingly, and in these novels especially, holds up a bleak picture of the human as an inert substance driven by a mechanical will (the driver's seat). This is the picture familiar enough to us in scientific naturalistic constructions of what it is to be human; however, Spark constructs a social imaginary, a world *lived* out though such a perspective, a world whose first person perspectives have disappeared entirely into the third. But even in facilitating a renewed understanding of this picture through a heightened and critical reflexivity, her fiction displaces that operant yet dysfunctional reflexivity that sustains and perpetuates the divided and mechanized contemporary experience of being. This method of critical and intelligent reflexivity has, of course, sometimes been misconstrued as a mandarin hauteur and indifference to her characters. Famously, in her essay on "The Desegregation of Art," Spark eschewed empathy and sentiment and advocated ridicule and irony as the only remaining effective literary weapons of disturbance. But her modes of double disengagement, by producing a *consciousness* of disturbance, a *consciousness* of the *feeling* of discomfort, allow her fictions to materialize in the reader feelings that are conspicuously absent in their mechanically driven worlds and characters. For, if art does not disturb, nothing changes.

This conception of the force and purpose of art informs the title that Spark chose for *Not to Disturb* (1971). Set in another heartland of the Reformation, Geneva, the novel portrays a group of modern-day servants busying themselves with the tools of technological mastery as they wait patiently for the Marxist-Hegelian plot to run its course and deliver their own redemption through the opportunities released in their aristocratic masters' self-destruction. But as in Doris Lessing's *The Memoirs of a Survivor* (1974), where a nuclear disaster destroys the culture of late capitalism, the new order that follows and promises genuine social and cultural revolution simply brings in more of the same. One disengaged and Hobbesian regime gives way to another, as the closeted upper-class engines of lust and landed inheritance run down to be replaced by the new engines of publicity, fame, and acquired wealth. The black carnival world is turned upside down, but its order and its models of human functioning and flourishing remain fundamentally undisturbed. The novel ends with another image of "unknowing": as the plainclothes man dozes in the hallway, the "household" (the enterprising retinue of the soon-to-be deceased Klopstocks), like some rough slouching beast, straggles up the back stairs (its hour come round again) seeking "the profound sleep of those who have kept faithful vigil all night, while outside the house the sunlight is laughing on the walls" (96).

Laughter, like the "cloud of unknowing" is an important weapon in Spark's armory, if not quite the anarchistic "bomb" advocated by Nicholas Farringdon after his vision of evil at the May of Teck Club in Spark's *The Girls of Slender Means* (1963). Baudelaire, whose stance of *dedoublement* and whose antisentimental and antibourgeois self-escalating acts of consciousness were an ironic precursor to Spark's own, argued in "The Essence of Laughter" (1855) that "the root of the Comic is to be sought in the sensation resulting from the observation of a thing becoming like a person. But from that point of view all men are necessarily comic: for they are all things, or physical bodies, behaving as persons" (154). In *The Driver's Seat*, humans explode and erupt like canisters of laughing gas (and also like schizophrenics as noted from the work of Bleuler and others since 1911). Similarly, the surrealist André Breton described laughter as the "mortal enemy of sentimentalism" (273); his categorizations of "black humor" also gave the machine precedence over the humanism of middle-distance realism.

Indeed, historically sentimentalism was closely entwined with the development of fictional realism. One of the requirements of an increasingly secular modernity was that it should find a way to place the moral life on a secular basis as a means of resisting the logic of the Hobbesian account of human nature. The empathetic and the sentimental needed to be heightened and disciplined to provide a secular substitute for the moral practices of the religious life, and the novel was an important vehicle for this process. For if the moral order can no longer be grounded in the transcendental, it must be discovered at the heart of the human and, in effect, in the human heart itself and its ability to be "touched" by the suffering and pain of others. As critics such as Michael Bell have observed, raising sentimentalism to a principle of virtue was important in that it elevated it above the contingencies of individual feeling into something approaching a metaphysical principle. In this sense, Spark's distance from realism also marks her resistance to sentimentalism as an adequate response to the mechanistic picture. In the "Desegregation of Art" (1971), she emphatically rejected the literature of empathy and sentiment for an art of ridicule, because she recognized that the assumption of empathy, the idea that one can see and feel the world through another's perspective, must always in some sense be a delusion: at the very best, the attempt to inhabit a different perspective carries with it a knowledge of itself as a strategy that already introduces a divisive splitting. Mostly, it simply leaves readers feeling that "their moral responses are sufficiently fulfilled by the emotions that they have been induced to feel," whereas a "derisory" art, an "art of ridicule" might "penetrate to the marrow. It can leave a salutary scar.

It is unnerving. It can paralyse its object" (36). By the middle of the nineteenth century, even Dickens, regarded as the great advocate of the novel as *the* vehicle for the education of moral sentiment, recognized the limitations of aesthetic sentimentalism in his damning portrait of Harold Skimpole in *Bleak House*. This ultra-sensitive aesthete quivers to the sweet music of peasant ballads while callously ignoring the needs of the suffering and mortally ill sweeper-boy, Joe, who lies languishing next door.

"To Me, Being Catholic Is Part of My Human Existence": Problems in "Theorizing" Muriel Spark

In *The Hothouse by the East River*, the city, Augustine's city of unholy loves, Baudelaire's city of dreams, a purgatorial Waste Land, seems poised at an Infernal tipping point. Elsa continues to sit, amused and unperturbed by it all, "well-dressed with her pretty hair-do and careful make-up, but sits solidly, as on valuable land-property painted up like a deteriorating building that has not yet been pulled down to make way for those high steel structures" (9).[3] Elsa's gaze drifts intermittently throughout the novel across the East River, toward the other side. Like Spark, she resides in a world of reductive materialisms, the consequences of a dualist outlook that Elsa herself sees beyond. Spark's own critique of the effects of a dualistic metaphysics, the dissociation of sensibility and the splitting of the human relation to the world into a delusory sentimentalism versus a mode of disengaged and over-explicit hyperreflexivity is also informed by the metaphysics of an alternative worldview, provided by the intellectual framework of Catholicism.

To what extent is knowledge of this framework a prerequisite for understanding Spark's work? What role, if any, does that framework play in her cultural and social understanding? Like Elsa, the Catholic Spark has recently come to be regarded like some valuable but underdeveloped piece of real estate awaiting demolition, high tech development and refurbishment. Like Elsa, always "away and [just] out of reach" (19), she is now a prime target for a new generation of critics wanting to claim her for their own. And like A. S. Byatt, whose novel *Possession* (1990) also played on the affinities between the premodern world of demonic enchantment and those of contemporary letters, Spark has always made much comic capital, particularly in her later novels, out of the theme of art as capital, literature as intellectual property, and unseemly wrangles for possession of writers as commodities. As we know from the various protracted legal battles, especially those over the publication of Martin Stannard's long-awaited biography, Spark was so highly protective of her cloud of unknowing that she was determined from the very beginning of her career to direct and control her critical legacy. For possessive individualism underpins the world of contemporary letters quite as much it does the world of real estate. Spark recognized only too well the characteristic hubris of the critic and the literary scholar: the tendency to assume that if you work on a writer, dig down into their soil, mingle your intellectual labor with the fruits of her own, then somehow she is yours, you have made her your own, you are pecu-liarly *licensed* to claim her as yours. So the literary critical "high steel structures" erected on her estate have continued to spring up and, of late, have been built with tools and materials drawn from critical theory. Such "theoretical" Sparks play with and foreground their own spectrality and that of their constructed object of analysis; is it for this reason that the "real" Muriel Spark, the embodied person (the "I" who parallels the one in "Borges and I"), has seemed remarkably unperturbed by them? Earlier critical commentaries often provoked her authorial wrath or defensiveness, especially those that sought to trap the cloud of unknowing with biographical facts, or to congeal into *lumpen* historical correspondence the finely wrought fabulist hermeneutics. She was determined that the famous smile on the ever-vanishing face should never be a fixed one. But as theoretical Sparks began to fly, she seemed more amused or bemused than litigious, assuming perhaps that their postmodern and often playful spirit was somehow akin to her own and, carrying all the performa-tive contradictions of the postmodern, offered no propositional threat to her fictional practice, which is premised on our inability to get to the bottom of things.

Playful and progressive as they might appear, however, not every attempt to bring the resources of critical theory to bear is so benign. The fully fledged project was launched with a strangely petty-minded and largely *ad hominem* attack on her earlier critics in the introduc-tion to Martin McQuillan's *Theorising Muriel Spark: Gender, Race, Deconstruction* of 2002. Whatever their real differences, these early Spark critics such as Frank Kermode, David Lodge, Malcolm Bradbury, and Peter Kemp, are here viewed as modernist mandarins—the kind that always look back nostalgically, ever in the shadow of T. S .Eliot, to a premodern world order that found its last and highest expression of a unity of being in the Middle Ages and especially in the writing of Dante. Malcolm Bradbury, for example, is held up as sexist and patriarchal and (anachronistically) pilloried simply for referring to her as "Mrs Spark" (although in fact the preface to every one of my first Penguin editions of her early to middle work refers to her as Mrs Spark; later editions politely refer to her as "Dame Muriel"). McQuil-lan then seeks to downplay the importance of Spark's Catholicism by listing the many twentieth-century writers who also happened to be Catholics. Unfortunately, the list includes writers such as Samuel Beckett, who was certainly Irish and a writer but was certainly never Catholic and Irish and a writer.

These might seem trivial quibbles, but the serious aim of the volume, as stated by McQuillan in his introduction, is to re-buff (in both senses of the word) Spark's "deteriorating" edifice as "Catholic writer" in order to reclaim her rightfully for the forces of political and intellectual progress. What is being attacked of course is the reading of Spark as part of the modernist legacy of T. S. Eliot, and the view that progressive politics are simply the impotent and ungrounded reflection of the break-up of a monumental Christian worldview. In such a world, all too easily, art is sought as a substitute for a purgatorially earned redemption and what Eliot refers to in his essay on Baudelaire (1930) as fragmentary Danteisms spring up in the vacuum left by the departure of authentic faith. The Infernal side of Dante's vision takes over: a grotesque and dark dandyism or a cult of sensation and death, embraced as a desperate and impoverished antidote to the stultifying routines of bureaucracy and petit-bourgeois anomie. Spark's Catholicism is normally read, in effect, as a desire to overcome such fragmentary Danteisms and such morbid aestheticism by drawing on the resources of irony to remind us of the greater importance of the Four Last Things.

The lure of this kind of reading of Spark has certainly been seductive. It might seem to make sense of many of her disturbingly strange fictions. Think of Lise in *The Driver's Seat* as she breaks out—with the awful daring of a moment's surrender—of the anomie of her rigid office life and the awful stasis of her functionally designed apartment; out of the set geometrical line of her mouth (not even a smile) and into maniacal (and mechanical) explosion, like the release of a canister of laughing gas, or the arrow from a bow. Soon, she is scenting the breeze, like a stag or, like Diana, hunting a stag, taut as a bowstring, her ruled mouth suddenly cracked open and expectant, scanning horizons with a recovered and intense purposefulness as she moves wilfully toward her death. She is in all respects a kind of Baudelairean hero: seeking sensation and the feeling of vitality in the paradoxical pursuit of "spleen," the cult of death, of crime and evil, seeking them as ends that give a patina of purpose to the flattened affective horizons of bourgeois life and its iron cage of reason: "the gleaming buttons of the policeman's uniforms . . . the holsters and epaulettes and all those trappings devised to protect them from the indecent exposure of fear and pity, pity and fear" (107).

It is true that earlier criticism of Spark was dominated by interpretations of her writing as narrowing and reshaping the Eliotic legacy into a critique of aestheticist ineffectuality. There seems no point in denying that Spark inherited this legacy; but what is important is that she consciously reworked it and found her own liberation from it by updating it as a vehicle for the interpretation of contemporary culture and its metaphysical assumptions. This reading of *The Driver's Seat*, for example, is entirely compatible with and could be gathered into the broader frame that I have been trying to sketch. At no stage of her career did she ever retract the view that her Catholicism had always been central to her activity as a writer. Yet McQuillan's tactic in his interview with her is to encourage her to play down her Catholicism and to play up her social and political engagement, as if the two were necessarily in contradiction. Spark comically and summarily derails the attempt. She appears (almost certainly disingenuously) to misunderstand the term *postmodernism* by bestowing upon it a meaning that is entirely compatible with the Roman Catholicism that she flatly insists throughout is central to her identity. McQuillan opens up: "One of the things I find distressing about much 'Spark' criticism is the way it tries to pigeon-hole you as a Catholic writer. . . . If you understand the penny catechism, you understand everything about Muriel Spark" (217). "I am a Catholic and I'm a believing Catholic. . . . [this is] bound to colour my narrative, inform my narrative approach. . . . Although I don't set out to be a Catholic Apologist in any form" (217), Spark replies, in an oft-rehearsed echo of almost every interview she has ever given. On being a postmodernist, the ironic qualifications are legion: "Maybe postmodernist. . . . They say postmodernist, mostly, whatever that means." "Do you know what that means?" prompts McQuillan. "Well, I think that it means that there is another dimension which is a bit creepy, supernatural . . . not supernatural, but not necessarily consequential. I always think that causality is not chronology . . . one thing doesn't necessarily lead to another inevitable thing, although it does lead to something else in actual fact."

What she means when she says again and again that being a Catholic for her means not being some kind of apologist, but arriving at a narrative form, is surely that for her being a Catholic and being a writer are inseparable and that at the level of form at least one cannot be understood without the other. Why else would she pluck out the rather odd reference to *causality* in her semi-acceptance ("they say") of the description of her as a postmodernist writer, in the McQuillan interview? Postmodernism hardly set out to reinstate the Aristotelian concept of teleology with the idea of a *final* cause, but it did much to challenge the idea that everything is reducible to the kind of purely *efficient* and chronological causality which is at the heart of scientific epistemologies; in challenging that assumption if not overturning it, postmodernism may at least have helped to even up the stakes so that other kinds of understanding are kept in serious circulation. Why indeed should she use the word *consequential* in this same context? Presumably because there are ways of thinking about actions and right actions that do not proceed from the utilitarian weighing up of outcomes, but from an axiomatic sense of what is virtuous and right, *in the first place*, and whatever the outcome, so that thinking begins from *ends* and not beginnings. In both instances, what is being opposed is the kind of calculative ratiocination that begins in science as an expression of secular dualisms and proceeds insidiously to support and direct moral outlooks. It's hard to see why McQuillan would disagree with this, but perhaps there is a tendency to see postmodernism as the only viable critique of modernity and to ignore critical, anti-hegemonic currents of thought and traditions that have continued from premodern sources in Aristotle and medieval and Renaissance thought.

Nothing is to be gained by claiming (wrongly) that early critics reduced Spark's work to the puerile jingle of a penny catechism, while ignoring the obvious point that the first step in correcting this bias (if it exists) might have been to explore more thoroughly and intellectually her very evident Catholic beliefs, rather than simply dismissing them as largely irrelevant to a newly fashioned and more theoretically informed reading (or image) of Spark. In this connection, it is important to grasp the broader, genealogical significance of Eliot's characterization of modernity as a dissociation of sensibility consequent upon modes of dualism, Cartesian and other. Granted, this characterization was put forward in Eliot's Clarke lectures and his early literary criticism, but developed more substantially in his later and more explicitly right-wing social thought in *Notes towards the Definition of Culture* (1948). But the provenance of Eliot's claims is not prima facie a reason for the abandonment or disinheritance of this tradition of thinking. Important elements of this tradition informed left-communitarian, feminist, postcolonial and multicultural thinking, especially the shaping of the New Left, in the late fifties and early sixties, when Spark was beginning to establish her reputation.

Similarly, the more phenomenological strains of postmodern "situated" thinking, especially its critique of modernity as an instrumental and hyperreflexive reduction of the world to a world-picture and of mind to a disengaged brain in a vat, are not at all incompatible with traditions of Catholic thought; to the contrary, this form of critique has actually at times engaged closely with the Catholic traditions which, if not exactly in Spark's bones (she is after all a convert), went a lot deeper than her fingernails. The most immediate *aesthetic* expression of this thought for Spark was undoubtedly in the writing of the Catholic philosopher Jacques Maritain (an important influence on T. S. Eliot too), and a key text in understanding Spark's own metaphysical perspective is Maritain's *The Philosophy of Art*, first translated and published in 1923, but extended and retranslated in 1949 as *Art and Scholasticism*. Central to its argument is the notion that an art withdrawn from responsibility to its historical and social contexts would be the "suicide of an angel—through forgetfulness of matter" (71). For Maritain, art is not a vision that resides in the angelic mind, aloof from history, but a practice thoroughly stained with the dye of the real. Spark always insisted that her perception of the Catholic acceptance of matter was central to her conversion, for at the back of the Incarnation, the belief in the resurrection of the body, and the meaning of the Eucharist, is Aquinas's understanding, derived from Aristotelian hylomorphism, of the paradoxical reality of the soul: that it is in the body yet contains rather than being contained by it. For a writer much preoccupied with the problems and perils of containment and of being inside and outside of plots, the attractions of this paradox are evident, but it also provides a perspective on, a different way of thinking about, the consequences of the Cartesian as it displaces the tradition of hylomorphism to set up the intellectual frame of modernity. The reason that, for Spark, as for Maritain, art does not reside in the "angelic mind," aloof from and removed from history, is because (in Maritain's words) "[i]t is subject in a soul which is the substantial form of a living body and which, by the natural necessity in which it finds itself of learning and becoming perfect slowly and with difficulty, makes the animal it animates a naturally political animal. Art is therefore fundamentally dependent upon everything which the race and the state, spiritual tradition and history transmit to the body and soul of man and his mind. By its subject and its roots, it belongs to a time and a country" (61). For Maritain, art was crucial in correcting the major defect of modernity—for him exemplified most acutely in the writing of Luther, Descartes, and Rousseau—which is seen as that overweening subjectivism that drains away the reality of the objective world. Art, in estranging us from habitual subjective experience, might liberate us by allowing us to see the object as other, and the self as subordinate to something outside itself of which it is also a part. Art must distance and disturb and create effects of the uncanny if it is to bring us back to the possibility of recognizing truth and experiencing fullness. Maritain referred to this repeatedly in his writing as *intelligence*.

Likewise, John Henry Newman's critique of the reformation and of Lutheran and Calvinist thought is essentially written from this perspective. Newman reads the Reformation as an event that begins the process of secularization that is carried forward through the Enlightenment and into what we would now recognize as the beginnings of our own modernity. At the heart of the Reformation, for Newman, was the project of overcoming belief in and the living of an enchanted worldview in which power resides outside, in forces, spirits, magical things, sacraments, and where the boundaries of inside and outside and flesh and spirit are always blurred (where black bile, for example, does not cause melancholy because it simply *is* melancholy). The Reformation thus began the process of "Enlightenment" that brought transferred power and agency to a self-regulating interiority that was compelled to live by rules, tastes, and customs while experiencing itself as a mind listening to its inner (universal) voice of reason. In short, Newman's critique suggests how by setting itself against superstition and magic, the new order required its own disciplinary regime, a rigid demarcation of inclusion and exclusion, of sinners and elect, the policing of marginals and the violent expulsion and sacrifice of subversives and scapegoats. As final causes wither and nature is autonomized, the universe becomes a kind of machine to be driven and harnessed by what Charles Taylor, in *A Secular Age*, refers to as the "buffered self" of modernity, with its "telos of autarky" (37-42).

Spark's best-known novel, *The Prime of Miss Jean Brodie* (1961), explores the effects of this disenchantment of the world and the dangerous political outcomes of an unleashed aesthetic sentimentalism that tries to stand in for its loss. Clothes are important commodities in the Sparkian world, for in a culture where the aesthetic so often stands in for the ethical, the fetishization of items of clothing confers on them a kind of tantric or sacramental power in spite and because of the secular regime. Throughout the novel, clothing is used as a culturally fetishized commodity that, in covering over and ultimately pointing to the grounding of "civilization" in human insecurity, exposes the territorialism and violence underlying a philosophy based on "taste" alone. The sacramentalization of the aesthetic as a response to an emptying out of the fullness of the world and its thinning down to regulatory regimes, is shown to be even more savage and dehumanizing in its possibilities than the regimes it seeks to displace.

At the Marcia Blaine School for Girls, "hatlessness" is "an offence," but "certain departures from the proper set of the hat on the head were overlooked in the case of fourth-form girls and upwards so long as nobody wore their hat at an angle" (6). Each of the "Brodie set," of course, has devised a way of tilting, folding, or balancing the school hat that manages to declare difference and belonging at the same time: "by the time they were sixteen, and had reached the fourth form . . . and had adapted themselves to the orthodox regime, they remained unmistakably Brodie" (6). But if we attend to the relevance of hats and sets in the context of the major themes of the novel, the trivial pursuits of schoolgirls carry the much weightier symbolism of the proprieties of Calvinistic Edinburgh and the sinister resonances of Fascistic uniform-ity. Within a Calvinistic plot of reward and punishment, election and damnation rule and there is no snakes and ladders game hanging on the possibility of grace or reversal for the sinner or nonconformist. Brodie's own set, of course, is as beset by *de registe* rules of inclusion and exclusion as both the Marcia Blaine school and Presbyterian polite Edinburgh of the thirties with its views of spinsters, sexual decorum, avoidance of display, and discreet codes of dress. All are ruled through codes of manners. Where the first re-quires conformity to Calvinistic ideas about moral (especially sexual) propriety, the second embeds itself through codes of aesthetic taste: knowing *as a fact* that Giotto is the greatest ever artist or that leaving windows open more than six inches is an offence against all canons of civilization. The Calvinist ethos of thirties' Edinburgh is presented in moral and antiaesthetic terms; those of the Brodie set in aesthetic and antimoral terms, but both are in fact codes of social conduct and taste and rules of conformity dressed up as ethical universals. They are there, like the practice of scapegoating and other forms of human sacrifice, to protect the identity of the group or "set," allay fears of mingling and contamination from without and subversion and revolt from within. The fences (between the boys and the girls) and the hats of the first page are signs of the rules and repressions and exclusivity of this Calvinistic world and of the rise of that expressive individualism which attempted to transcend or circumvent its polic-ing of the body while remaining broadly within its boundaries. It has shaped Jean Brodie as thoroughly as it has shaped Miss Mackay or the sewing sisters. Even before Sandy's betrayal of her, the reversal of Miss Brodie's fortunes rests on the discovery of a misplaced item of her wardrobe—the *crêpe de chine* nightdress already so out of place in this most Puritan of environments, is found farther out of place, and, shockingly, under Mr. Lowther's pillow.

Spark's fiction poetically explores many of the same themes narrated by Charles Taylor (2007) in his monumental history of secu-larization. Taylor painstakingly traces the rise of this modern notion of secular autonomy from the Calvinistic imposition of "plot" to the emergence of a modern self, with new confidence in its own powers of ordering and self-fashioning, its capacities to plot, shape, and create worlds, and its self-control and inward constitution through modes of self-reflexivity. Freud noted in *Civilization and Its Discon-tents* (originally published in 1930) that we have become prosthetic Gods who seem to control nature absolutely, but who seem to have lost our own natures in our internalization of technological efficiency.

Modern technologies, bio-regulatory regimes, and the cultivation of manners, all aspects of the secularizing process, also intensified the effects of philosophical dualism, from the Calvinistic interpretation of Augustine's view of the fallen body, to the rise of "manners" and taste as modes of social control of the body, to the utilitarianism of mass culture, where the body may come to be regarded as so much waste and dirt if it cannot be absorbed efficiently into the regulatory machine. Spark herself comments in an early piece of 1953, entitled "The Religion of an Agnostic," on how such dualisms have even crept into and taken over contemporary Christianity. Spark writes: "it could be abundantly demonstrated that present day Christian creative writing, that which is most involved in an attempt to combat materialism, reflects a materialism of its own; this takes the form of a dualistic attitude towards matter and spirit. They are seen too much in moral conflict, where the Spirit triumphs by virtue of its disembodiment. This is really an amoral conception of the spirit" (Spark 1). Fear of the body as *waste* within capitalist economies further gives rise to those ergonomic regimes of bodies as efficient systems, thermodynamic machines, informational bio-feedback systems, which must regulate their own orders (the metaphor appears increasingly in management parlance as it does in the biological sciences). This view of the body becomes increasingly central to Spark's work. As suggested in *The Driver's Seat*, the body is a casing for that motor engine which is the mechanical will or instinct; in *Hothouse,* where worms crawl out of bosoms and where a couple dance "like manicured ladies' fingers," the body is incorporated into a vast electro-chemical circuit that flows through human and metropolis like a postindustrial version of Wordsworth's correspondent breeze; and in *Not to Disturb*, the bio-semiosis of the digital age transforms world and human into flows of information in a relentless publicity machine where the human and the virtual are brought uncannily close in the new technological sublime of the media age.

"I Intend to Stand Aside and See If the Novel Has Any Real Form Apart from This Artificial Plot": Confirmation Bias, Delusion, and the (Secularized) Critic

All of Spark's twenty-two novels are concerned with plotting, instrumental logics, group psychologies, and the ubiquity and dangers of sets or elites and exclusive groups.[4] But if her interrogations focus self-reflexively on the nature of plots and plotting, her narratives also pre-empt any attempted strategy of premature narrative closure (on the part of the reader or the characters). Her famously intrusive use of prolepsis (for example, in *Brodie* and *The Girls of Slender Means*) throws the narrative emphasis away from suspense and toward curiosity, away from the empathetic seductions of limited or perspectival focalization at the level of story and character and towards an "anticipation of retrospection" that engages a wider and more impersonal and detached interrogation of how a story's manner of telling shapes what is told. This formal technique is fundamental to Spark's rejection of sentiment and empathy. For in pedagogic terms, her fiction is a vehicle for the moral and epistemological education of its readers out of the perils of reading according to our own plots rather than attending to the words of the text. Spark (presumably echoing Maritain and using the word specifically in the sense that he brings to it) has sometimes referred to the capacity that she seeks to enhance in her readers simply as "intelligence"; part of its application is in the use of fiction to enhance critical thought in a world that functionally depends on the widespread habit of delusional thinking facilitated by radical disembedding from the environments in which we act and interact.

Though adaptational advantage appears to accrue to those who practice and thrive on deceit, self-deception, and manipulative and self-enhancing behaviors, delusional thinking and the kinds of amoral fictionalizing encouraged in situations of cultural disembeddness, which are likely to encourage Hobbesian territoriality and insecurity, are also seen to be the source of our sickness and maladaptedness, our violences and dangerously totalizing political thought. Although Spark acknowledges the postmodern for its greater openness to pluralistic ontologies, in no way is this reflected in a requirement that we suspend the ordinary propositional truth claims of the worlds of history: art, as in Maritain's understanding, is to provide us with ways of overcoming subjectivism and the means to strive toward the seeing of objects in themselves as they are. Although she provides her own sense of the limitations of positivism, her position here is in some ways quite close to the Popperian idea of critical reasoning developed in his thinking of the forties and fifties and central to works such as *The Open Society and its Enemies* (1962) and *Conjectures and Refutations* (1963). Karl Popper's very influential idea of pseudoscience was used by him to describe a discourse where an aesthetic design, betraying the desire for a perfect order, is presented under the mantle of a rationalist metaphysics masquerading as science, as, in his view, in the writing of Hegel, Marx, and Freud. As art is not open to the kind of disconfirmation or proof required by scientific thought, such aesthetic "grand narratives," presented as scientific accounts of the universe, or as the laws of history, are simply sophistic shadows projected onto the real with disastrous consequences. This idea, along with Hans Vaihinger's exploration of the uses of plots and fictions in his *The Philosophy of As If* (originally published in 1921), was the starting point for Frank Kermode's *The Sense of an Ending* (1965) with its exploration of fictionality as the desire to project consolatory plots and fictions onto history in the form of degenerate myths. A little earlier in the 1960s, in essays published as *The Dyer's Hand* (1963), W. H. Auden had also discussed the responsibilities of the writer in contemporary mass society, warning against abuses of the magical in art, and the potential ethical dangers of unrestrained aestheticism. His views were close to those of his friend, the philosopher Hannah Arendt, whose controversial *Eichmann in Jerusalem: A Report on the Banality of Evil* also appeared in 1963; this text can be read as, in part, a continuation of Arendt's preoccupation with the human craving for meaning expressed in the need to tell stories. But Arendt had also warned (like Auden) about the dangerous potential when mythopoeic craving finds release in the construction of world-historical logics and utopian thinking which project perfect aesthetic orders onto the contingency and muddle of history.

Hence, in *The Prime of Jean Brodie*, for example, though Sandy Stranger initially admires Miss Brodie's reckless aestheticizing of experience, Sandy very quickly begins to recognize and stand back even farther from the irresponsibility and dangerous enchantments of Brodie's delusional transformations of the real. After listening to Miss Brodie's enchanted versions of Mussolini's politics and her identification with the vision of an aesthetically perfected sphere of the political, Sandy receives her revelatory glimpse of the actual ugliness and horror of poverty as she witnesses the "snaky creature" (40), the shivering and straggling file of the unemployed moving jerkily and desperately through Lauriston Place. She is filled with an acute dread that drives her home to seek warmth and comfort. Sandy's growing detachment and critical refusal of Brodie enchantment is honed through her ability to stand back and reflect detachedly on her own predilection for transfiguring the commonplace, and it is intensified once she discovers the science room, where lessons are called "experiments," and where Miss Lockhart begins the first lesson by informing her class that she has enough gunpowder to blow up the school. The lesson continues as a "naming of the most impressive objects in the science room" with an ever-present sense of the dangerous consequences of their misuse. Yet, although Sandy learns to respect the thinginess of objects and to detach herself from the dangerous enchantments and consolations of art, her tortured grip on the bars of her cell at the end of the novel suggests that, even as Sister Helena, she has not quite shaken off a haunted obsession with the aesthetic seductiveness of the prime of Miss Jean Brodie. Truth does not necessarily console.

What Sandy recognizes from the first is that Miss Brodie suffers acutely from what cognitive and social psychologists now refer to as *confirmation bias*: a term used to indicate a mode of thinking characterized by errors of inductive inference, evidenced in the tendency to approach and to interpret new information in ways that simply confirm existing preconceptions and to ignore or deselect information that challenges any such worldviews, so that hypotheses are confirmed or disconfirmed in the light of unknowing prejudice rather than the careful weighing up of evidence. Persistent confirmation bias is an early indicator of paranoia and is always present in full-blown psychosis: those suffering from psychotic delusions are notoriously closed to reasoning or evidence proving them false. From her very first novel, *The Comforters* (1957), Spark's work has shown a persistent fascination with the relations between art and delusional behaviors and their relation to the economic, cultural, and intellectual formations of modernity: a fascination with the dangers of aesthetic consolation and a determination that her readers should be disturbed and not consoled. For Spark, the responsible critic or reader of the novel, like the enduring artist, is one who, like Nicholas Farringdon in *The Girls of Slender Means*, has to learn to live with and respect the provisionality of any fictional hypothesis or aesthetic vision—to use a more critical and ironic awareness to test out hypotheses and hone something closer to and more understanding of the texture of the real. Nicholas, we are initially informed, is "enamored" of the May of Teck Club "in only one exceptional way, that stirred his poetic sense to a point of exasperation, for at the same time he discerned with irony the process of his own thoughts, how he was imposing on this society an image incomprehensible to itself" (71). To impose any image is always in some sense to disengage from what is being imagined, but to impose an image on a world which is "incomprehensible to it" is dangerously close to a sentimentalism that wants to retrieve and mollify the real, or an instrumental logic that desires to subdue and mold it into some other order.

In Spark's novel, both sentimentalism and instrumentalism are shown to be vehicles of confirmation bias, transforming the world in the image of one's desire and then reimposing that desired image upon the world. Nicholas's critical intelligence tells him that to set up his fanciful and poetic image of the residence for the girls of slender means as a utopian space of pastoral anarchism is a skewed and wilful obscuration of its very real ethical impoverishment, its survivalist savageries and careless egotisms. But his critical intelligence is paralyzed by his infatuated and sentimental feelings for the beautiful

Selena, whom he chooses to regard as the vehicle for and symbol of his ideal moral order, a kind of Rousseauian economic and pastoral republic of simple needs that is actually as far removed from Selena's consumerist lusts as can be imagined. Clued in via narrative prolepses to Nick's later conversion and martyrdom, the reader looks on his moral education through the lens of dramatic irony. But even though we possess early on the knowledge of Nick's final moral turnaround and his tragic demise and have thus viewed with deepening irony his infatuation with the superficial and monstrously selfish Selena, there can surely be no first-time reader who has not gasped with horrified surprise when Nick's heart turns dark as he witnesses Selena emerge triumphant out of the apocalyptic fires of the burning building in the novel's closing pages. Here Spark uses the same narrative technique of focalized retardation employed so effectively in Conrad's earlier allegory of darkness, whereby Kurtz comes into gradual focus through the telescopic lens from which Marlow gets his first glimpse of Kurtz's encampment. Kurtz is revealed to be surrounded not by what Marlow at first takes to be "ornamental balls" decorating the railings around the Central Station, but by what Marlow (along with the reader) soon after discovers are the shrunken human heads that are the final evidence of Kurtz's cannibalistic self-dissolution. Interestingly, of course, Marlow's own narrative is then employed to rescue Kurtz even in the face of the overwhelming and indubitable evidence of his brutality and debauched behaviour, so that the darkness is once again transfigured, aesthetically, into a picture of moral enlightenment and overcoming of evil.

Situated in a kind of Marlovian perspective, Nick pulls himself up level with the glass skylight of the burning building and through its narrow frame gazes on Selena approaching along the smoky corridor with what appears to be the long and limp body of a rescued human being. As she slides through to safety with all the grace of one for whom "poise is perfect balance," and ever will be, the human form caressed in her arms comes into focus as the Schiaperelli dress, the coveted item of luxurious adornment in a time of economic constraint, with its coat hanger dangling, uncannily and horrifically, "like a headless neck and shoulders" (125). Unbeknownst to the purposeful Selena, somewhere in the cloud of smoke just behind her, Joanna begins to burn to death. It is one of the most disturbing moments in a very disturbing oeuvre because it articulates so directly the key Sparkian theme that this essay has explored: the ethical consequences of expanding a reduced conceptualization of matter into a metaphysics of materialism and the kind of intelligence required to critique that process without falling prey to nostalgia or sentimentalism.

Notes

1. The quotation in the heading above comes from *The Hothouse by the East River*, p. 140.

2. The quotation in the heading above comes from *The Driver's Seat*, p. 71.

3. The quotation in the heading above comes from *The Bachelors*, p. 79.

4. The quotation in the heading above comes from *The Comforters*, p. 105.

Works Cited

Arendt, Hannah. *Eichmann in Jerusalem: A Report on the Banality of Evil.* New York: Viking, 1963.

Auden, W.H. *The Dyer's Hand.* London: Faber and Faber, 1963.

Baudelaire, Charles. "On the Essence of Laughter." *The Painter of Modern Life.* Trans. Jonathan Mayne. London: Phaidon, 1995. 147-65.

Bell, Michael. *The Sentiment of Reality: Truth of Feeling in the European Novel.* London: G. Allen and Unwin, 1983.

Breton, André. *Anthology of Black Humor.* Trans. Mark Polizzitti. San Francisco: City Lights, 1997.

Borges, J. L. "Borges and I." *Labyrinths.* Trans. Donald A. Yates and James E. Irby. Harmondsworth: Penguin, 1970. 282-84.

Brooks, Peter. *Reading for the Plot: Design and Intention in Narrative.* Cambridge, MA: Harvard UP, 1992.

Byatt, A. S. *Possession: A Romance.* New York: Random, House, 1990.

Conrad, Joseph. *Heart of Darkness.* Ed. Paul B. Armstrong. New York: W. W. Norton, 2006.

Eliot, T. S. "Baudelaire." Ed. John Hayward. *Selected Prose.* Harmondsworth: Penguin, 1953. 185-196.

———. *Notes towards the Definition of Culture.* London: Faber and Faber, 1948.

Freud, Sigmund. *Civilization and Its Discontents.* Trans. James Strachey. New York: W. W. Norton, 1961.

Kermode, Frank. *The Sense of an Ending: Studies in the Theory of Fiction.* Oxford: Oxford UP, 1966.

Laing, R.D. *The Divided Self.* London: Tavistock, 1960.

Lessing, Doris. *The Memoirs of a Survivor.* London: Octagon, 1974.

Maritain, Jacques. *Art and Scholasticism and Other Essays.* Trans. J. F. Scanlan. London: Sheed and Ward, 1949.

MacIntyre, Alasdair. *After Virtue: A Study in Moral Theory.* London: Duckworth, 1985.

McQuillan, Martin. Ed. *Theorising Muriel Spark: Gender, Race, Deconstruction.* Basingstoke: Palgrave, 2002.

Orwell, George. *The Collected Essays, Journalism and Letters.* Vol. 2. Eds. Sonia Orwell and Ian Angus. London: Secker and Warburg, 1968.

Plath, Sylvia. *Ariel.* London: Faber and Faber, 1965.

Popper, Karl. *Conjectures and Refutations: The Growth of Scientific Knowledge.* London: Routledge and Kegan Paul, 1963.

———. *Open Society and Its Enemies.* London: Routledge and Kegan Paul, 1962.

Sartre, Jean-Paul, *Sketch for a Theory of the Emotions.* Trans. Philip Mairet. London: Routledge, 2002.

Sass, Louis A. *Madness and Modernism: Insanity in the Light of Modern Art, Literature, and Thought.* Cambridge, MA: Harvard UP, 1992.

Sechehaye, Marguerite. *Autobiography of Schizophrenic Girl.* Trans. Grace Rubin-Rabson. New York: Grune & Stratton, 1951.

Spark, Muriel. *The Comforters.* 1957. Harmondsworth: Penguin, 1963.

———. *Curriculum Vitae.* Boston: Houghton Mifflin, 1993.

———. "The Desegregation of Art." 1971. *Critical Essays on Muriel Spark.* Ed. Joseph Hynes. New York: Hall, 1992. 33-37.

———. *The Driver's Seat.* 1970. Harmondsworth: Penguin, 1974.

———. *The Girls of Slender Means.* 1963. Harmondsworth: Penguin, 1965.

———. *The Hothouse by the East River.* 1973. Harmondsworth: Penguin, 1975.

———. *Not to Disturb.* 1971. Harmondsworth: Penguin, 1974.

———. *The Prime of Miss Jean Brodie.* 1961. Harmondworth: Penguin, 1965.

———. "The Religion of an Agnostic: A Sacramental View of the World in Writings of Proust." *Church of England Newspaper,* 27 Nov. 1953, 1.

Taylor, Charles. *A Secular Age.* Cambridge, MA: Harvard UP, 2007.

Vaihinger, Hans. *The Philosophy of As If.* Trans. C. K. Ogden. London: Routledge and Kegan Paul, 1935.

Wiener, Norbert. *Cybernetics: Or Control and Communication in the Animal and the Machine.* New York: John Wiley, 1948.

CHAPTER 4

MURIEL SPARK AND THE

MEANING OF TREASON

Marina MacKay

The whine in her voice—". . . betrayed me, betrayed
me"—bored and afflicted Sandy. It is seven years, thought
Sandy, since I betrayed this tiresome woman. What does
she mean by "betray"?

—Muriel Spark, *The Prime of Miss Jean Brodie*

What are we talking about when we speak of betrayal?

—Gabriella Turnaturi, *Betrayals*

"If you did not betray us it is impossible that you could have
been betrayed by us," Sandy Stranger tells her former teacher in
Muriel Spark's *The Prime of Miss Jean Brodie:* "It's only possible to
betray where loyalty is due" (135–36). One of Miss Brodie's "set" and
an ally in the running battle with the traditionalism of Marcia Blaine's
School for Girls, Sandy Stranger has betrayed her mentor by bringing
Miss Brodie's fascist allegiances to the attention of the headmistress,
Miss Mackay. Sandy's act of treason repays the betrayed in her own
currency: Miss Brodie has betrayed the stolidly conservative school
of which she is a part and Sandy has betrayed Miss Brodie; in both
cases the reader is meant to concede Sandy's point about the limits
of due loyalty. What this essay sets out to do is, first, to suggest
that this question of what makes calculated treachery legitimate, a
question most explicitly asked in *The Prime of Miss Jean Brodie*, is
the central problem addressed in the first half of Spark's career, and,
second, to argue that the recurrent idea of treason in her novels offers a way of understanding in both historical and literary-historical
terms a writer more usually read in relation to theological than historical inquiries.

The Midcentury Context

Spark shared her preoccupation with disloyalty with another famous midcentury woman writer, Rebecca West, whose studies of Second World War and Cold War traitors, *The Meaning of Treason* and *The New Meaning of Treason* (1964), give my essay its title and its guiding assumption that to think about treason is to think less about a moral problem than about the ways in which moral problems acquire their contingently cultural and historical significance: what, after all, does treason mean, and how does it accrue new meanings? Long understood in relation to theological and ethical preoccupations identified with her well-known conversion to Roman Catholicism in 1954 and now increasingly theorized in more secular terms, Spark's writing is seldom read historically and contextually, almost certainly because her narrative experiments seem to operate almost exclusively in the conceptual space where the more abstract preoccupations of Roman Catholic theology overlap with the metafictional and fabulist concerns of postmodernism. Spark's focus on essentially ontological rather than cultural questions—and the ontological is where religious inquiry and self-conscious textuality meet in her work—makes her writing resistant to being read in relation to those questions of cultural reference more usually identified in Spark's own time with the turn, after modernism, toward realist forms of fiction.

By this I mean that midcentury British fiction famously demonstrates a sense of division over the formal futures of the novel: the terms by which the era would largely be defined were set by Spark's more earth-bound contemporaries, writers such as the polemically realist C. P. Snow, John Cowper Powys, and the so-called Angry Young Men, all intent on restoring fiction to a condition of panoramic social documentary that obtained (at least for their polemical purposes) before the generation of Joyce and Woolf transformed the novel as a form. However, this was also the era of the domestic *nouveaux romanciers* B. S. Johnson and Christine Brooke-Rose, keen to extend modernist and modernizing aspirations into the second half of the century. Seen in relation to these starkly divided possibilities, Spark, along with contemporaries like Henry Green and Iris Murdoch, is an amphibious figure. "They say postmodernist, mostly," Spark told Martin McQuillan in a 1998 interview, "whatever that means" ("The Same" 216); at the same time as Spark acknowledges how poorly she corresponds to the norms of midcentury realism, she slyly registers her own unease with the dominant alternative of postmodernism—a critical/taxonomical alternative rather than a creative/literary one. This is a crucial ambivalence: a novelist like Spark is scarcely a realist, but to align her unproblematically with the emergent postmodernism of the *nouveau roman* would mean underplaying the capacious sociability, the meticulous curiosity about the specificities of mid-century manners that distinguishes her so clearly from continental counterparts. Rather than come down on one side or the other of this problematic binary, what I propose in this essay is that Spark's interest in treason is intractably real-worldly and historical, intimately connected to the political contexts in which she began her career as a novelist, but, importantly, that it also offers a different way of thinking about those concerns with the textual, fantastical, and world-making force of the imagination that point toward an incipient postmodernity: treason, for Spark, is always aligned with forms of political and social creativity.

It would be easy to assimilate to her moral preoccupations Spark's characteristic attention to duplicity, backstabbing, and decep-tion. On this conventional reading, novels that superficially resemble the ordinary social world are finally reducible to a Catholic novelist's Augustinian parables of human frailty. Hélène Cixous rather surpris-ingly took this orthodox line when, in 1968, she remarked that the "play of evil" in Spark's fiction is "comically modern": "it proceeds mechanically and anonymously, often by telephone or threatening letters," and is advanced by "some Judas who stands above the aver-age thanks to his intelligence and who exerts occult powers, either by blackmail, or profession (if he is a medium), or a gift for second sight" (206). So far so familiar, you might say: Spark the penetrat-ing moralist; Spark the Catholic novelist. Nonetheless, the timeliness that Cixous noticed when she called Spark's idea of evil "comically modern" is potentially significant. There is, after all, something more contingently historical than metaphysically universal in a Cold War preoccupation with knowledge that is illegitimately obtained and inappropriately exploited.

And the illicit acquisition and deployment of information is the central obsession of Spark's early work. Her first novel, *The Com-forters,* describes a pathologically attentive young man spying on his diamond-smuggling grandmother and a young woman being driven toward nervous collapse by the realization that her author watches her every move. In *Memento Mori*, the gerontologist Alec Warner wards off his horror at the approach of old age by corruptly accumulating information on his elderly cohort ("one had to use spies and win allies" [62]). In another early novel, *The Bachelors*, a forensic graphologist investigates a spiritual medium, while the central character of *The Ballad of Peckham Rye* is the demonic Dougal Douglas, whose profes-sional pastime of "human research" (18) means compiling secret dos-siers on those around him: "I would make an excellent informer," he admits with entertainingly evil candor, "for gathering information and having no scruples in passing it on you could look farther than me and fare worse" (130). Even Spark's ostensibly more serious and realistic *The Mandelbaum Gate* has as one of its main characters a Jordanian travel agent/insurance broker/trafficker in prostitutes whose various enterprises allow him to gather blackmail-worthy intelligence on the British residents of Jerusalem: "To be a spy of some sort was the respectable thing for any literate Arab," his son Abdul muses (100). (But espionage is not so neatly racialized in the novel; there is also a treasonous Englishwoman.) *The Abbess of Crewe* (1974) is often bracketed off from the rest of Spark's oeuvre as a witty but slight satire on the Watergate scandal, but its concern with illegitimate inquiry, with knowledge that is surreptitiously obtained and unfairly advantageous, is everywhere in Spark's fiction, and was very much in the midcentury air when she wrote her early novels. "Sandy will make an excellent Secret Service agent," Miss Brodie predicts, "a great spy" (*Prime* 116–17).

Where Sandy's dubious gift ultimately takes her speaks as much to the 1960s of the novel's publication as to the 1930s of its setting. The problem of treason, or the individual's readiness to resist the claims that the nation-state makes on its citizens, was a matter of pressing urgency in the middle of the twentieth century, during the years when the end of the Second World War shaded into the first half of the Cold War. The impetus for Rebecca West's forensic studies of treason—"The Better Mousetrap," *The Meaning of Treason*, *The New Meaning of Treason*, and *The Vassall Affair*—came from the procession of British traitors who appeared in the Old Bailey in the years after the Second World War. First to be tried was William Joyce, the famous "Lord Haw-Haw" of wartime German radio, hanged for broadcasting Nazi propaganda intended to undermine British morale; he was followed by John Amery, the black-sheep son of distinguished parents, who recruited for the Germans among the British soldiers detained in German prisoner of war camps. Then came, one after the other, the Communist scientists, embassy staff, and defense clerks who passed secrets to the Soviet Union: Allan Nunn May, Emil Klaus Fuchs, William Marshall, and William Vassall, among others. Meanwhile, the 1951 defection of the British diplomats Guy Burgess and Donald Maclean was stage-managed in such a way as to maintain, in one of those familiar Cold War paradoxes, maximum obscurity and maximum publicity. What makes West's case studies of all those famous midcentury figures so compelling is that she is interested less in how particular traitors betrayed, than in why anyone interested in the nature of the ties that bind individuals to communities should care about the Joyces and Amerys, Burgesses and Macleans.

Perhaps not surprisingly in view of West's own long career as a novelist, though strikingly enough in view of her increasingly conservative politics, her studies of treason reveal an amused fascination with the traitor's ability to construct and live in alternate realities. Although West never goes so far as to propose romantically that artistry and treason are exactly interchangeable forms of dissidence—as, say, her near-contemporary James Joyce had done when he allowed his authorial surrogate Stephen Dedalus to take as his artistic credo the "non serviam" of the first traitor (126, 260)—but she certainly attributes treason to fictive and fabulatory impulses that find expression in the construction of parallel worlds. The traitor "hates the real world," West proposes in *The Meaning of Treason*: "His power of fantasy enables him to build any country which is the declared enemy of his fatherland into an ideal and beloved world" (242). And then there is her attentiveness to those seductions of plot that link the traitor to the creator and consumer of fiction: "Nothing was simple in that world of espionage and counter-espionage, treachery and counter-treachery, vengeance and vendetta; and complication is to the soul what condiments are to the palate." Throughout *The Meaning of Treason*, political disloyalty becomes a kind of artistry for the disempowered: "the life of the political conspirator offers the man of restricted capacity but imaginative energy excitements and satisfactions which he can never derive from overt activities" (21). In this respect Spark's best-known heroine resembles West's prototypical traitor: an ordinary Edinburgh schoolmistress—"there was nothing outwardly odd about Miss Brodie"—who makes her life extraordinary through fantasy; "Inwardly was a different matter, and it remained to be seen, towards what extremities her nature worked her" (*Prime* 45).

Imagining the War

To move between the literal, large-scale acts of treason that West records and the small-scale betrayals of Spark's invention is perhaps simply to register that, as the German journalist Margret Boveri wrote in her 1956 study of modern treason, "for us treason has become a concept which permeates every day of our own lives" (5–6). Although the Cold War prolonged such wartime preoccupations as covert and overt allegiance, the containment of dissent, and the legitimacy of the state's command on its citizens, Spark had also known treason first hand during the Second World War. This is crucial in view of how central the war is in the novels of the first half of her career. So, for example, the novel that follows *The Prime of Miss Jean Brodie* is another story of treachery, but set in the context of the war's endings rather than its beginnings: *The Girls of Slender Means* concludes with a knife slipped into the back of a member of

the crowd gathered in London to celebrate the end of the war, a lit-
eralizing of the metaphor driving the novel's main story of a savage
betrayal in a bombed hostel—a betrayal that derides any complacent
belief in the moral righteousness of the war's British victors. The war
is even more necessarily central to *The Mandelbaum Gate*; set in
Jerusalem during the trial of Adolf Eichmann, it is another novel in
which the victorious British prove treacherous and unreliable allies.
And in Spark's most opaque novel, *The Hothouse by the East River*,
characters in 1960s New York are tormented by memories of war work
that required them to enlist German prisoners for the British cause.
The novel is centered on a mystery: the reappearance of Helmut
Kiel—a German prisoner of war, possibly a Nazi double agent, the
former lover of the novel's heroine Elsa, and supposedly sent to his
death in prison by her jealous husband Paul. The novel begins with
the sighting of Kiel in New York looking not a day older than he did
in the POW camp twenty years earlier. By the end of the novel the
reader has learned that not only is Kiel a ghost but also that Paul
and Elsa are themselves long dead, killed by a V-2 rocket in London
in the spring of 1944.

Derived from her own war work, *The Hothouse by the East
River* captures, Spark said, some of the "surrealistic, mysterious"
qualities of that time (*Curriculum* 159). The organization referred
to as the Compound in the novel is based on what, in her interim
autobiography *Curriculum Vitae*, she called "Delmer's Compound,"
where she absorbed "a whole world of method and intrigue in the
dark field of Black Propaganda or Psychological Warfare, and the
successful and purposeful deceit of the enemy" (147). The journalist
Sefton Delmer's black propaganda unit at Milton Bryan in Bedfordshire
was run under the auspices of Britain's new Political Warfare Execu-
tive; in the words of Spark's estranged former collaborator Derek
Stanford, this operation "might have come intact out of one of her
own novels" (43). The unit produced radio programs that masquer-
aded as authentically and loyally Nazi in order to communicate their
deeply subversive messages to the Germans. To create convincingly
German-sounding broadcasts the unit resorted to devious means
of gathering and manipulating information: bugging the prisoner of
war camps for authentic-sounding idioms, reading the dead letters
addressed by their families to missing German soldiers (and counter-
feiting heartless replies intended to undermine civilian morale), and
recruiting its personnel from prisoner of war camps. "Traitors" is the
word Spark conscientiously avoids when she writes, in *Curriculum
Vitae*, about the captive personnel with whom she worked; on the
contrary, these were "truly patriotic Germans" eager to volunteer
for a role in which "they could oppose Hitler and the Nazis" (151). A

treasonous personnel, then, was used to impersonate loyalty, to mimic the pro-German stance that it was attempting to overturn: "grand fellows," Sefton Delmer calls them with appropriately double-edged irony in his autobiography, "with tremendous *esprit de corps* and a truly German pride in their work" (112).

Spark describes with warmth "those brave POWs, who were risking so much to smash Hitler" (*Curriculum* 155). It perhaps goes without saying that the German and British causes were hardly morally equivalent, but it is worth noting, all the same, how Spark redefines German traitors as true German patriots here—as she would have known perfectly well, British nationals who succumbed, or encouraged others to succumb, to comparable inducements in the corresponding circumstances of German prison camps were put on trial for their lives at the end of the war (this was the crime for which John Amery was hanged). But despite that the autobiographical account of her war work offers such an uncomplicated justification for the acts of treason that were both mimicked and elicited at Milton Bryan—hence those "truly patriotic Germans"—Ian Rankin was surely right to suggest that Spark's work in black propaganda "proved crucial to the writing career that followed" in view of the emphasis in her novels on "forgeries and fakes . . . creators of fiction" (45). Importantly, the very self-consciously fabulatory novel that arose out of these experiences is more troubling and resonant than anything in the autobiography. Now, in *The Hothouse by the East River*, the prisoners of war who have turned informant, "whatever the degree of conviction that has led them to work for the enemy," are made uneasy by "a nagging knowledge that they have deserted their native forces" (54), while it is the possible S.S. man Kiel who may be the "loyal German at heart" (118). The double lives at issue in the novel are not just those of the suspected double agent Kiel—doubled again in what is either a literal resurrection or a coincidental resemblance to innocent Mueller, a New York shoe salesman—but also those of the guilty, tormented Elsa and Paul, who proved themselves the falsest of friends to him. The undead guilt that haunts the present is not simply that of the evil German Kiel, spectrally alive in the 1960s, but that of the supposedly loyal war workers, the ghostly Elsa and Paul.

Unreality and indeterminacy are the keynotes of *The Hothouse by the East River*; its creative response to the all-too-historical lies and masquerades of wartime double-dealing is antirealist fantasy. In an act of metafictional world making, the guilty and tormented intelligence worker Paul brings the characters from his wartime career back into life: "These people are not real," Paul tells a policeman on a thoroughly solid seeming New York street; "My son, my wife, my daughter, do not exist" (93). Paul and Elsa are "ghosts twice removed from reality," as Alan Bold puts it, because "they are, after all, only literary creations and so hover between the existence the reader grants them and the illusion the author asserts" (98). As Bold's comments suggest, the novel is far more complicated than a ghost story because of how continuously it underscores the flickering spectrality of all literary invention. Instead of asking the reader for one initial suspension of disbelief, *The Hothouse by the East River* forces us to keep in mind, at the same time, both the solid verisimilitude of the literary illusion and the insistently fictional status of Elsa and Paul, Spark's haunted and haunting, innocent and culpable war criminals. The metafictionality of the novel resides in the same kind of self-consciousness about the malleability of the real and the true as that which sustains traitors impersonating treason at the Compound.

Imagining the Nation

The Hothouse by the East River is a typical Spark novel in that it is set in an artificially enclosed community. Invariably, the self-contained collectivities of her fiction are ripe for betrayal from within, and perhaps treason is almost an inevitable plot outcome of her characteristic institutional settings. Nonetheless, what makes *The Hothouse by the East River* a particularly telling treatment of disloyalty is that its wartime origins indicate most explicitly how Spark's microcommunities might be seen to intersect with and model the wider community of the nation-state. And insofar as treason is a rejection of what Spark, in *Curriculum Vitae*, calls the "crowd emotions" elicited by nationalism, it clearly has an emancipating function (63). The specific context in which the phrase appears is her discussion of the antinationalism instilled in her by Miss Brodie's original, Christina Kay. She was, Spark explains, a member of the generation of women made permanent spinsters by the epic-scale loss of their male contemporaries in the First World War: a "war-bereaved spinsterhood," she calls it in *The Prime of Miss Jean Brodie* (43). But the implications of Spark's autobiographical anecdote about her former teacher are as much political as psychosexual in underscoring how the Great War was a highpoint of chauvinistic and imperialist public nationalisms:

> For instance, she felt "Land of Hope and Glory" was basically anti-Christian. And we were expressly forbidden to join in any singing of the lines "Wider still and wider Shall thy bounds be set; God who made thee mighty, Make thee mightier yet." Of course, she was quite right. Such teachings, the sheer logic of the contradiction inherent in

them to the moral culture we honoured, sank in. Miss Kay recommended to us, instead, the lines of Kipling's "Recessional": "The tumult and the shouting dies; The captains and the kings depart; Still stands thine ancient sacrifice; An humble and a contrite heart." More than once, Miss Kay brought home to our attention exactly *what* we were singing so lustily. We were taught not to be carried away by crowd emotions, not to be fools. (*Curriculum* 62–63)

The Marcia Blaine School in *The Prime of Miss Jean Brodie* makes a telling idol of the nation-building Garibaldi, but the novel's radical skepticism about the demand for solidarity that national communities enforce appears in Miss Brodie's proclamations about the school's catchwords: "Phrases like 'the team spirit' are always employed to cut across individualism, love and personal loyalties," she tells the girls, who "would as soon have entered the Girl Guides as the team spirit" (82, 83).

Just as in *The Hothouse by the East River* Spark ties politically motivated falsifications and betrayals to acts of world-making fantasy, what the treacherous Sandy learns from the treacherous Miss Brodie is that it is possible to reshape the world according to her own needs and desires. "Sandy was never bored, but she had to lead a double life of her own in order never to be bored," the narrator explains; Sandy wonders if "Jenny, too, had the feeling of leading a double life" (*Prime* 20, 19). Miss Brodie turns her girls into artists by showing them that the world in which they live is intractably multiple and endlessly rewritable. With no more self-consciousness than the children she teaches, she makes an alternative reality for herself out of all the materials that are available to her as a cultured Scotswoman. To return for a moment to the novel's Great War background, Miss Brodie's dead lover, the soldier Hugh Carruthers, an early object of her pupils' fascination, is far more textual than fleshly:

> Season of mists and mellow fruitfulness. I was engaged to a young man at the beginning of the War but he fell on Flanders Field. . . . He fell the week before Armistice was declared. He fell like an autumn leaf, although he was only twenty-two years of age. When we go indoors we shall look on the map at Flanders, and the spot where my lover was laid before you were born. He was poor. He came from Ayrshire, a countryman, but a hard-working and clever scholar. . . . Hugh was one of the Flowers of the Forest, lying in his grave. (9–10)

Hugh is a composite of the prematurely dead: John Keats ("Season of mists . . ."), Robert Burns ("from Ayrshire, a countryman . . ."),

Wilfred Owen ("fell the week before Armistice"), the dead boys of John McCrae's patriotic war poetry ("In Flanders Fields"), and lost lovers from Scottish folk ballads ("Flowers of the Forest"). Jean Brodie is a textual bricoleuse and improviser, composing out of whatever is available. Both already attuned to the complex possibilities of conducting multiple lives in fantasy, Sandy the spy and the actress Jenny will come instinctively to understand Miss Brodie's methods of overwriting one reality with another: "the two girls listened with double ears, and the rest of the class with single" (76).

Sandy's fantasy life, however, will take her from outlaw heroine to heroine of law enforcement. When, for example, Sandy and Jenny write their novel about the return of Miss Brodie's Hugh—in their rendering, a character from Robert Louis Stevenson, with a touch of Brontë's Rochester—they position themselves as romantic, righteous rebels like Miss Brodie herself:

> He had not been killed in the war, that was a mistake in the telegram. He had come back from the war and called to enquire for Miss Brodie at school, where the first person whom he encountered was Miss Mackay, the headmistress. She had informed him that Miss Brodie did not desire to see him, she loved another. With a bitter, harsh laugh, Hugh went and made his abode in a mountain eyrie, where, wrapped in a leathern jacket, he had been discovered one day by Sandy and Jenny. (17)

For all its hilarious precocity, the narrative that Jenny and Sandy create is very much a testament to the seductive charms of Miss Brodie's world-transforming habits. Learning from Miss Brodie that women, too, can be the heroines of adventure stories, Sandy and Jenny will save the day for the sexy Hugh Carruthers. But an encounter between Jenny and a flasher introduces the unnamed policewoman who develops a powerful command on Sandy's imagination: Sandy will later invent the character of Sergeant Anne Grey and embark on a campaign "to eliminate sex from Edinburgh and environs." Although the ensuing fantasy is as funny as any of the others, it is also a telling foreshadowing of her betrayal of Miss Brodie to the forces of the law for which the puritanical Miss Mackay has, in Sandy's imaginative life, previously stood: "And another thing," Sandy tells the imaginary Sergeant Anne Grey in a patchwork of euphemisms cribbed from the local newspapers, "we've got to find out more about the case of Brodie and whether she is yet in a certain condition as a consequence of her liaison with Gordon Lowther, described as singing master, Marcia Blaine School for Girls." "All we need are a couple of incriminating documents," replies the imaginary Sergeant Anne Grey—and Sandy, the traitor in the making, offers to supply them (72). The prefiguring of the final betrayal is clear, though the creativity ironically originates with Brodie.

And creativity means casualties. When Sandy starts imagining herself a policewoman, we know that Miss Brodie will suffer for it, just as the girls who comprise Miss Brodie's "fascisti" (31), as Sandy comes to think of them, are put at risk by the fantasy life of their teacher. Thanks to their mentor's work of unifying a heterogeneous group of children, they are "all famous in the school, which is to say they were held in suspicion and not much liking" (2). While one is famous for sex appeal and others for more conventional talents, Sandy Stranger is "famous for her vowel sounds"—half-English in a Scottish school, Sandy's accent marks her as the "stranger" her name implies—and, more troublingly, she is "merely notorious for her small, almost non-existent eyes" (3). These all-seeing eyes, "tiny eyes which it was astonishing that anyone could trust" (106), signify a talent for spying that Miss Brodie thinks can be harnessed to her own ends: lovely Rose is to be Teddy Lloyd's lover in her teacher's stead, while Sandy "with her insight" is to be the "informant" who keeps Miss Brodie up to date on the progress of her vicarious ro-mance (116). "Almost shrewdly" (112), she chooses Sandy as her agent-spy, but Sandy's protest against this autocratic allocation of the girls' destinies will be to sleep with Teddy Lloyd and to turn that gift for acquiring and manipulating knowledge, so often praised by Miss Brodie, on Miss Brodie herself. Initially a patriot and spy for Miss Brodie, Sandy ultimately defects because her loyalty enables insight; and her insight, treason. And Spark is insistent that the leader has created in her follower the conditions of her own betrayal; after all, she prides herself on being the descendant of Edinburgh's much-mythologized Deacon Brodie, a respectable cabinetmaker by day and a robber by night: Willie Brodie "died cheerfully on a gibbet of his own devising" (93). The traitor Sandy is both the gibbet that executes its architect and the symbolic cancer or "internal growth" that finally kills Miss Brodie (58).

Insofar as Sandy-as-traitor is represented as both a "stranger" or outsider and an almost inevitable byproduct of the Brodie cult, she conforms to the psychology of treason that West hypothesized in her report on what is perhaps the most famous of the cases of real-world disloyalty that gripped midcentury British culture. The 1945 trial for high treason of William Joyce, "Lord Haw-Haw," raised the most resonant questions about the precise nature of the claims and expectations that make treason possible and punishable. It emerged during the course of his prosecution that Joyce had never in fact been a British subject, and that, unknown perhaps even to himself, Joyce was the American-born son of formerly Irish (at that time British) and now naturalized American citizens who had returned to Ireland in Joyce's childhood without renewing their British citizenship. Yet despite being indicted for betraying a country that was never his own, Joyce was hanged in January 1946 because although his discovered citizenship seemed to render null the expectation of loyalty that would make treason possible, it was outweighed by another technical circumstance: that he owned a British passport and thus owed allegiance for the protection it gave him. In support of this indictment, West's *The Meaning of Treason* quotes Edward Coke's maxim "Protectio trahit subjectionem, et subjectio protectionem" (22)—"protection draws allegiance and allegiance protection"—another way of saying, as Spark's traitor does, that it's only possible to betray where loyalty is due. Inevitably, the controversy outlived Joyce's execution because no case could more comprehensively have denaturalized, so to speak, the seemingly "natural" claims of national allegiance—right after a war among nations that had killed sixty million people—than that of a deracinated Irish-American hanged for betraying a country whose only legal claim on him arose from a passport he should never have possessed and that would never, were the fraud discovered, have given him the protection that proved the grounds of his hanging.

You could say that this already resembles the world of darkly ironic contingency in which Spark's fiction operates: a real-life *nouveau roman* of absurdist plot twists in which the critical knowledge about the protagonist that will save or hang him is withheld even from the main actor himself. This was, West concluded, "a peculiarly nonsensical doom" and "the most completely unnecessary death that any criminal has ever died on the gallows" (8, 28). What gives the story of William Joyce its particularly Sparkian turn of the screw, though, is that the war's most notorious British traitor turned out to have been the most naïvely ardent of British patriots. As a working-class Catholic teenager in Ireland, he had acted as an informant for the Royal Irish Reserve Force, better known as the notoriously brutal and undisciplined paramilitary outfit the Black and Tans, an experience he would later invoke in support of a failed attempt to become an officer in the British Army: living in his own world, internally coherent but unrelated to any recognizable historical reality, Joyce had almost certainly misunderstood the embarrassing reputation of the Black and Tans. Hyper-patriotic fantasy makes traitors, West argued, when she looked for the roots of Joyce's treason in the pro-British fanaticism of a reluctantly Irish and unknowingly American youth. His fascism, paradoxically, proved to be the outcome of his capacity for patriotism rather than a contradiction of it: "his love of an obsolete England . . . made him a fascist," as West puts it (17–18). Boveri took a similar line in her study of treason. As a German nationalist who had continued to work under Nazism, so not exactly ill-placed to understand the attractions of romantic nationalism, Boveri proposed that Joyce was driven to treason by his "love of a romanticized fatherland which never existed, but which he was determined to create" (148). But whatever Joyce's political ambitions, West writes, his slender command of reality was such that he "could never have been trusted not to make a mistake of such grossness as the mistake which led him, loving England, to plan her salvation through subjugation to the architects of Belsen and Buchenwald" (*Meaning* 41).

Echoing this continuity that West and Boveri posit between political treason and idealist fantasy, characters betray in Spark's novels not because they care too little for their victims, but because they care too much. Indeed, in some of her novels treason is presented as morally obligatory. Perhaps the exemplary "necessary betrayer or good Judas figure," to borrow Bryan Cheyette's characterization (75), is Jean Taylor in *Memento Mori*, who frees the elderly Charmian Piper from debilitating guilt over her unearned moral advantages by knowingly divulging the ancient secret of Charmian's adultery: "There is a time for loyalty and a time when loyalty comes to an end," Jean Taylor says, sounding like Sister Helena of the Transfiguration at her most gnomic (175). Sandy's treason, though, is less like Jean Taylor's loving betrayal and more the kind of treason West and Boveri envisage when they propose that treason is the product of a capacity for imaginative transformation that renders the real inadequate—a "transformation of the commonplace," as it were, as in the famous title of Sandy's "odd psychological treatise on the nature of moral perception" (*Prime* 35). In the end, Sandy will betray Miss Brodie for failing to be what Sandy thought she was. "Friendship?" asks one of Lord Lucan's former accomplices in Spark's *Aiding and Abetting*, another novel about misplaced loyalties: "Yes, but there can be too severe a strain on friendship. In friendship there is a point of collapse—a murderer revealed, or a traitor—they are people-within-people hitherto unknown" (56). Shortly before the betrayal Sandy will wonder whether it is she or Miss Brodie who has changed over the years, but the reader already knows that "the principles governing the end of [Miss Brodie's] prime would have astonished herself at the beginning of it" (*Prime* 45). Miss Brodie never saw in herself the Nazi she would become, and Sandy's eventual betrayal will hold her accountable to what Sandy used to think her. For Spark, as for West and Boveri, treason is a crime of passion.

A Better Mousetrap

Seen from one angle, treason liberates: an unthinking collective like the Marcia Blaine School for Girls deserves the shake-up Miss Brodie gives it, and the Brodie set, too, has solidified into a force for ill. Seen from another angle, however, treason entraps. Miss Brodie's flight from 1930s-style conservatism, exemplified in the novel nationally by Stanley Baldwin and locally by the stalwart Miss Mackay, takes her directly to fascism; Sandy, in turn, will walk out of the increasingly oppressive Brodie set and right into the Roman Catholic Church, "in whose ranks she [will find] quite a number of Fascists much less agreeable than Miss Brodie" (134). This is the problem Rebecca West was getting at when she titled her essay on the traitor William Marshall "The Better Mousetrap." "The trouble about the British Embassy in Moscow," West writes, "is that people there are apt to feel as if they were in a mousetrap" (258–59); she goes on to describe the grim atmosphere of claustrophobia, remoteness, and acute visibility pervading the lives of the British diplomatic staff stationed there. The real danger, though, is that those expatriates who "*give way to this fancy* of being in a mousetrap may find themselves inside a real one" (259; emphasis added). Ultimately the Soviet espionage ring in which the lonely radio operator William Marshall becomes embroiled proves to be, simply, a more effective prison than the "mousetrap" of his own imagination. Throughout *The Prime of Miss Jean Brodie*, traitors build themselves better mousetraps, and fascism is to Spark's account of treason what Communism is to West's.

Catholicism, though, is a mousetrap of a more complex kind in this novel, as becomes clear when Spark characterizes the tension between the allure and the danger of imaginative rebellion through the relationship between Miss Brodie and the science teacher Miss Lockhart, her rival for the affections of Gordon Lowther and the Brodie set. Miss Lockhart captures the attention of the girls with her preliminary demonstration of the potential risks of the science room: "I have enough gunpowder in this jar to blow up this school," she tells them (*Prime* 79); Jean Brodie is intent on blowing up the school in her own way, of course, but Miss Lockhart's is a "lawful glamour" (24). Prefiguring Sandy's rejection of the lawless Miss Brodie, nice Mr. Lowther will ultimately choose the science teacher who "could . . . blow up the school with her jar of gunpowder and would never dream of doing so" (121). This echo of the Gunpowder Plot, the treasonous 1605 conspiracy of the Catholic Guy Fawkes, indicates that the significance of Roman Catholicism in the novel is as much political as spiritual—a significance oddly occluded even in accounts of Spark that foreground her Catholicism.

Of course, Catholicism is superficially implicated in treason to the extent that Sandy's betrayal of Miss Brodie partly takes the form of her conversion to a religion that her teacher despises: "Do you think she did this to annoy me?" Miss Brodie asks; "I begin to wonder if it was not Sandy who betrayed me" (66). More important, though, is the extent to which Catholicism is treason in the more literal sense that to become a Catholic in this novel is to embrace what the novel explicitly presents as foreign and alien. Thus Miss Brodie, denouncing Catholicism, "bring[s] to her support a rigid Edinburgh-born side of herself when the Catholic Church was in question, although this side was not otherwise greatly in evidence" (90), whereas Sandy, in contrast, is like her author insofar as "both were born and raised in Edinburgh, but not entirely of it" (Murray and Tait 116). Sandy increasingly comes to recognize herself as an outsider: in a novel dominated by the Scottish capital, Sandy realizes that "her fifteen years might have been spent in any suburb of any city in the British Isles" and that "some quality of life peculiar to Edinburgh and nowhere else had been going on unbeknown to her all the time" (115). West argued in *The Meaning of Treason* that "people do not become traitors unless they are unable to fit into the society in which they were born" (228), and what Sandy has missed out on is "the religion of Calvin . . . something definite to reject" (*Prime* 115). It is in order to reject a Scottish culture to which she never really belonged that Sandy embraces what Spark represents as the suspect foreign identity of the Catholic.

Miss Brodie's own characterization as "Roman" throughout the novel implies at the same time her foreignness, her attraction to fascism, her unacknowledged affinity with Catholicism, her imperial glamour and coercive power, and her vulnerability to treachery: "As soon expect Julius Caesar to apply for a job at a crank school as Miss Brodie," the girls loyally believe. "If the authorities wanted to get rid of her she would have to be assassinated" (6). Miss Brodie is also associated, and associates herself, with the beautiful, tragic, Roman Catholic, and only in the most arbitrary sense Scottish, Mary Queen of Scots, who was, like Miss Brodie, both accused of treason and herself betrayed. During what Spark summarizes as a decade of crank obsessions, Miss Brodie is one of those high-minded and intellectually curious unmarried women who "called themselves Europeans and Edinburgh a European capital" (44); in one way, then, she represents the attractive side of internationalism, a cosmopolitan freedom from narrow-minded nationalisms, but in another she evokes the more sinister transnational ideologies of old (Roman) and new (Fascist) imperialism. Seen in this light, Catholicism's own transcendence of national divisions is both emancipating and treacherous, as well as being associated—and here Spark knowingly resurrects a longstanding anti-Catholic slur—with secret knowledge, surveillance, and espionage. The "deracinated" Jew (Spark herself identified as part-Jewish) serves a similar function in *The Mandelbaum Gate*: a creatively transgressive and a culturally suspect figure because her comprehensive knowledge may be covertly accumulated, and her allegiances are always open to question. When she finishes the novel as Sister Helena of the Transfiguration, Sandy embraces what is paradoxically a dissident, outsider status. Just as Jenny will show her debt to the theatrical Miss Brodie by becoming an actress, Sandy, in taking on literally a new identity as a Roman Catholic nun, will follow—in the idea if not the detail—her seemingly rejected mentor.

In short, what creative fiction-making and political treachery have in common in Spark's novels is their shared skepticism about orthodoxy, their resistance to consensual and monolithic understandings of what constitutes the real. This is as true of Sandy's betrayal of Miss Brodie as it is of Miss Brodie's betrayal of the Marcia Blaine School for Girls. Indeed, when the sociologist Gabriella Turnaturi argues that disloyalty has its own creative pleasures, she brings us strikingly close to the idea of fiction at work in a writer like Spark:

> For the betrayer—for all betrayers, and not just spies—the world that surrounds us loses its obviousness and appears as simply one of many possible versions of reality and truth. In a certain sense, the person who betrays and is aware of his own duality—of the disconnect between what is and what appears to be—enjoys the epistemological privilege of glimpsing possible worlds and probing behind and beyond appearances. He becomes aware of realities more complex than apparent reality, which is in itself complex and multiple. This epiphany of the possible can make the game of betrayal positively voluptuous. (34)

Throughout Spark's writing the imagination tends toward treason, toward an "epiphany of the possible" that is inherently subversive. "In each act of the imagination is a repetition of Satan's original rebellion against the Almighty," writes Cairns Craig in his discussion of how the Calvinistic fear of the imagination has shaped the modern Scottish novel (200): it is, Craig argues, her dawning realization that fantasy is dangerous that leads Sandy to put herself behind bars rather than become the woman she so closely resembles (202).

But even if Spark agreed with Sandy that the imagination is evil, and with the novelist surrogate of *Memento Mori* who says that the art of the novel "is very like the practice of deception" (192), she knew that policing the imagination meant the death of fiction. Beginning her career in an era when the scope of the British novel was essentially being circumscribed by antimodernists who had appointed themselves custodians of the real, and in an era when the novel was being mourned as a dead form by literary critics who took those writers at their own somewhat inflated evaluation, Spark would present a more expansive view of the possibilities of fiction. In *The Comforters*, another novel about fiction-making and parallel existences, the heroine is writing a book on narrative form in the modern novel. When asked about its progress, Caroline admits that she is "having difficulty with the chapter on realism" (57). Forty years later, her author would describe in an interview her own very profound "difficulty with . . . realism": "I find," she said, "that realistic novels are more committed to dogmatic and absolute truth than most other varieties of fiction" ("An Interview" 147). What I have tried to suggest in this essay is that Spark's postmodernist—"whatever that means"—concern with realities that are plural, contingent, provisional, and amenable to creative transformation are nowhere more evident than when she draws in miniature the political betrayals that dominated midcentury British culture. In the end, I think, Spark would have endorsed the conclusion West reached in *The Meaning of Treason*, that treason is as necessary as it is inevitable: "All men"—and all women— "should have a drop or two of treason in their veins" (306).

Works Cited

Bold, Alan. *Muriel Spark*. London: Methuen, 1986.
Boveri, Margret. *Treason in the Twentieth Century*. Trans. Jonathan Steinberg. New York: Putnam, 1963.
Cheyette, Bryan. *Muriel Spark*. Tavistock: Northcote, 2000.
Cixous, Hélène. "Grimacing Catholicism: Muriel Spark's Macabre Farce." *Theorizing Muriel Spark: Gender, Race, Deconstruction*. 1968. Ed. Martin McQuillan. Basingstoke: Palgrave, 2002. 204–07.
Craig, Cairns. *The Modern Scottish Novel: Narrative and the National Imagination*. Edinburgh: Edinburgh UP, 1999.
Delmer, Sefton. *Black Boomerang: An Autobiography*. Vol. 2. London: Secker, 1962.
Joyce, James. *A Portrait of the Artist as a Young Man*. Harmondsworth, UK: Penguin, 1992.
Murray, Isobel, and Bob Tait. *Ten Modern Scottish Novels*. Aberdeen: Aberdeen UP, 1984.
Rankin, Ian. "The Deliberate Cunning of Muriel Spark." Ed. Gavin Wallace and Randall Stevenson. *The Scottish Novel Since the Seventies: New Visions, Old Dreams*. Edinburgh: Edinburgh UP, 1993. 41–53.
Spark, Muriel. *Aiding and Abetting*. 2000. New York: Anchor, 2001.

————. *The Ballad of Peckham Rye*. 1960. New York: New Directions, 1999.

————. *The Comforters*. 1957. New York: New Directions, 1994.

————. *Curriculum Vitae*. 1992. London: Penguin, 1993.

————. *The Hothouse by the East River*. 1973. Harmondsworth, UK: Penguin, 1975.

————. "An Interview with Dame Muriel Spark." By Robert Hosmer. *Salmagundi* 146–7 (2005): 127–58.

————. *The Mandelbaum Gate*. 1965. New York: Welcome Rain, 2001.

————. *Memento Mori*. 1959. New York: New Directions, 2000.

————. *The Prime of Miss Jean Brodie*. 1961. Harmondsworth, UK: Penguin, 1965.

————. "'The Same Informed Air': An Interview with Muriel Spark." By Martin McQuillan. *Theorizing Muriel Spark: Gender, Race, Deconstruction*. Basingstoke, UK: Palgrave, 2002. 210–29.

Stanford, Derek. *Muriel Spark: A Biographical and Critical Study*. London: Centaur, 1963.

Turnaturi, Gabriella. *Betrayals: The Unpredictability of Human Relations*. Trans. Lydia G. Cochrane. Chicago: U of Chicago P, 2007.

West, Rebecca. "The Better Mousetrap." *A Train of Powder: Six Reports on the Problem of Guilt and Punishment in Our Time*. 1955. Chicago: Ivan R. Dee, 2000. 253–310.

————. *The Meaning of Treason*. New York: Viking, 1947.

CHAPTER 5

READING SPARK IN THE AGE

OF SUSPICION

Bran Nicol

"I don't say that such and such a person lived and such
and such a person crossed the road, simply because I write
it—in a court of law it wouldn't carry any weight."
—Muriel Spark

In his well-known essay "Muriel Spark's Fingernails," Malcolm
Bradbury argued that Spark's 1970 novel *The Driver's Seat* was
part of a "distinct aesthetic phase" in which the author, "by localis-
ing certain aspects of a once broader artistic endeavour, made [her]
forms conspicuous" (272). Although Bradbury's essay has fallen into
disregard of late, largely as a result of the problems surrounding
its labelling of Spark as a "Catholic Novelist" (McQuillan, "Introduction" 1–7), this is a persuasive idea. *The Driver's Seat* depicts in a
particularly powerful way one of the key elements that preoccupied
Spark as a writer, which was, as the metaphorical connotation of
this novel's title suggests, a fascination with the question of one
individual's control over another—especially the curious, uncanny,
"battle" between an author and her fictional creation, the character,
for control of a novel.

On the face of it, this is not to say anything new. Bradbury
notes that "a preoccupation with the relation of an author to a fiction
and its agents" is central to Spark (Bradbury 272), while her "cruel"
treatment of her characters, as demonstrated most famously by her
matter-of-fact, proleptic anticipations of their deaths, has been long
acknowledged. However, the analogy between this aspect of Spark's
writing and the idea of the "God-like" writer, raised frequently in relation to Catholic writers, needs to be reassessed. Bradbury argues that
the "paradoxical analogy, between God and the novelist, is the basis

112

of much of [Spark's] fictional speculation and the stuff of her stories" (Bradbury 271). But I find little justification for this within the novels themselves. Unlike those of her contemporaries, such as Iris Murdoch or Graham Greene, Spark's novels do not offer a sustained meditation on religion or spirituality (even though the topic of Catholicism crops up frequently). God is not one of her "themes." Considering her approach to authorship in relation to the idea of God rather than other paradigms of power and control makes sense only—and this is the source of recent objections to Bradbury's discussion of Spark's Catholicism—in the unsatisfactory terms of "biographical criticism."

On the contrary, the detached, disciplined, often cinematic way Spark tells her stories and the anxious, self-interested, behavior of her characters, makes the Sparkian universe a godless one, similar in spirit (and at times in style) to the atheistic world of the *nouveau roman*. In this essay I want to take a fresh look at Spark's self-reflexive treatment of authors in her fiction, especially *The Driver's Seat* but also *The Comforters* (1957) and *Loitering with Intent* (1981), in the light of characterizations of her approach to authorship that are more recent than Bradbury's. I suggest that the figure of the author in Spark is in fact far from God-like. What we have instead is a deposed, humanized figure rather than a transcendent one; a small-scale, prurient, menacing entity, more like a stalker than a deity.

The Comforters and Self-consciousness

Spark's most God-like presentation of authorship comes right at the beginning of her career, in a very literal struggle between author and character that is at the heart of her first novel, *The Comforters*. Even then, though, the figure is more spectral than divine, not to mention fallible and ultimately defeated. The story tells of the haunting of the heroine Caroline Rose by the author who writes her into the novel. Once Caroline has guessed what is going on, once she has interpreted the persistent ghostly tapping of the typewriter keys and choruses of voices speaking her own thoughts, the author responds aggressively. She interrupts the narration of events to announce that "[a]t this point in the narrative, it might be as well to state that the characters in this novel are all fictitious, and do not refer to any living persons whatsoever" (*Comforters* 69). When this merely leads Caroline to decide she must counter the will of the author with her own, and try to "hold up the action of the novel" (105), the novelist retaliates by involving Caroline and her fiancé in a serious car crash, injuring them both.

But Caroline is capable of giving as good as she gets, and as she lies in her hospital bed she goads the phantom writer, complaining about the lack of "lively details" about her surroundings, suggesting bitchily that it is because "the author doesn't know how to describe a hospital ward" (161). This forces the author to produce, a page later, a passage describing what the ward includes in detail so rich as to be obviously overdone. The author addresses the reader directly again, confessing, "It is not easy to dispense with Caroline Rose. [. . .] When her [broken] leg was not too distracting, Caroline among the sleepers turned her mind to the art of the novel, wondering and cogitating, those long hours, and exerting an undue, unreckoned, influence on the narrative from which she is supposed to be absent for a time" (137).

At this point it is clear that the balance of power has shifted and where a character was initially haunted by the author, now the author is haunted by her character. Where the novelist has previously been described as "tuning into" Caroline's life (96), now Caroline is described at one point as having " 'picked up' a good deal of the preceding passage" (139), written by the author. In fact the two identities begin to merge. Caroline has been working out what the contents of the novel are likely to be by transcribing the echoed conversations she hears. She becomes convinced that "the narrative could never become coherent to her until she was at last outside it, and at the same time consummately inside it" (181). In practice this means taking over the writing of the novel itself. Having completed the book on the "twentieth-century novel" she has been working on, *Form in the Modern Novel* (pointedly, she is "having difficulty with the chapter on realism" [57]) she announces that next she is going to write a novel about "[c]haracters in a novel" (202). The next passage describes the actions of "the character called Laurence Manders" (202)—Caroline's fiancé, with whom *The Comforters* begins. The suggestion is therefore that the novel we have been reading, *The Comforters*, is itself the narrative over which Caroline has taken control.

The painful awareness of both spectral author and determined protagonist of their novel-boundedness makes *The Comforters* typical of what is known as metafiction. A fondness for using writers as central characters and deploying the sudden intervention of the author into the fictional world feature as standard characteristics of metafictional texts, which thereby explore the nature of fiction itself. Metafiction, or postmodernism, has been among the main contexts for reading Muriel Spark, along with Catholicism or, most recently, in the collection *Theorizing Muriel Spark*, "the philosophy and theory of the contemporary scene" (McQuillan, "Introduction" 6). In the period from the mid-1970s to mid-1980s, when metafiction began to be the subject of sustained analysis by literary theorists (Alter, Scholes, Waugh, Hutcheon), the trope of self-consciousness was used to describe fiction that seems *as if* it is aware of its existential status, of being read by a reader, and offering an in-built critique of itself or offering the reader a number of pointers on how to interpret it.

Behind such accounts is a notion of authorship that transforms the imaginative writer into a *critic* or *theorist*, one who builds into his or her fiction a critique or commentary on the work itself. The implication, curiously at odds with the post-Barthesian disrespect for the author as transcendent figure that took hold during the same period in criticism, is that this author is aware of what his or her text *is* in its entirety, how it works and how it will affect readers in advance of its being read. Thus Robert Scholes defines metafiction as fiction that "assimilates all the perspectives of criticism into the fictional process itself." A work of metafiction, he writes, "may emphasize structural, formal, behavioral, or philosophical qualities, but most writers of metafiction are thoroughly aware of all these possibilities and are likely to have experimented with all of them" (Scholes 29). Patricia Waugh describes metafictions as texts that incorporate an in-built "critique of their own methods of construction" (Waugh 2). Linda Hutcheon argues that "the point of metafiction is that it constitutes its own first critical commentary, and in so doing [. . .] sets up the theoretical frame of reference in which it must be considered" (Hutcheon 6).

However, the notion of self-consciousness on which these early definitions of metafiction depend has come under scrutiny. Mark Currie, for example, has noted that "the idea of self-consciousness is strangely inconsistent with most postmodern literary theories that would attribute neither selfhood nor consciousness to an author, let alone a work of fiction" (Currie, "Introduction" 1). Nicholas Royle argues—appropriately enough, in a reading of Spark's *Memento Mori*—that "[w]hat is distinctive about 'metafiction' is a logic not so much of self-consciousness [. . .] but of self-referring," and this is something that involves a "strange logic," for the moment of self-referring simultaneously belongs and does not belong to the fiction. Thus, he argues, the act of referring to oneself, which defines metafiction in the 1960s, forms part of the "dislocation of the sovereignty and authority of the figure of the author and of authorial self-consciousness" (Royle, "*Memento*" 192) that has taken place in twentieth-century fiction.

Spark's writing in the first three decades of her career was, naturally enough, given the kind of themes explored in *The Comforters*, considered as part of the debate about the role of the author as a paradoxical God-like figure in contemporary metafiction (as in Coover's *Pricksongs and Descants* [1969] or Fowles's *The French Lieutenant's Woman* [1969]). In her book, *Metafiction: The Theory and*

Practice of Self-Conscious Fiction, Waugh discusses a self-referential passage in *Not to Disturb* (1971) and argues that it "fits in with the larger designs of the novelist playing God" (Waugh 18). For other critics, such as Bradbury, the added value here was Spark's Catholicism. The implicit analogy between the author-character relationship and that between God and his creations seemed especially pertinent in the case of a writer who believed in God and portrayed him as a plotter (Bradbury 271).

Royle's provocative reading of *Memento Mori* puts forward another candidate for the kind of author that operates in Spark's fiction, one that can replace both the novelist-as-Catholic-God and the self-conscious novelist-critic of "orthodox" metafictional theory. He suggests that the self-referential aspects of Spark's *Memento Mori*—principally the repetition of the novel's title by an unidentified voice on the telephone—expose the *telepathic* foundations of narrative fiction. Third-person narrative fiction, as Royle has also argued elsewhere (Royle, *Telepathy*; *After*; "Telepathy"), is actually telepathic in operation rather than "all-knowing" because it is "based on the fiction of a narrator who is able to inhabit the bodies, thoughts, and feelings of different characters: this is what is sometimes, and quite misleadingly, referred to as 'omniscient narration'" (Royle, "*Memento*" 193). The author is thus neither omniscient nor God-like nor a theorist, but uncanny and telepathic.

As *The Comforters* shows, with its ghostly repetition of Caroline's thoughts and its conception of writing fiction as "tuning in" and "picking up" the thoughts of characters, this is a highly plausible reading. It is also supported, to an extent, by a novel Royle does not consider, *Loitering with Intent* (1981). The treatment of authorship in this novel accords with Royle's more general purpose of using Spark to demonstrate how strange and uncanny narrative fiction is, especially its central activity—which we tend to take for granted through familiarity—of one person "creating" other people and a world to put them in, animating them, reporting their words, and interpreting their thoughts. The act of authoring is presented in this novel as an uncanny activity, bordering on magical, with effects that elude the control of the author.

Along the way, however, another version of the author is constructed by the novel, one that has the effect of undercutting the idea of the telepathic novelist as much as it might support it. Where the telepathic novelist still figures as a transcendental being, superior to the characters it invades and animates—much in the way a psychic presents himself or herself as the conduit for God through the ability to channel the energies of the afterlife—this "other" novelist portrayed in *Loitering with Intent* appears as a figure worthy of suspicion, someone up to no good, predisposed to criminal behavior.

Plotting and Planning: *Loitering with Intent*

Loitering with Intent masquerades as the memoir of a well-known novelist, Fleur Talbot, which details its author's growing conviction that the people around her and the events in which they are involved are starting to resemble those in her first novel, *Warrender Chase*. She is alarmed, as it seemed her writing is uncannily shaping reality. But then she comes to a more mundane conclusion and suspects the manuscript has been stolen by the disreputable Sir Quentin Oliver, her employer at the Autobiographical Association, in order to "appropriate the spirit of my legend for his own use" (Spark, *Loitering* 114),that is, use her novel—whose eponymous hero is a thinly veiled version of Sir Quentin himself—as a kind of script for his own behavior. She observes that Sir Quentin seems to be "conforming more and more to the character of my Warrender Chase; it was amazing, I could have invented him, I could have invented all of them—the lot" (77–78). Later, however, once she has recovered the purloined draft of her novel, her original suspicion about the mysterious power of her writing seems to be reaffirmed. She experiences a kind of ambivalent epiphany about the predictive power of her novel:

> My thoughts went like this: Warrender Chase was killed in a car crash while everyone is assembled, waiting for him. Quentin Oliver's destiny, if he wants to enact Warrender Chase, would be the same. It was a frightening thought, but at the same time external to me, as if I were watching a play I had no power to stop. It then came to me again, there in the taxi, what a wonderful thing it was to be a woman and an artist in the twentieth century. It was almost as if Quentin Oliver was unreal and I had merely invented him, Warrender Chase being a man, a real man on whom I had partly based Sir Quentin. (140)

Sure enough, she soon receives news—and shows no signs of remorse—that Sir Quentin has been killed in a car accident (161).

Fleur's and Sir Quentin's grappling for control of *Warrender Chase* echoes the battle of wills between spectral author and protagonist in *The Comforters*. In the later novel, though, the figure of the novelist has descended onto the level of the fictional world. Rather than someone with a God-like view of events, who is capable of altering characters' lives from "above," this version of the novelist is down amongst the characters she observes "loitering with intent."

The eponymous phrase is used on two occasions. The first is when the scene that begins the novel is returned to in the final chapter. Fleur is sitting on a gravestone in a disused Kensington graveyard eating her lunch when she is approached by a young policeman who asks her what she is doing. In the first account all she tells us about their conversation is that "[h]e stopped to talk awhile, then he said good-bye, the graves must be very old, and that he wished me good luck and that it was nice to speak to somebody" (Spark, *Loitering* 1). In the second, however, more details of their conversation are provided: "I asked him: suppose I had been committing a crime sitting there on the gravestone, what crime would it be? 'Well, it could be desecrating and violating,' he said, 'it could be obstructing and hindering without due regard, it could be loitering with intent'" (155).

This passage raises the possibility—absent from the earlier version—of whether, in this scene, Fleur is actually being treated as suspicious by the policeman. It thus taps into an undercurrent of distrust for Fleur that is likely to have been lingering in the reader's mind throughout the novel. The replaying of this scene, besides satisfying a fondness for aesthetic closure through circularity, has an uncanny effect which is more than just the familiar reappearing as the unfamiliar (as Freud's classic formulation would have it): it gives the reader the sense that something he or she had been aware of unconsciously has suddenly come into the light. The effect of the second account of the scene is that it resembles the elaboration of a lie given, say, as part of a police statement, with added details such as the exact date and the weather designed to give the impression of veracity. We know, too, that embellishment is one of Fleur's particular skills. Her job at the Autobiographical Association is officially to type up and correct the manuscripts of aging *grandé(e)s*, but what this really amounts to is acting as ghostwriter for the memoirists, improving their texts, or, as she puts it, "making them expertly worse."

It is therefore appropriate that the charge the policeman mentions should be "loitering with intent." The offence "loitering with intent to commit a felony," introduced in 1783 as one of a "class of crimes regarded by the law as of a graver character than misdemeanors" (OED), has always been a controversial one. Regarded by some as unconstitutional, a convenient way of policing something (homosexuality in the nineteenth century, for example) that is considered necessary to police but for reasons that are difficult to justify, the charge has typically been used in relation to theft. Crime lurks at the edges of Fleur's story: Sir Quentin's theft of her manuscript and his attempts to prevent its being published, her friend Dottie's breaking into Fleur's house to obtain it, Fleur's retaliatory housebreaking to get it back. In the more precise context of "loitering," Fleur's group of friends have developed the habit of whistling "Auld Lang Syne" in the street outside each other's windows as a code to let each other in.

But a more specific connotation applicable to Spark's novel is suggested when the eponymous phrase is used for the second time. *Warrender Chase* is eventually published and is a sudden and unexpected success. This prompts Dottie to accuse Fleur "of having plotted and planned it all. 'You know what you were doing,' she said. I agreed I had been loitering with intent" (170). This suggests, then, that "loitering with intent" figures in the novel as a definition of authorship.

Rather than the transcendent God-like author or mysterious telepathic being, *Loitering with Intent* depicts the novelist as a figure who has the whiff of something criminal about her, is capable of committing a crime. Whether the crime is actual (e.g., housebreaking or even loitering in graveyards) or magical (e.g., causing the death of Quentin Oliver), the business of authoring is a matter of "plotting and planning," acting with menace. Authorship is presented as an indistinct crime, in other words, a crime that is hard to identify but that involves hanging around "everyday life," considering what one can use for one's fiction, and affecting events adversely as a result, even exploiting the dead.

Narrator as Stalker: *The Driver's Seat*

The starkest and most sustained portrayal of the author as menacing figure is provided by *The Driver's Seat*—as befits its status as the text that "makes Spark's forms conspicuous," to return to Bradbury's point in "Muriel Spark's Fingernails." In this novel, Spark's famous authorial coldness and detachment (Bradbury's title is an allusion to the line in *The Portrait of the Artist* about the artist remaining "within or behind or beyond or above his handiwork, invisible, refined out of existence, indifferent, paring his fingernails" [Joyce 181]) is taken to new levels. *The Driver's Seat* has often been considered, quite justifiably, in the context of the *nouveau roman* (Bradbury; Roof; Day) because it is narrated throughout in the opaque, present-tense style characteristic of writers such as Robbe-Grillet and Sarraute. It resembles a screenplay, setting out the movements of characters and reporting the words they utter, but leaving unclear any sense of the individual interiority so central to traditional realism, such as a character's motivations.

The Driver's Seat details the last few days of the life of its protagonist, a neurotic and alienated woman called Lise, during which time she plans and executes her own murder. Scrupulously mean in its economy, the narrative follows her as she chooses the dress she will wear (one that must reveal a stain), selects the manner and location for her death (a stabbing following a car journey, which is the literal explanation for the novel's title), ensures that appropriate witnesses have seen enough to help police retrospectively construct the narrative of her death, and, most of all, sets about finding and enlisting the services of a murderer, a young man in a business suit, who remains nameless throughout the novel.

At a basic level, *The Driver's Seat* might be considered a murder mystery in which the basic coordinates of the genre are rearranged. It is a detective story in reverse: it ends with a murder instead of beginning with one; we have a murderer and a victim, though both of their roles merge into one another, as Lise is complicit in her own murder; and the killer, although he commits the act of his own free will, is strongly influenced by his "victim." Absent, of course, is the figure of detective, though we might argue that, to some extent, Lise plays this role, too, for it is she who lays down the clues leading to the discovery of the crime. In his 1966 essay "The Typology of Detective Fiction," Tzvetan Todorov builds on an observation in Michel Butor's *nouveau roman Passing Time* (1960) about there being *two* narratives in a work of detective fiction and argues that the detective story foregrounds the basic distinction on which all narrative is founded, story and plot (*fabula* and *szujet*) by dividing its narrative into two. On the one hand there is the story of the crime (which corresponds to *fabula*), and, on the other, the story of the investigation (which corresponds to *szujet*). Todorov's argument is that in classic "whodunnit" detective fiction the *fabula* is effectively suppressed while the narrative is given over purely to the *szujet*. The story of the crime is always absent yet significant, while the story of the investigation is present yet insignificant. Spark's "detective story" turns this around so that the investigation remains offstage, still to come; what we are presented with is the story of crime, the part of the narrative that is normally left to the detective to reconstruct.

The novel's proximity to the detective genre is something that Spark, in a typically enigmatic self-referential statement, draws attention to. For most of the story Lise carries around with her a novel, on the cover of which are a boy and a girl on vacation, which at one point she "seems to display[—]deliberately" (39), as if to emphasize its significance to her story. When she gives it to a porter toward the end of the novel she tells him "You can have the book as well; it's a whydunnit in q-sharp major and it has a message: never talk to the sort of girls that you wouldn't leave lying about in your drawing room for the servants to pick up" (101).

If we were to take this enigmatic comment seriously (even though we don't know whether Lise has actually read the book), what might it mean? It would underline the fact that Spark's novel is not driven by the investigation to find out who is responsible for the murder, but rather the question of *why* the murder takes place. Who did it—at least in legal terms—is never in doubt, but the mystery that remains as we finish the novel is why Lise should arrange her own death and how she is able successfully to persuade the young man to carry it out.

The claim about the whydunnit novel's "message" is based upon two equations that seem to pertain throughout. The first is that a girl (like Lise) is equivalent to an object, perhaps to something one could select and *read*, like picking up a book. But "pick up," of course, refers most obviously to sexual seduction, a sense used in Spark's novel. Lise tells Bill, one of her fellow passengers on the plane, that "I'm not looking to pick up any strangers" (35). This leads us to consider the novel's connection to another set of crime-fiction conventions, those of *noir*. At the heart of the *noir* narrative is the conflation of sexual attraction and death, an equivalence embodied in the *femme fatale*. In *The Driver's Seat*, the young man's chance encounter with Lise, as well as her continual references to whether or not someone is her "type" are reminiscent of the love story, yet in this case they appear to relate to death. This means, then, that the peculiar libidinal economy that operates in *The Driver's Seat* equates "pick up" with "death." Seduction, as Jean Baudrillard's use of the term suggests, is more than simply sex; more generally and fundamentally, it is a process by which one is confronted by unexpected things and "rush[es] towards them with an energy equal to that with which, in other circumstances, we would oppose them" (Baudrillard 105–6). Lise functions as the *femme fatale* in the life of the young man in that her role is to lead him to his downfall, his destiny. Thus she signals the double meaning of *fatale*: fatal as in "leading to death," but also as in embodying *fate*, or *destiny*. From the point of view of the novel's nameless murderer, from the moment he sets eyes on the *femme fatale* his destiny is clear, and the narrative resembles the distinctive "trap" plot of *noir* (as in Cain's *Double Indemnity* or *The Postman Always Rings Twice*) in which the protagonist is unable to alter the course toward his death upon which he is set. Like the archetypal *noir* couple he and Lise traverse the text as a kind of living dead.

These connections to the motifs of crime fiction are suggested by the enigmatic comment about the "whydunnit." Evocations of crime-fiction motifs are common in modern and contemporary fiction. Spark's novel is one of the numerous literary fictions in postwar writing (e.g., Beckett's *Molloy*, Pynchon's *The Crying of Lot 49*, Martin Amis's *London Fields*) that turn to the conventions of crime fiction strategically in order to access deeper themes about the nature of writing and reading—but without going so far as to structure the novel more systematically as a parodic crime story, along the lines of Eco's *The Name of the Rose* or Auster's *City of Glass*. The enigmatic moment of self-reference in *The Driver's Seat* would seem to signal that if this is a variation on the classic "logic-and-deduction" novel, it is written in an impossible key, one that cannot make sense. The most intriguing effect of the "whydunnit" reference in *The Driver's Seat* is not how it enables us to conceive of the underlying textual economy, important as this is, but the way it points to key elements in the triangular relationship between author, character, and reader. It reminds us that, for all her efforts to retain control of her destiny, to remain in "the driver's seat," Lise remains part of someone else's plan.[1] She is imprisoned in Spark's "whydunnit."

Detective fiction is commonly regarded as a genre that demonstrates the novelist's capacity to control his or her narrative and manipulate the reader's responses. In the homology Todorov uses to explain how the plot unfolds—"author : reader = criminal : detective"—the author is significantly allied with the criminal rather than the detective because his or her task is to plan and cover-up the crime in order to prevent the reader from discovering it too quickly. More precisely, s/he uses the narrator to aid and abet him or her in this criminal act. As Pierre Bayard has said:

> *All mystery fiction in effect implies the narrator's bad faith.* The genre dictates that even when this narrator is not the murderer or even a character but simply the vaguely embodied act of stating, his job, for most of the book, is to lead the reader astray. Not only does the narrator refrain from telling everything he knows, but by a highly selective presentation of the facts [. . .] he ensures that the reader will be led off in the wrong direction. (54, emphasis in the original)

As well as trading in stories of crime, detective fiction itself demonstrates how writing fiction, if not exactly "criminal" in the legal sense, is an activity which requires deviousness and involves the seductive positioning of the reader in order to arrive at the outcome desired by the author. This function of the narrator is invoked by *The Driver's Seat*'s moment of self-reference.

The economy of Spark's prose in *The Driver's Seat* means that its narrator is far from "dramatized," but equally far from the dumb gaze of the surveillance camera. Its narrator is more like the mobile camera, tracking the heroine wherever she goes. The narrator does not attempt get inside Lise's mind, but concentrates on recording her movements and actions, occasionally offering a poetic interpretation. Early on, for example, we read: "Her hair is pale brown, probably tinted. [. . .] She might be as young as twenty-nine or as old as thirty-six, but hardly younger, hardly older" (18). The narrator notes that "She *seems* not to see [the porter] [my italics]." Later we are told "Her lips are slightly parted and her nostrils and eyes, too, are a fragment more open than usual; she is a stag scenting the breeze, moving step by step" (73). These descriptions may plausibly be the focalized perspectives of people who notice Lise, or even those of Lise herself, captivated by her own sense of destiny. Yet the cumulative effect is that Lise's actions come across as being *observed* by someone following her. In *The Driver's Seat* we gradually become aware of the presence of the author, accessing the world of the text through the narrator, as a shady, hidden, menacing presence.

Rather than acting out a fantasy of telepathy, in other words, the narration here resembles a less supernatural, more sinister, voyeuristic practice, like stalking. While Royle's highlighting of the "telepathic" elements of Spark's writing is persuasive—because of her sense of the uncanny and not just because her texts exemplify a widespread phenomenon—*The Driver's Seat* actually confounds the notion of Spark as a "telepathic" novelist. It demonstrates the degree to which Spark's style aspires to the cinematic, offering a perspective on a character from the outside rather than from within. This is indeed what she argued was one of the main influences of the *nouveau roman* on her development as a writer, its potential for showing how to avoid reporting the thoughts and feelings of a character—an aim of hers, she says, as far back as *The Ballad of Peckham Rye* (Spark, "Same" 216). Spark might conform to Royle's depiction of the author's fantasy of telepathy insofar as she, like all novelists, plays the fictional game of creating and inhabiting imaginary beings, but in an important sense *The Driver's Seat*, the pinnacle of her achievement in the "*nouveau roman*" phase of her career, is dedicated to resisting the telepathic element entirely, and this is what gives the novel its compelling appeal.

"A Woman and an Artist in the Twentieth Century": Suspicious Writers and Suspicious Readers

The self-referential dimension in Spark, then, contributes to the diminishing of the aura of the novelist, a key effect of the work of metafictional writers in the postwar period. What emerges from her fiction is a vision of the author as "loitering with intent" rather than fulfilling any loftier ambition. This vision is a more subtle complement to contemporary presentations of the author as a dislikeable, prurient, vaguely menacing figure, such as the moment in Fowles's *The French Lieutenant's Woman* when the novelist enters a train carriage and sizes up his sleeping hero in a way which "suggest[s] something unpleasant, some kind of devious sexual approach" (Fowles

389). One might compare, too, the despotic author in Coover's "The Magic Poker," who brings two sisters to the island he has invented and notes how easily he has "dressed them and may well choose to undress them" (Coover 25).

This deflationary conception of authorship generates a complementary model of reading. Once the author becomes a suspicious figure, then the reader's role needs to alter in response. The reader is invited, required, to become a kind of detective-figure, trying to make sense of the inconsistencies, gaps, and contradictions in the narrative. This, too, is clarified implicitly by the oblique reference to the detective genre in *The Driver's Seat*. Detective fiction has traditionally been synonymous with a particular method of reading. The literary critic, like the detective, is in the business of decoding signs and interpreting narrative. Jorge Luis Borges once stated that Edgar Allan Poe, in inventing the detective story in the 1840s, really invented the *reader* of the detective story. At issue is "a reader who reads with incredulity, with suspicion, with a special kind of suspicion" (Borges 16).

Spark's fiction, and more precisely its fondness for constructing novels around enigmas, demands this same attitude from its readers. Readers of Spark realize that they must look behind and beyond what her fiction might be telling or showing us, in search of the meanings lurking beneath. *The Comforters*, for example, ends with an apparently decisive (albeit fantastical) development, as Caroline "takes over" the writing of the novel. But is it actually sufficient to assert simply, as some critics have done, that *The Comforters* "turns out to be the novel Caroline is writing" (McQuillan, "Introduction" 3; McHale 122–23)? Although it may seem like it, *The Comforters* cannot be an example of what Steven G. Kellman once termed the "self-begetting novel," "an account, usually first person, of the development of a character to the point at which he is able to take up his pen and compose the novel we have just been reading" (Kellman 1245). For if *The Comforters* is Caroline's novel, then why is she not in control of *all* the words—that is, the words that she hears accompanying the sound of the typewriter? Who was the original "Typing Spook" (191), and where has she gone now that Caroline has assumed control of the narrative? If it is Spark "herself" then surely we are not to believe that the novel is written by a fictional character? Or are we to assume that author and protagonist are one and the same, and Caroline is recording her own thoughts? Whatever the conclusion, it renders the author a more deceitful, unreliable figure than before.

The ending of *The Comforters* further complicates the conundrum. Laurence writes a letter to Caroline protesting the inaccuracy of the notes about himself and others Caroline has been making for

the book (presumably her version of *The Comforters*) and complaining that he "dislike[s] being a character in a novel" (203). He has
second thoughts and tears up the letter, scattering the pieces in the
wind on Hampstead Heath. However, he is surprised when the letter
appears in the finished version of the book. We know this, as it is
quoted in full. But how can Caroline have read the letter, if she were
not some spectral being herself—or simply mendacious? How could
Laurence have read the end of the novel before she has even finished
it? Where it had seemed for much of the novel as if the fictional
world was becoming aware of its own fictionality once it gradually
began to recognize the narrative endeavors of a real author, now,
by contrast, it seems as if the fictional has triumphed, emphasizing
that the real author is fictional. The circular logic of the self-begetting
novel, whereby finishing the novel invites readers to begin it again,
this time in the light of their knowledge of why it has been written,
is here turned into an endless, twisting spiral.

In *Loitering with Intent* a mystery reigns over what is apparently
the more straightforward of the two tasks Fleur claims her memoir
is to fulfil (besides exposing Sir Quentin's crimes): namely, giving
an "account of that small part of my life and all that happened in
the middle of the twentieth century, those months of 1949–50." It is
never clear why she is at such pains to pinpoint the "changing-point
in my life" (155) as the middle of the century—the exact midpoint,
in fact, the 30th of June 1950. Nor is it apparent why it should be
the seemingly inconsequential scene in the graveyard which should
mark this turning-point, "the last day of a whole chunk of my life
but I didn't know that at the time" (1)—other than that this scene is
where the idea of authorship as "loitering with intent" first occurred
to Fleur.

Similarly, what lies behind Fleur's repeated assertion about
"what a wonderful thing it was to be a woman and an artist in the
twentieth century"? On one level the explanation would be that she,
a "woman artist," has been able to overcome the masculine brutality that threatened to derail her writing career before it had begun.
But Fleur's remark separates the status of being an artist from that
of being a woman, "a woman and an artist." What does it mean to
be an *artist* at this point in the century, and how does Fleur's story
show this? Is it that fiction has an uncanny power, the capacity to
turn her successful defence against Sir Quentin's attempts to ruin her
career into his literal death? Given the context, it is difficult to take
this repeated statement as anything other than a kind of obscure
threat, an assertion of power.

However we interpret Fleur's words, the counterpoint between
suspicious author and suspecting reader underlines Spark's own

position as artist writing in the second half of the twentieth century. A more contextualized assessment of the influence of the *nouveau roman* on Spark would need to take into account how her writing is unmistakably the product of what Nathalie Sarraute once called (in 1963) the "age of suspicion," the cultural moment when the traditional realist forms of writing became regarded incredulously by both reader and writer, following the lessons they had absorbed about the complexity of human psychology from Freud and modernist writers like Proust, Kafka, and Joyce. The automatic investment of faith in the realist writer by his or her reader that typifies the nineteenth-century novel is replaced in the late twentieth century, Sarraute suggests, when author and reader establish a more productive relationship based on mutual suspicion. In this relationship, the writer denies his reader a "familiar" position, that of the reader of traditional realism and instead reminds him or her of the constructed, artificial quality of the text. One of the outcomes of this new sensibility, in turn, is the dominance of what Sarraute describes as a new kind of narrator: "an anonymous 'I,' who is at once all and nothing, and who as often as not is but the reflection of the author himself, has usurped the rôle of the hero, occupying the place of honor" (Sarraute 56).

In searching for models of this kind of literary practice, Sarraute looks to the refusal of the realist paradigm in Proust, who boasted that "[n]ot once does one of my characters shut a window, wash his hands, put on his overcoat, utter a phrase of introduction" (quoted in Sarraute 69). She also looks to Kafka and Joyce, who name their heroes with initials (K and HCE, respectively), so that the reader is constantly reminded of these figures' dependence on the person doing the naming. The value of this "dispossession of the reader" is that he or she becomes "entice[d . . .] into the author's territory" so that the reader "is on the inside, exactly where the author is, at a depth where nothing remains of the convenient landmarks with which he constructs the characters" (Sarraute 71).

The narrators of the *The Driver's Seat* and *Loitering with Intent* are, respectively, more and less dramatized than the kind of narrators Sarraute is referring to. But the modes of narration used in each text, the opacity of the former and the enigmatic inconclusiveness of the latter, mean that the reader of these novels is similarly denied the "external" perspective of the reader and ends up "inside," in the position of the author. Judith Roof has noted that the reader of *The Driver's Seat* is denied the suspense typical of the detective story because of the sheer obviousness of its clues, as well as Spark's characteristic prolepsis (we are left in no doubt, early on, concerning what will become of Lise, because of a reference to a future crime-scene photo of her [18]). This reduces the story's suspense and means that the reader's engagement with the text becomes voyeuristic, as we are simply waiting to see the worst. Hence Lise's pursuit of the young man is shadowed by the reader. The reader has had no option but to become a willing accomplice in the author's crime.

As is the case with the dubious goings-on in the world of *Loitering with Intent*, no one comes out of *The Driver's Seat* with their hands clean—only, this time, that includes the reader. Spark's fiction contains a fascinating illustration of the postwar deposition of the God-like author, a complement to the direct expression of this idea in essays like Sarraute's "The Age of Suspicion" or Barthes's "The Death of the Author." Where modernists such as Joyce retain a sense of the author as a transcendent deity, albeit a cruel, indifferent one, late twentieth-century writers—not just Spark and her contemporaries like Fowles or Coover but also writers of subsequent generations like Auster in *City of Glass* or Bret Easton Ellis in *Lunar Park*—present the author as voyeuristic and prurient, someone predisposed to "loitering with intent."

The most obvious explanation for this postwar attitude toward authorship is the postmodern decline in the power of metanarratives of authority, especially religion. Whether or not we consider it legitimate to take Spark's own religious beliefs into account when exploring this question in relation to her writing, attending more closely to the depiction of the author in Spark produces a curious effect. By presenting her professional, and to some extent personal, identity as fundamentally grubby and disreputable, as is the case in her fiction from *The Comforters* to *Loitering with Intent*, Spark engages in what amounts to an implicit admission of guilt, maybe even a confession. Hence, if we were to consider afresh what Bradbury calls Spark's "Catholic aesthetic" (271), we might begin with her *practice* of writing, how its forms and discourses relate to Catholic ones, rather than try to find evidence of the author's underlying beliefs.

Note

1. Taking his cue from the reference on the last page of the novel to the typing-out of the young man's statement, Martin McQuillan concludes that *The Driver's Seat* is actually the police report of Lise's death and therefore a comment on "the reporting of women's experience by men" (McQuillan, "Introduction" 3). This is unconvincing, however, as there is no direct indication that the writer is male. Nor, surely, would any police report feature the kind of poetry we find at key moments in *The Driver's Seat*.

Works Cited

Baudrillard, Jean. "Please Follow Me." Trans. Paul Foss. *Art and Text* 23.4 (March–May 1987): 103–14.

Borges, Jorge Luis. "The Detective Story." Trans. Alberto Manguel. *Descant* 16.4 (1985): 15–24.

Bayard, Pierre. *Who Killed Roger Ackroyd?* London: Fourth Estate, 2000.

Bradbury, Malcolm. "Muriel Spark's Fingernails." *No, Not Bloomsbury.* London: Arena, 1987. 268–78.

Coover, Robert. "The Magic Poker." *Pricksongs and Descants.* New York: Grove, 2000. 20–45.

Currie, Mark, ed. *Metafiction.* London: Longman, 1995.

———. "Introduction." *Metafiction.* London: Longman, 1995. 1–18.

Fowles, John. *The French Lieutenant's Woman.* London: Vintage, 1996.

Hutcheon, Linda. *Narcissistic Narrative: The Metafictional Paradox.* Waterloo: Wilfrid Laurier UP, 1986.

Joyce, James. *Portrait of the Artist as a Young Man.* 1916. Oxford: Oxford UP, 2000.

Kellman, Steven G. "The Fiction of Self-Begetting." *Modern Language Notes* 91 (December 1976): 1243–56.

Kermode, Frank. "The House of Fiction: Interviews with Seven Novelists." *The Novel Today: Contemporary Writers on Modern Fiction.* Ed. Malcolm Bradbury. Manchester: Manchester UP, 1977. 117–46.

McHale, Brian. *Postmodernist Fiction.* London: Methuen, 1987.

McQuillan, Martin, ed. *Theorizing Muriel Spark: Gender, Race, Deconstruction.* Basingstroke: Palgrave, 2002.

———. "Introduction: 'I Don't Know Anything about Freud': Muriel Spark Meets Contemporary Criticism." McQuillan 1–31.

Roof, Judith. "The Future Perfect's Perfect Future: Spark's and Duras's Narrative Drive." McQuillan 49–67.

Royle, Nicholas. *After Derrida.* Manchester: Manchester UP, 1995. 78–81.

———. "*Memento Mori.*" McQuillan 189–203.

———. *Telepathy and Literature.* Oxford: Blackwell, 1990.

———. "The Telepathy Effect: Notes towards a Reconsideration of Narrative Fiction." *The Uncanny: An Introduction.* Manchester: Manchester UP, 2003. 256–76.

Sarraute, Nathalie. "The Age of Suspicion." *The Age of Suspicion: Essays on the Novel.* Trans. Maria Jolas. New York: George Braziller, 1963. 51–74.

Scholes, Robert. "Metafiction." In Currie 22–38.

Spark, Muriel. *The Comforters.* London: Macmillan, 1957.

———. *The Driver's Seat.* 1970. Harmondsworth: Penguin, 1974.

———. *Loitering with Intent.* 1981. London: Virago, 2007.

———. "The Same Informed Air: An Interview with Muriel Spark." McQuillan 210–29.

Todorov, Tzvetan. "The Typology of Detective Fiction." *The Poetics of Prose.* Trans. Richard Howard. Oxford: Blackwell, 1977. 42–52.

Waugh, Patricia. *Metafiction: The Theory and Practice of Self-Conscious Fiction.* London: Methuen, 1984.

CHAPTER 6

STYLISH SPINSTERS: SPARK,

PYM, AND THE POSTWAR

COMEDY OF THE OBJECT

Hope Howell Hodgkins

[S]ay what your beauty means to you or your plainness,
and what is your relation to the ever-changing and turning
world of gloves and shoes and stuffs. . . .
—Virginia Woolf, *A Room of One's Own*

[A]n artist is only an artist on condition that he is a double
man and that there is not one single phenomenon of his
double nature of which he is ignorant.
—Charles Baudelaire, "D'Essence de la rire"

It is style that makes us believe in a thing—nothing but
style.
—Oscar Wilde, "The Decay of Lying"

"The position of the unmarried woman—unless, of course, she
is somebody's mistress, is of no interest whatsoever to the reader
of modern fiction." So comments Barbara Pym in her diary. Then
she adds cheerfully, "The beginning of a novel?" (*Very Private* 269).
Certainly by the mid-twentieth century the classic British spinster
seemed a relic of the past associated, as George Orwell noted, with
nostalgia for an England of "old maids biking to Holy Communion
through the mists of the autumn morning" (75). And yet unmarried
women, including spinsters, abound in modern fiction, and in modern
fiction by women the spinster often takes pride of place as never
before. This essay analyzes the uses of fashion, narrative style, and
the spinster in novels by Muriel Spark and Barbara Pym, especially

129

noting those fictions' intersections with the post–World War II literary world of Great Britain. The question of why Spark, in particular, has not been regarded as a "Movement novelist" (despite her similar use of an ironic, understated narrative style) may be answered through examining her use of such trivia as dress both to celebrate individual female perception and to satirize traditionally grand literary ideals. Comedy's necessary self-objectification (*dédoublement*, as Baudelaire called it) is amply illustrated when the spinster—usually the object of pity, neglect, or scorn—becomes the subject of a novel.

On the surface, few women look less alike than the self-drama-tizing Jean Brodie and the modest Mildred Lathbury. Where Spark's famous novel describes *The Prime of Miss Jean Brodie*, Pym allows her humble spinster to be subsumed into the unenviable category of *Excellent Women*. Where Miss Brodie celebrates her prime, Mildred pours tea and observes the romantic vicissitudes of others. And where Jean Brodie romanticizes her own sex in a kind of myth-making gigan-tism, Mildred engages in comic deflation of all pretensions—including idealized gender stereotypes of any sort. Nevertheless, each woman is a spinster surprised by her own longings. And just as the style of each spinster presages her substance, whether Brodie's splendid "Roman profile" (6) or Mildred's "mousy" plainness (7), so female self-presentation through fashionable dress serves as a cameo for each narrative's style.

In following fashion, a willing self-objectification is a neces-sary component, as Karen Hanson has noted: "A personal interest in dress and open responsiveness to the changing whims of fashion depend upon a recognition that one is seen, that one is—among other things—an object of others' sight, others' cognition" (70). And of course modernist fiction entails a vexed interpretation of subject-object relations. Thus Spark constructs her stylish novel as a complex free indirect confessional. The narrative never tells us Jean Brodie's thoughts, always showing her through the speculations of her young students or a bemused larger world. Yet Miss Brodie, so ostensibly the risible object rather than the narrating subject of Spark's book, triumphs through her own overtly ridiculous, vivid style: "I wore my silk dress with the large red poppies which is just right for my colouring," she tells her girls. "Mussolini is one of the greatest men in the world" (46). The inappropriate juxtaposition shows the teacher's delusive charm as well as the book's juggling of affections and ethics. In contrast, Pym's novel, with its more straightforward first-person narration, indeed is plain, but its protagonist both observes and seeks to validate her own subjectivity. To the condescending salesgirl behind the makeup counter, Mildred insists that she has a right to vividly colored lipstick: "'Thank you, but I think I will have Hawaiian

Fire,' I said obstinately, savouring the ludicrous words and the full depths of my shame" (*Excellent* 130). Again an incongruity, here that of casting a lipstick purchase as a milestone, links that novel's plot to Mildred's own style, including an all-too-conscious sense of herself as potential object of ridicule. Thus both books, through their monumental trivialism, take the subject-object dilemma to new heights (or depths). Finally, too, the girls in Spark's *The Girls of Slender Means* seem to follow Virginia Woolf's admonition: they overtly acknowledge their "beauty" or their "plainness" through their relation to the "everchanging and turning world of gloves and shoes and stuffs" (Woolf 88)—and, in so revisioning the postwar world, put paid to the succession of proud louses that populate the postwar Britain of male-authored fiction.

Postwar Styles

Even to speak of style in the same breath as war is to mix the seemingly frivolous and transient with that which is serious, tragic, and perhaps even epic. In this case, it also links a reputedly female domain—that of dress—with the traditional arena of male grand action. And yet the Second World War created a negative apotheosis of British style in the categories of dress and of literature. First, during the war, fashion, and especially women's dress styles, were recognized as overt political markers, simultaneously applauded and critiqued for their statements about the depths or limits of wearers' political commitments. In 1941, British *Vogue* told women, "Now if ever, beauty is your duty" to encourage the troops (qtd. in Wilson 44); at the liberation of Paris in 1944, war correspondent Lee Miller was shocked to see the extravagant and colorful dresses flaunted by the supposedly oppressed Parisiennes (62). Spark would spell out the classic rejoinder to Miller's shock through her character Selina, who at the war's end wears a "high hoop-brimmed blue hat and shoes with high block wedges; these fashions from France, it was said, were symbols of the Resistance" (*Girls* 83). Resistant or collaborative, however, fashion in the 1940s also increasingly became a venue for women to exercise an independent thought. As James Lauer points out, English woman accepted the clothes rationing instituted early in the decade even as they quietly fought off efforts to reinstate the corset (248–52). But after the war, despite the economic troubles and social upheavals of the later 1940s in Britain, the standard utilitarianism of women's dress took a sharp turn with Christian Dior's "New Look." Where some Austerity designers had created wartime dresses using less than two meters of cloth per garment, Dior's longer, fuller skirts, and petticoats shockingly consumed dozens of meters of material. And advertisers flaunted them even in the aftermath of the February 1947 fuel crisus. While *Daily Express* headlines screamed "LESS . . . LESS . . . LESS," postwar British women seemed to want more—but a more that joined expenditure with traditional feminine modesty and restraint: those rejected corsets reappeared. All could be purchased in mass-produced versions, as Harry Hopkins observed, enabling feminine style to say more for less (94–95).

Meanwhile, in a parallel break with high style, the late 1940s in Britain gestated a new postwar literature that provided a second version of modest style, saying more for less through rhetorical minimalism. This minimalism, often associated with Philip Larkin, Kingsley Amis, and the Angry Young Men or Movement poets of the 1950s, employed a plain, deliberately anti-eloquent language espe-cially suited to a leveling, comic fiction. Oddly enough, the Movement is rarely referred to in analyses of Spark's fiction, and never, to my knowledge, in studies of Pym. Yet these women writers too, writing after the war and about its effects, developed a leveling aesthetic, the ostensibly shallow surface of a deep structure of protest. For the Movement's literary subjects, one need only think of Larkin's most famous topoi—empty churches where "there's nothing going on" ("Church Going" line 1), or a cold and lonely sexual revolution that descends to a quest to find "Words . . . not untrue and not unkind" ("Talking in Bed" lines 11–12). But for a summary of the Move-ment's philosophy, as well as a prose example of its anti-eloquent eloquence, one could hardly do better than the musings of Pym's Letty on her spinsterhood: "might not the experience of 'not having' be regarded as something with its own validity?" (*Quartet* 25). As Michael Cotsell noted, Pym's fiction typifies mid-twentieth-century British self-perception: "the 'minor events in minor lives' . . . belong to the postwar context in which 'something major—Britain—became minor'" (qtd. in Little 78).

"Becoming minor" characterizes, in general, the styles of post-war fiction. From the Movement poets to Alan Sillitoe's working-class *Saturday Night and Sunday Morning*, British literature turned away from high-modern experimentation—partially in response to more than eighty years of Flaubert-inspired artistic efforts to kick free of earth's constraints. The French novelist had boasted of writing "a book about nothing" (154). His early twentieth-century heirs often seemed, like James Joyce's young artist Stephen Dedalus, to draw "less pleasure from the reflection of the glowing sensible world . . . than from the contemplation of an inner world of individual emotions mirrored perfectly in a lucid supple periodic prose" (180–81). For the high-modern aesthete, style was in itself a major subject. By 1959, however, Kingsley Amis was complaining about the "nostalgia for style nowadays among people of oldster age-group," by which he meant "a personal style, a distinguished style . . . with wow from imagery, syntax, and diction" as in "Donne, Pater, [and] Virginia Woolf" ("She" 635). Postwar literature, in keeping with its writers', diminished expectations, punctured, deflated, mocked, and refused to emulate elaborate stylistics.

In fact the Movement did not disdain careful style but overblown importance: "What is needed," *Poetry London* editorialized in 1950, "is not so much the inspired poem as a revival of style: first-class workmanship rather than the prophetic tone" (Bergonzi 160). And the two new postwar styles—sartorial and literary—parallel one another in their understated triviality, as in their seemingly ordinary texture. Spark's and Pym's uses of details of dress and appearance may be specifically "female," but they also typify the minimalism of postwar British fiction. Amis's Jim Dixon finally lands his dream job because of his negatives rather than his positives: "It's not that you've got the qualifications, for this or any other work," his millionaire employer remarks, "You haven't got the disqualifications, though, and that's much rarer" ("Lucky Jim" 234). Amis's gleeful celebration of lack is not so different from the non-evidence provided by Miss Brodie's nightdress of crêpe de chine, which damns her in the eyes of her fellow teachers not by its presence under Mr. Lowther's pillow but through its subsequent absence: "She's that brazen" (99). Not so different, that is, except that the one instance involves a man's career and the other a woman's love affair, substantiated through details of dress. And these novels' minimalizing similarities raise a question: If dress in the twentieth century was considered largely a woman's domain— both commonplace and ephemeral, concerned with surface rather than depth—then why could not a comic literature that deliberately spoke a quotidian vernacular become, at last, equally the possession of men and women?

That is to say, the postwar, masculine relinquishment of epic grandeur might have enabled a full appreciation of feminine trivia as well. But this appreciation never developed. Indeed it is my contention that the two sorts of style in these postwar novels by Spark and Pym point up the still-large gulfs between male and female understand-ings of literature and the sexes. Above all it is each woman's comic treatment of the stylish spinster—needlessly fashionable, it would seem, since she lacks a man—that demonstrates these novelists' self-objectifying gifts, gifts that include a delicate mockery of all male expectations of female style.

Fashion and Women

Why should clothing style serve both to define and to dismiss these spinsters and these novels? The concept of fashion offers a trope for gender subjectivity in ways that intertwine feminine and narrative styles. Theories of fashion have, in recent decades, focused on psychological, historical, or gender-based interpretations, and yet it has become evident that a monological approach will not serve. We have long graduated from Georg Simmel's comfortable claim that "if we have the adorned body at our disposal, we are masters over more and nobler things" (344); we may adorn our bodies, but we cannot master how others perceive us or what each of us may inadvertently reveal through our clothing. Rather "when we dress," Elizabeth Wilson writes, "we wear inscribed upon our bodies the often obscure relationship of art, personal psychology, and the social order" (247). But in what ways is this relationship inscribed, and which audiences does our clothing address? For what those inscriptions say varies drastically in different places and in different eras. If fashion provides a handy interpretative grid for many aspects of our culture, it is not so easily defined itself.

Certainly Wilson is correct that fashion reflects our inner selves and their relation to the outer world, and, just as certainly, fashion's transient manifestations matter. The constant flux of styles—what was fashionable last month is not in style today, as any Paris Hilton knows—has become intrinsic to the definition of fashion along with its necessarily exclusive nature: if we all dress in the height of fashion, then the concept of fashion has become nonsense. Dress style's necessary transience is one of fashion's aspects that so fascinated nineteenth-century poets Baudelaire and Mallarmé, in addition to clothing's potential for masking the image one presents to the world. Hence Ulrich Lehmann, in his study of those poets' writings on dress, argued that fashion reflects the modern condition in its self-conscious obsession with a self in flux. In response, some theorists have speculated that fashion, in enabling us to choose our dress, may offer a way to resolve the cruxes of modernity; as Joanne Finkelstein sums up, "fashion succeeds by promising to annul the fragmented condition of modernity with the imposition of a coherent subjectivity" (47). Hence Jean Brodie, in choosing her red dress with poppies and magisterially announcing its effects, endeavors to impose her subjective self-vision on her students and so to control her body as perceived object.

However, the modernist reading of dress style is complicated (not contradicted) when we recall that the idea of exclusive, fashionable clothing has been around since antiquity. The differences lie, in the modern centuries, in three characteristics. First, material availability has made fashionable dress, in more prosperous nations, available to most classes rather than (as in the past) to a tiny court-centered ruling class; the distinctions necessary to maintain the exclusivity of fashion therefore proliferate rather than fade away. Second, the speed of change, in moving information and material goods, has multiplied exponentially in a way hard to imagine in earlier centuries and cultures. It is not, as in medieval Europe, the last century's or last decade's fashions that we must avoid, but last month's. Third, and most important for this study, in the nineteenth century, fashion—hitherto the sign of a leisure class, whether male dandy or lady of leisure—came to be regarded as the province of women for reasons that are still debated today. The change did little to advance respect either for fashion or for women. This is not to say that men were not still frequently the rulers of fashion, whether as designers or publicists, but when Mallarmé produced *La Dernière Mode* or Oscar Wilde edited *The Woman's World*, they were understood to be serving as needed male authorities for women who craved fashion leadership. Similarly, as costume historian James Lauer describes, the designer Charles Frederick Worth revolutionized fashion design in 1858 but substantiated the gender status quo in requiring for the first time in history that his female customers come to him as the recognized dictator of Paris fashion (186).

There was, in any case, little to design creatively in men's clothes by the mid-nineteenth century, which is why the very idea of a hypothetical Victorian *Men's World* or a "Latest Mode" magazine for males makes us chuckle now. Following Beau Brummell's epochal proclamation in Regency England, all men now needed was "fine linen, plenty of it, and country washing" in order to be "correct"—the new sartorial ideal for the Western male (Moers 21). Appropriately, the province of the best men's dress clothes became not Paris couturiers but London's Saville Row tailors. Variations on the dark suit have been with us ever since, however spruced up by Baudelaire's red cravats or Wilde's hand-held lilies. Indeed, even the dandies' concerns with proper dress became sexually suspect in the later 1800s, increasing into the twentieth century when an occupation such as Worth's, or Mallarmé's and Wilde's editing of fashion magazines, would come to be seen as evidence of gender transgression. In a typical instance of this twentieth-century stereotype, one of Pym's protagonists recognizes immediately that a new acquaintance is homosexual when his gaze moves over her figure, appraising not her body but the cut and price of her clothes (*Sweet Dove Died* 144–45). Real men, it is believed, do not care about clothes, whether their women's or their own.

The reasons for this gender migration in fashion identity—one that would have startled a medieval ruler and amused a Renaissance courtier—are debatable. In a much-disputed analysis, J. C. Flügel, in *The Psychology of Clothes* (originally published in 1930), argued that "The Great Masculine Renunciation" of decorative dress stemmed from the leveling influences of the French Revolution and the increasing respectability of work—hence "the projection of the [male] exhibition-istic desire onto a person of the opposite sex" (118). Thus bourgeois wives became—in their increasingly elaborate and nonfunctional corsets, petticoats, and frills—vicarious symbols of their husbands' successes. While Flügel has been criticized for oversimplifying and crankiness (he argues that, if only men dressed better, women would escape narcissism), he clearly is correct about certain economic roots. Just as important as the causes, however, are the results for fashion, dress references, and their associations with women.

A circular logic comes into play when fashion becomes the arena of female performance; even as "the fashionable" increases its speed of change and new clothing becomes more widely avail-able across the social spectrum, dress style is pigeonholed as trivial because it is radically temporal. Fashion becomes associated, as the rate of change increases, with stereotypical female fickleness and shallowness—hence the hand-wringing from early feminist leaders who sought to liberate women from shallow displays of style. In the late eighteenth century, Mary Wollstonecraft concluded bluntly that "the fondness for dress, so extravagant in females, arises from . . . want of cultivation of mind" (285). Over a century later Germaine Greer would concur, elaborating: "While her mate toils in his factory, [woman] totters about the smartest streets and plushiest hotels with his fortune upon her back and bosom, fingers and wrists" (52). These thinkers sought a high moral purpose and seriousness for their campaigns, one that seemed at odds with style. And, in fact, philoso-phers and high-minded thinkers traditionally have scorned fashion, as Karen Hanson documents, ostensibly because "the instability of the fashionable choice may seem to some a proof of [its] emptiness and confusion" (60). Clearly, fashion and women each damage the other's good name.

However, as Hanson also shows, the philosophical disdain for fashion also may involve fears of change, of the temporal physical body, and of the welter of desires that drive human existence—all aspects of life that, again, often have been attributed to the female mind and world. Fashion directly confounds our longings for unchang-ing categories: "if, as Kant says, the satisfaction determined by the beautiful is unrelated to inclination, then one who would judge some fashionable dress beautiful will clearly have to cope with some dif-ficult problems of desire" (Hanson 65). The very act of dressing our bodies exemplifies change and acknowledges embodiment; if that act is attended by a desire to dress fashionably, it then is "somehow, somewhat, influenced by the dynamics of others' desires" (68). That is to say, in getting dressed in the morning I am implicitly acknowledging my body as an object to myself, but if I then begin to consider it as an object of others' consideration, I plunge into a swamp of considered desires and relative objectivities. It is no wonder that Joanne Finkelstein has concluded that fashion in its turbulence is not a language but (after Fred Davis) a complex "aesthetic code" (27). Nor is it surprising that this code traditionally has been labeled a female enigma, one more wrinkle in that famous Freudian question, "What do women want?"

For these reasons, fashion and dress in fiction by women have become not merely a topic but a rhetorical instrument for examining desires in and for females. Thus we find Jean Brodie linking dress and literature in order to present herself as an object of desire (both sexual and emulative); as her student Sandy perceives, the teacher self-consciously employs her personal style to create fiction, "making patterns of facts" (76). But it is her identity as a stylish spinster that makes her a pathetic if not oxymoronic cliché. Or perhaps even a monster; as Pym suggests, what alarms the public about spinsters is the fear lest "all passion should not be spent!" (*Very Private* 75). The stylish spinster in these texts presents us with the question of female desires in their starkest form.

Stylish Spinsters

Spark's *Miss Jean Brodie* is more experimental in structure than Pym's fiction and thus commonly seen as more serious literature. Nevertheless, Pym's *Excellent Women*, often denigrated as merely a woman's novel, offers first a foil but then a more radical demonstration of why style and the spinster are key to comprehending both the place of women in, and their contribution to, twentieth-century fiction. I am here both making a claim—that the eponymous style of each character is tied to the substance of the novel about her—and asking a question: in what ways are these details of dress and appearance specifically female, and in what ways do they typify post–World War II British fiction? The very titles describe both a female and a narrative style: Jean Brodie is in her "prime," suggesting a peak of excitement; Mildred is "excellent," of straightforward and consistent quality (despite all her comic efforts to differentiate herself from other drab spinster types). Spark's rhetoric, like Miss Brodie herself, is both dramatic and ironically twisted; hence those bright poppies on the teacher's dress, the color of passion, also evoke drugs and death (as we know, the poppies bloom on Flanders Field, where Jean's youthful lover Hugh "fell like an autumn leaf" [9]). And it is her grand affinities with Mussolini and with Caesar, as Miss Brodie flattens those who scorn her "beneath the chariot wheels of her superiority" (56), that bring her student Sandy to betray her to the school authorities and yet also put Sandy behind iron bars at the novel's end. The complex time frames of Spark's novel (at least six) signify its ironic moral complexities as well. For Miss Brodie, as for her creator, "Safety does not come first" (7).

In *Excellent Women*, on the other hand, the narration is cautiously plain and apologetically ironic: "I couldn't help noticing . . ." Mildred frequently murmurs, preparatory to another devastating deflation of human pretension. Nor does she spare herself, slipping effortlessly from observing subject into a crowd of objects—that is, insecure females. After her hard-won lipstick purchase, for instance, Mildred takes her Hawaiian Fire to the ladies' room and meditates on the seriousness of makeup: "Inside it was a sobering sight indeed and one to put us all in mind of the futility of material things and of our own mortality. *All flesh is but as grass* . . . I thought, watching the women working at their faces with savage concentration, opening their mouths wide, biting and licking their lips, stabbing at their noses and chins with powder-puffs" (131). Here, the grand language is employed only for parodic deflation—a straightforward irony we might call it, especially in contrast to Spark's slipperiness. Frequently we are amused by the contrast between Mildred's words and her thoughts and especially her clear-eyed understanding of male-female differences: "'You see,'" the vicar comments sadly of Allegra, "'I thought her such a fine person.' She was certainly very pretty, I thought, but I did not say it" (211). Yet the satire is gentle, like Mildred herself, perhaps because she refuses to romanticize her own story. Where *Miss Jean Brodie* offers sly allusions to Brontë's *Jane Eyre*, Mildred announces bluntly, "I .J. . with my shapeless overall and old fawn skirt . . . am not at all like Jane Eyre, who must have given hope to so many plain women who tell their stories in the first person" (7).[1] And indeed, Pym's tolerably happy ending is hardly like Jane's final blissful union with Mr. Rochester: "So, what with my duty there and the work I was going to do for Everard, it seemed as if I might be going to have what Helena called 'a full life' after all" (256).

Mildred's diminished romantic expectations—and Jean Brodie's diminished ending—do typify post–World War II fiction. Each woman longs for an exciting, unattainable object—for Mildred, it is her handsome and charming neighbor Rocky, while Jean Brodie is in love with Teddy Lloyd, the married, one-armed art-master (shades of Rochester, who also has a heroically maimed arm). Each woman must settle for less. Both novels too are explicitly postwar in plot. *Excellent Women* refers to continued rationing as well as bomb damage in the London churches and the difficulties of displaced persons finding lodgings prompt Pym's plot. Spark's 1961 novel, on the other hand, suggests a symbolism verging on political allegory: Miss Brodie's most cherished memories are of the Great War where Hugh died; she flourishes as an Edinburgh spinster of the 1930s (with fewer men available but more freedom than previously), while naively celebrating the rise of fascism on the Continent. Appropriately, then, Jean Brodie's downfall comes in 1939, and she dies of cancer in 1946. If the first war serves as locus of the Romantic for Spark's teacher, the second delineates the destruction of Britain's, along with Miss Brodie's, glory. Early on, she sits "nobly like Britannia with her legs apart" in Mr. Lloyd's art class (50), but she will hunch "shriveled and betrayed" after the war's end (58). Like Cotsell's Britain, she is "something major . . . becoming minor."

But are Spark and Pym "Angry Young Women"? Perhaps Amis's denigratory "wow" quite well describes Jean Brodie's melodramatic personal style, "head up, like Sybil Thorndike, her nose arched and proud" (*Prime* 27). But such a label ignores the elaborate novel's complex sympathy for the doomed teacher. Similarly, Pym's piling-up of trivial details (at one point, Mildred actually meditates on old laundry lists) may appear to be, as A. S. Byatt has claimed, not an effective postwar style but being "petty about pettiness" (862). The women do write differently. The telling details of dress, so significant for Spark and Pym, are quarantined by Amis into the space of female bad taste. In *Lucky Jim,* Dixon's hysterical girlfriend Margaret is characterized repeatedly by her hideous green Paisley frock and low-heeled, quasi-velvet shoes (11, 19, 155), while the idealized Christine is notable only for her blond beauty and her large breasts. (The style of Dixon's ripped pants is never detailed.) Clearly Spark employs a different framework when she uses small details for the grandiose Miss Brodie.

If the details of dress are petty, too trivial even for postwar fiction by men, we may turn to the truism that the use of trivia typifies fiction written by women. Feminine values, as Virginia Woolf noted, commonly are called "trivial," since they naturally must deal with all the unrecorded details of everyday life (73). The small is writ large in their lives; as Pym's Mildred puts it, "The burden of keeping three people in toilet paper seemed to me rather a heavy one" (10). Pym is the natural employer of the small telling detail for very practical reasons. To focus on the trivial is to focus on the real conditions of our lives and, perhaps, to acknowledge our own smallness. "[A]fter all, life was like that for most of us," Mildred remarks, "the small unpleasantnesses rather than the great tragedies, the little useless longings rather than the great renunciations and dramatic love affairs of history or fiction" (101). A trivial style is, then, a humble style. It also is a style that signifies nonsignification: "The ideology of the trivial," Judy Little writes, "is that it has no significant ideology, belongs to no master narrative, no great codes of quest or romance, and no *sermo patrius*" (76)—that is, no traditionally male genre of worthwhile literature.

Spark's fiction, however, does not incline us to sympathy with those who fret over toilet paper. Her style plays with signification in the fondly ominous way that she claimed to play with her characters: "I love them most intensely, like a cat loves a bird. You know cats do love birds; they love to fondle them" (qtd. in Stannard 104). Likewise she fondles the trivia, always with an ironic edge. As Ian Gregson comments, "The pleasures of her fictions arise from the consequent fun she has with the incongruous weight which her characters attach to trivia" (5–6). That is, the narratorial perspective is skewed for us: the peripheral is made to appear important, and the most significant pushed to the margins. "I'm not really interested in world affairs," says Sandy, "only in putting a stop to Miss Brodie" (134). But we know that Sandy should be concerned with world affairs in contrast to which the affairs of Miss Brodie are trivial indeed.

We also know, however, that trivia is a metonymic art in Spark's novel: the part stands for the whole, Miss Brodie stands for Mussolini and Caesar. In other words, the trivial does (like Jean Brodie herself) possess a significant ideology here, because it comprises a true style of small things with not only social and philosophic significance but aesthetic roots. Like Ezra Pound's Image, the trivial detail "presents an intellectual and emotional complex in an instant of time" (Pound 253). So in accordance with modernist Imagism, Spark employs small metaphors for large meanings, or—as another modernist poet put it—"For all the history of grief / An empty doorway and a maple leaf" (MacLeish, "Ars Poetica" lines 19–20). We might recall, then, the ways in which a leaf stands for Miss Brodie's dramatized history of grief: as Mary Schneider has noted, the teacher's account of Hugh's death (which sets her entire class weeping) is permeated with references to autumn leaves (424). In this scene Miss Brodie quotes from Keats's ode "To Autumn" and then says that her lover "fell like an autumn leaf," and when the headmistress unexpectedly appears, the errant teacher catches "a falling leaf neatly in her hand" (9, 10). This insistent image is not only a textbook exemplar of New Critical aesthetics but also, in its overdetermination and its sly humor, suggests the totalitarian potential of an airtight formalism. We do not cry with the little girls; we merely notice that Miss Brodie herself is in a mellow and fruitful autumn—another implication of the leaf, though one that she cannot control. In another ironically precious image, Jean Brodie in her prime is seen to wear newer clothes and "a glowing amber necklace" with magnetic properties that she enjoys demonstrating to her girls (55). Her own attraction for the two male teachers at the school is a patent analogy, but we also know what amber truly is and that Miss Brodie is caught, surely as any insect, in a grotesquely frozen beauty. In self-staging herself, as a "prime" object of desire, she inadvertently dresses herself in the signs of her own desires and ultimate end. Spark has reworked—and mocked— the vestiges of high-modern artistic tenets in the service of her own complex style.

In a very different vein, but with a similar play on modernism, the much-scorned trivia of *Excellent Women* offer an example of realism with its grandeur erased. When Mildred, negotiating between her secret attraction to Rocky and her pragmatic self-view, buys yet another brown hat, we are offered a serious trope for stagnation. Even "brown" may signify in modernist poetry: Eliot's *Waste Land* is a "brown land" of "brown fog" (175, 61). And we may recall J. Alfred Prufrock, whose potential love-interest repels him by her arms, "downed with light brown hair!" (63). In Pym's narrative, however, the color brown is neither tragic, nor grim, nor strikingly repulsive. Mildred's brown dresses and coats exemplify merely the drabness of trivia, the dullness summarized by Byatt as "brown frocks, knitted socks in clerical grey and cauliflower cheese" (862). Pym's Realism is real rather than a complex of aesthetically stunning symbols.

Yet the color brown bears one important association for Pym and for her style. In a comic riff in her journals, she foresaw her life as "this old brown spinster" (*Very Private* 68–69), and the question of spinster-style haunts and concludes the stories of both Mildred and Jean Brodie. "Oh, Mildred," Rocky says, "there were so *many*"—that is, so many lonely Wren officers that he romanced during the war (137). And indeed there were so many unmarried women in England from the 1920s through the 1940s—an historical reality but also a crux. The spinster, writes Laura Doan, "is defined by absence. . . . What the spinster lacks is an 'other' to be defined against or in relation to" (5–6). Spinsterhood traditionally suggests lack and frustration, but it may also imply the freedom to define oneself. Certainly the motif dominates the self-styling of both our protagonists; even their fictions' titles signify spinsterhood. Miss Jean Brodie explicitly views her single state as integral to her "prime": "If I were to receive a proposal of marriage tomorrow from the Lord Lyon King-of-Arms I would decline it," she tells her girls. "I am dedicated to you in my prime" (22). Her little girls understand this link; as they observe to one another, their parents "don't have primes"—"they have sexual intercourse"

(15). In the end, spinster-style crowns the futility of Miss Brodie's much-vaunted "prime." She is brought down to brownness, sitting "shriveled and betrayed in her long-preserved dark musquash coat," as she admits, "I am past my prime" and "Hitler *was* rather naughty" (58, 131). Now the non sequitur is pathetic not comic—and less of a non sequitur to our understanding. As with her protagonist, Spark's complex narrative spins down to a conclusion that is chronological after all, leaving us with Miss Brodie's grave and Sandy clutching "desperately" at the bars of her nun's grille, heir to barrenness (137). Miss Brodie both shows the attraction of high literary grandeur and illustrates the inevitable end of Romantic signification.

If *Miss Jean Brodie* looks back in time, Mildred looks forward and so perhaps succeeds in breaking out of the spinsterish stereotype of the "excellent woman." We are told repeatedly that "It was not the excellent women who got married" (170), and Mildred responds in surprise to Everard: "You would consider marrying an excellent woman? But they are not for marrying" (189). Her possible escape from brown spinsterhood is signified when, at the novel's end, she buys a black dress and changes her hair. She then anticipates that "full life," which may include marriage with Everard and certainly will include doing his indexing. When Everard makes the tentative suggestion, during the novel's concluding romantic dinner, that Mildred might help index his scholarly tome, we as readers are left in a quandary. We may interpret his remark either as a coded romantic proposal (he already has mentioned that indexing is what anthropologists' wives do) or as a deflationary revelation of his crass motives. But Mildred herself is neither deluded nor cynical; rather than responding as the stereotypical spinster, desperate for marriage at any price, she considers his proposal an interesting option. In so doing, she realistically redefines the term "full life"—as she has redefined her style—against Romantic stereotypes, against the modernist great narrative, perhaps against even the significance of small things as anything more than a comic marker for others' pretensions, including male perceptions. Here is a typical compliment from Mildred's suitor: "'You seem to be very nicely dressed,' said Everard without looking" (146). And here is another male friend after Mildred changes her style: ". . . an improvement on the way you usually look? But how do you usually look? One scarcely remembers" (251). The jokes are not only on the men, who ignore the small details, but also on the smallness of the details in which women place so much stock.

In fact, the joke is on all of us, for Mildred's unobserved details are as integral to her experience as Miss Brodie's poppy dress to hers, but the diminished style of Pym's spinster appears, to certain observers, too painfully small to contemplate for long. Philip Larkin

read the very funny *Excellent Women* as "a study of the pain of being single, the unconscious hurt the world regards as this state's
natural clothing . . . time and again one senses not only that Mildred
is suffering, but that nobody can see why she shouldn't suffer, like
a Victorian cabhorse" (Letter 368). Against which we may set Pym's
own remark, "Why is it that men find my books so sad? Women don't
particularly" (*Very Private* 223). This interpretative gulf between the
sexes also may be read as the chasm between perceiving subject
and comic object, categories breached by and through these fictional
spinsters. The chasm looms large when we consider Spark's *Girls of
Slender Means* as a final explication of female style in response to
male-authored postwar fiction.

The Comedy of the Object

That expectations are diminished is a given for these postwar
spinsters, but it is a given that men have struggled to take in. The
lives of spinsters are small and their stories conclude in minor keys.
Where then lies the comedy of happiness and laughter? The unex-
pectedness of Spark's destructive undercurrents "would be comic if
we could laugh," John Updike mourned when he reviewed *The Girls
of Slender Means*. Yet anyone who has read portions of Spark's fiction
aloud or watched the stage or film interactions of Miss Brodie with
her class can attest that Spark is often hilarious. It is the implication,
Updike explained, "that the farcical world of her portrayal is the *real*
world"— the world of 1945 London, where a boarding house and an
innocent young woman are about to be blown to shreds—that should
sober us ("Between a Wedding" 311). We may well be shocked to
find that Spark's climax hinges on choosing a fashionable dress over
a human life, but the very disjunction between trivia and serious
events precipitates the comedy of the object in her novels.

Spark has been the queen of detached objectivity from the
first; when Caroline of *The Comforters* is haunted by voices narrating her thoughts and life, she eventually uses them to re-objectify
herself: "[S]he possessed a large number of notes, transcribed from
the voices, and these she studied carefully . . . the narrative could
never become coherent to her until she was at last outside it, and at
the same time consummately inside it" (181). Caroline also finds her
lover Lawrence, and men in general, secondary if not dispensable:
"Where else," Updike uneasily asks, "in the fiction of the fifties, do
we find a heroine whose heterosexuality is so calmly brought forward
and assigned a secondary priority . . . ?" ("From the Forties" 148).
Certainly not in men's novels of this period. Even those that entertain
a woman's perspective assume sex and romance are feminine pre-

occupations, as in Amis's *Take a Girl Like You* (1960), or they find, as in Larkin's beautifully imagined *A Girl in Winter*, that the plight of the single woman is unutterably sad. In the Larkin novel, Katherine, an Angry Young Woman haunted by romantic dreams, fields a half-hearted marriage proposal: "I mean, if I asked you, for instance, to marry me, you'd refuse, wouldn't you . . . wouldn't you?" (247). Finally she accepts a devastatingly lessened consolation. Larkin's conclusion may seem to resemble Pym's diminished happy endings. But it is not comic; the emphasis is on irony and loss, far from Mildred's consoling hope for "a full life." In an opposing vein, *Lucky Jim*'s Margaret, because always presented as an object, is never other than hilariously appalling: she is forever the stereotypical man-obsessed yet frigid spinster, and to sympathize too much with her, Dixon concludes, would mean nothing but sharing her misery.

Certainly, as Pym discovered in portraying spinsters like herself, the comic object is a large risk when the mockery seems directed at oneself. In Baudelaire's analysis of the comic, laughter is linked with human fallibility (149); therefore, a "man who trips would be the last to laugh at his own fall, unless he happened to be . . . one who had acquired by habit a power of rapid self-division and thus of assisting as a disinterested spectator at the phenomena of his own ego" (154). This "self-division" or doubling (*dédoublement*) is necessary for the sort of laughter willing to view oneself as a comic object, and perhaps the humor of Spark's novels, especially, depends on the reader's own capacity for *dédoublement*, a self-doubling that resembles Eliot's mystical desire "to care and not to care" ("Ash-Wednesday" I.38). Pym's fiction does not fully acknowledge the harshness of this division: she makes us sympathize with her characters and then claims no conflict between caring and amusement. It is Spark's gift, however, to move us between sympathy and disinterested laughter, using her glossy, impeccable surfaces.

In *The Girls of Slender Means* we find this comic objectivity even in the trivia that, until the climax, constitutes most of the plot. The narrative begins as a fable: "Long ago in 1945 all the nice people in England were poor, allowing for exceptions" (3). But Spark smoothly proceeds to puncture any fairytale expectations, observing that the bombed buildings look "like the ruins of ancient castles" only until one observes the lavatory chains dangling over ruined walls (7). Likewise, the May of Teck Club, where the girls of slender means dwell, is not the Golden Age microcosm that the self-obsessed litterateur Nicholas imagines, yet the petty glamours and greeds it contains propel him to a Catholic martyrdom. The catalyzing "action of savagery so extreme" itself is wrapped up in feminine small-mindedness (60): Nicholas sees his lover, beautiful Selina, return as the fire looms, slipping through that bathroom window that only very slender girls can manage (as usual, Spark's title is a pun). Selina risks her life not to help the other girls, but in order to steal a beautiful Schiaparelli ball gown. Meanwhile Joanna, the saintly rector's daughter who is a kind of Pym-ish excellent spinster, perishes along with her recitations of classic, idealistic literary verses. In their place we are left with the vapid Two-Sentence mantra that Selina has daily repeated, emphasizing "elegant dress" and "immaculate grooming" (57). As usual, Spark suggests a wittily allegorical interpretation, here centered on the opposing recitations and the amazing dress with its prewar avant-garde exoticism: "It was made of taffeta, with small side panniers stuck out with cleverly curved pads over the hips. It was coloured dark blue, green, orange and white in a floral pattern as from the Pacific Islands" (108). Just as Joanna's death reminds us that the era of elaborate Romantic poetry is over, the dress represents the coffin lid on the happy comic dream of infinite self-making: its disappearance is synchronized with the war's end, but already we knew that it was a sham, borrowed by each girl in turn in order to stage herself as stylish and desirable.

Only one girl never borrows the Schiaparelli dress: Jane, because it does not fit her. "Fat but intellectually glamorous" to her housemates (32), this observant character has some commonality with other male postwar protagonists: Jim Dixon; John Wain's Charles Lumley in *Hurry on Down* (1953); Sillitoe's Arthur Seaton in *Saturday Night and Sunday Morning* (1958); John Braine's Joe Lampton in *Room at the Top* (1957). All are sharp, tough-minded observers, ambitious to achieve their desires and not above a little dishonesty. Only the Spark and Amis characters, however, are outwardly unprepossessing (most Movement novelists chose big, handsome men as their fictional alter egos). And only Jane and Jim triumph in the ends of their stories. However, where Dixon's is a fairytale triumph, a classic comic conclusion—he gets the princess and the kingdom through luck—Jane has sweated her way to an ideal job of gossip columnist, but never to a happy love life. Significantly, Jane never really learns "that literary men, if they like women at all, do not want literary women but girls" (91); she is never a suitable object of male desires. Nor are the other handsome postwar heroes blissfully happy in the end, though they usually, like Dixon, get the job and the desired girl. Originally these protagonists dream of fairytale happiness: "the fairy came down from the Christmas tree, the straw was spun into valuable gold," Charles exults (Wain 123). And even climber Joe Lampton sees the rich girl he courts as "the princess in the fairystories" (Braine 68). But each man ends in disillusionment. For Lampton especially, a grisly tragedy reveals the price paid for his climb, resulting in a concluding *dédoublement* far from comic: "I didn't like Joe Lampton. He was a sensible young accountant. . . . Why, he even made a roll in the hay with a pretty little teen-ager pay dividends. I hated Joe Lampton, but he looked and sounded very sure of himself sitting at my desk in my skin" (Braine 280).

Why should an objective view of oneself be a grim discovery in the male-authored novels? Each of the representative postwar books exemplifies a petty, desperate materialism; the young protagonist counts his cigarettes, adds up the costs of drinks, informs us of his specific wages, and frequently worries about his loss or delights in his increase. (What is Jean Brodie's salary? Who has ever thought to ask?) The plots offer elaborate details of drunken and post-drunken states and sexual encounters, carefully kept separate from the princess the hero hopes to obtain. In contrast to the feminine trivia of dress style, with its complex codes for self-presentation, nearly everything has a price in these novels, including, in a nice irony, fashionable clothing itself. Arthur Seaton, we are told, dresses carefully and is in fact a "Teddy Boy"—the 1950s version of the Victorian dandy (Sillitoe 73). Yet we hear little of Arthur's clothing, except that his suits are "the good hundred pounds' worth of property hanging from an iron-bar. These were his riches, and he told himself that money paid-out on clothes was a sensible investment because it made him feel good" (66). Joe Lampton, on the other hand, carefully describes both male and female dress but always relates it to money and upward mobility. A coworker feels Joe's suit and comments, "Highgrade worsted. . . . My goodness, Mr. Lampton, however do you manage on your coupons?" (Braine 138). Even the coveted little rich girl Susan, wearing "a black taffeta skirt and a white *broderie anglaise* blouse," prompts a reference to economics: "If anyone ever needed a justification of the capitalist system, I thought, here it was" (160). Certainly Joe is an accountant whose ambitions are being satirized and will be chastened, but Braine's novel is only a more conscious version of these 1950s narratives in which (*Lucky Jim* aside) each concluding material success finds a sadder-but-not-wiser protagonist who cannot see where his detailed materialism went wrong.

In *The Girls of Slender Means*, however, postwar life for the girls means not a desperate struggle for pounds and shillings, or against class barriers, but unromantic acceptance of circumstances. Despite the penury indicated in the title, most girls have prospered through attention to the club's unwritten interests, "Love and money. . . . Love came first, and subsidiary to it was money for the upkeep of looks and the purchase of clothing coupons at the official black-market price of eight coupons for a pound" (27). In this formulation, clothing is not for the sake of making money, but money serves to get clothes.

The girls acknowledge that clothing is, in itself, a trivial concern, and once again we find the established categories of perceiving subject and comic object overturned. For the comedy of the object teaches women to laugh at their own desires as well as at men's.

The stylish spinster is disturbing because she seems (like Spark herself) to choose style over any realized substance, if substance means only measurable material advancement. Nevertheless, she refuses to play the games in which female style is only a code for male desires, erotic or monetary. Not that the stylish spinster necessarily views the world purely in terms of traditional female desires: as Updike noted, *eros* is secondary for most of Spark's women, and this circumstance puzzles her male characters. Jane, like Sandy Stranger, bears a commonality with postwar male protagonists in caring about power and fame, but at the price of being frequently interpreted as bisexual or simply de-sexed. On the other hand, Barbara Pym's spinster world is both simpler and more absolute. Pym refuses to relinquish her heroines' fascination with the male sex, even as her spinsters learn that "becoming minor" and living a life of trivial satisfactions is no great tragedy. Nevertheless, Pym ruefully maintained to the end that a huge gulf lies fixed between male perceptions of women and the reality of female existence. In her journal she comments, after giving a ride to a pair of elderly spinsters in her village, "Looking at one of them with her hairy chin and general air of greyness one couldn't help thinking that this was as much a woman as a glamorous perfumed model" (*Very Private* 306). Pym was all too aware that most men of her era would disagree. And, in her fiction, however much comic insight the women achieve into their own selves, the men never move beyond seeing the women as objects.

Spark however refused to give up the fight. And finally the question of Muriel Spark's place among the male postwar novelists is figured metaphorically, as the author preferred, by the conclusion of *The Girls of Slender Means*. Only Jane is left a spinster at the book's end—yet she is no pathetic single woman, but a tough observing consciousness like the author herself. After watching the wild celebrations of V-J night, Jane stands in the park pinning up her hair and comments, "Well, I wouldn't have missed it, really." Nicholas, who soon will exile himself from both self-centered literary ambitions and erotic desires, marvels at her, and it is not the Schiaparelli-stealing Selina but the unalluring Jane that he recalls "years later in the country of his death—how she stood, sturdy and bare-legged on the dark grass, occupied with her hair—as if this was an image of all the May of Teck establishment in its meek, unselfconscious attitudes of poverty, long ago in 1945" (176). In concluding thus, Spark too leaves us with a persistent image, beyond diminished literary style and Romantic hopes, of the resilience of the stylish spinster.

Note

1. Miss Brodie reads *Jane Eyre* to her girls during their sewing class, leading Sandy to an elaborate fantasy in which Mr. Rochester is courting Sandy herself. And, in typically twisted Sparkian ironies, Jean Brodie is like Jane, an erotically questing spinster teacher in love with a married man. For allusions to Brontë's novel in *Excellent Women*, see Janice Rossen. In both books, *Jane Eyre* serves as a touchstone for unrealistically romantic expectations.

Works Cited

Amis, Kingsley. *Lucky Jim*. 1954. London: Penguin, 1992.

———. "She Was a Child and I Was a Child." *Spectator* 6 Nov. 1959: 635–36.

Baudelaire, Charles. "D'Essence de la rire." *The Painter of Modern Life and Other Essays*. Trans. Jonathan Mayne. Greenwich, CT: Phaidon, 1964. 147–65.

Bergonzi, Bernard. *Wartime and Aftermath: English Literature and Its Background, 1939–60*. Oxford: Oxford UP, 1993.

Braine, John. *Room at the Top*. Boston: Houghton, 1957.

Byatt, A. S. "Marginal Lives." *Times Literary Supplement* 8 August 1986: 862.

Doan, Laura, ed. *Old Maids to Radical Spinsters: Unmarried Women in the Twentieth-Century Novel*. Urbana: U of Illinois P, 1991.

Eliot, Thomas Stearns. *The Complete Poems and Plays: 1909–1950*. New York: Harcourt, 1971.

Finkelstein, Joanne. *Fashion: An Introduction*. New York: New York UP, 1998.

Flaubert, Gustave. Letter to Louise Colet. 16 January 1852. *The Letters of Gustave Flaubert, 1830–1857*. Trans. Francis Steegmuller. Vol. I. Cambridge, MA: Harvard UP, 1980. 154.

Flügel, J. C. *The Psychology of Clothes*. London: Hogarth, 1950.

Greer, Germaine. *The Female Eunuch*. New York: McGraw, 1971.

Gregson, Ian. "Muriel Spark's Caricatural Effects." *Essays in Criticism* 55 (2005): 1–16.

Hanson, Karen. "Dressing Down Dressing Up: The Philosophic Fear of Fashion." *Aesthetics: The Big Questions*. Ed. Carolyn Korsmeyer. Malden, MA: Blackwell, 1998. 59–71.

Hopkins, Harry. *The New Look: A Social History of the Forties and Fifties in Britain*. Boston: Houghton, 1963.

Joyce, James. *A Portrait of the Artist as a Young Man*. 1916. Ed. Seamus Deane. New York: Penguin, 1993.

Larkin, Philip. *Collected Poems*. Ed. Anthony Thwaite. New York: Farrar, 2004.

———. *A Girl in Winter*. 1957. New York: St. Martin's, 1963.

———. Letter to Barbara Pym. 14 July 1964. *Selected Letters of Philip Larkin. 1940–1985*. Ed. Anthony Thwaite. New York: Farrar, 1992. 368.

Lauer, James. *The Concise History of Costume and Fashion*. New York: Abrams, 1969.

Lehmann, Ulrich. *Tigersprung: Fashion in Modernity*. Cambridge: MIT Press, 2000.

Little, Judy. *The Experimental Self: Dialogic Subjectivity in Woolf, Pym, and Brooke-Rose*. Carbondale: Southern Illinois UP, 1996.

MacLeish, Archibald. *Collected Poems, 1917–1982*. Boston: Houghton, 1985.

Miller, Lee. "The Liberation of Paris." *The Forties in Vogue*. Ed. Carolyn Hall. New York: Harmony, 1985. 62.

Moers, Ellen. *The Dandy: Brummell to Beerbohm*. Lincoln: U of Nebraska P, 1978.

Orwell, George. "The Lion and the Unicorn." *The Collected Essays, Journalism and Letters of George Orwell*. 1941. Ed. Sonia Orwell and Ian Angus. Vol. 2. Harmondsworth, UK: Penguin, 1970. 74–134.

Pound, Ezra. "A Retrospect." *Early Writings: Poems and Prose*. 1918. Ed. Ira B. Nadel. New York: Penguin, 2005. 253–56.

Pym, Barbara. *Excellent Women*. 1952. New York: Penguin, 1978.

———. *Quartet in Autumn*. 1977. New York: Harper, 1980.

———. *The Sweet Dove Died*. 1978. New York: Harper, 1980.

———. *A Very Private Eye: An Autobiography in Diaries and Letters*. Ed. Hazel Holt and Hilary Pym. New York: Random, 1985.

Rossen, Janice. "On Not Being Jane Eyre." *Independent Women: The Function of Gender in the Novels of Barbara Pym*. Ed. Janice Rossen. New York: St. Martin's, 1988. 137–56.

Schneider, Mary W. "The Double Life in Muriel Spark's *The Prime of Miss Jean Brodie*." *Midwest Quarterly* 18.4 (1977): 418–31.

Sillitoe, Alan. *Saturday Night and Sunday Morning*. 1958. New York: Knopf, 1959.

Simmel, Georg. "Adornment." *The Sociology of Georg Simmel*. New York: Free Press, 1950. 338–44.

Spark, Muriel. *The Comforters*. New York: New Directions, 1957.

———. *The Girls of Slender Means*. New York: Knopf, 1963.

———. *The Prime of Miss Jean Brodie*. 1962. New York: Harper, 1999.

Stannard, Martin. "Nativities: Muriel Spark, Baudelaire, and the Quest for Religious Faith." *Review of English Studies* 55 (2004): 91–105.

Updike, John. "Between a Wedding and a Funeral." *Assorted Prose*. New York: Knopf, 1965. 310–14.

———. "From the Forties." *New Yorker* 8 June 1981: 148–58.

Wain, John. *Hurry on Down*. 1953. New York: Viking, 1965.

Wilde, Oscar. "The Decay of Lying." *De Profundis and Other Writings*. London: Penguin, 1986. 55–87.

Wilson, Elizabeth. *Adorned in Dreams: Fashion and Modernity*. Rev. and Updated. New Brunswick, NJ: Rutgers UP, 2003.

Wollstonecraft, Mary. *A Vindication of the Rights of Men* and *A Vindication of the Rights of Woman*. Ed. Sylvana Tomaselli. Cambridge: Cambridge UP, 1995.

Woolf, Virginia. *A Room of One's Own*. 1929. Orlando: Harcourt, 2005.

CHAPTER 7

THE MANDELBAUM GATE:

MURIEL SPARK'S APOCALYPTIC

GAG

John Glavin

Why revisit *The Mandelbaum Gate*, Muriel Spark's 1965, large-frame novel of Jerusalem and its environs? With the notable exception of Frank Kermode, it has rarely been admired. Indeed, Spark seemed effectively to minorize it by characterizing herself as a writer of short (her word was *minor*) fiction. She was not nor did she wish to be seen as, in her own words, Mrs. Tolstoy (Hynes 30). No more big books, I recall her insisting, when we met in 1987. If she were to be remembered, she assumed—and preferred—that it would be for her short stories. Certainly not for her single big and historical novel.

And yet I have come to think that *Mandelbaum Gate* is actually the cardinal novel of her long career, cardinal in its literal sense of *hinge*, the novel on which the career pivots. There's a typical sort of Spark novel before *Mandelbaum Gate*—those high-modernist innovations of the 1950s and the early 1960s. *The Comforters. The Girls of Slender Means. The Ballad of Peckham Rye.* Supremely, *The Prime of Miss Jean Brodie*, the one that made her world-class. We can think of that Spark novel as something like the work of a tougher Sylvia Townsend Warner crossed with a more accessible Henry Green: 150-250 pages, elegant in prose, middle class to shabby in subject, a realistic verging on absurd comedy of very English manners crossed and complicated by a mystic's Macguffin, often outré but never rude or outraged. And then there's a typical sort of Spark novel after *Mandelbaum Gate*. The novels of the remaining forty or so years. *The Driver's Seat. The Hothouse by The East River.* All the way through to *Aiding and Abetting* and *The Finishing School*. Novella length, weird, elliptical, opaque, derisive, mysterious, utterly unclassifiable in terms that apply to any of her contemporaries. Hardly novels at all, really, or perhaps just the kind of novel Medusa would have written to while away the interval between stares. Nevertheless, this is the fiction for which I think, *pace* Spark, Spark will ultimately be remembered.

Mandelbaum Gate works the passage from the first manner to the second. It is literally the gate, this chapter argues, through which she transforms her practice of fiction. I concede its many flaws: it disproportion, its bland and unengaging heroine, its failure to integrate the lengthy Abdul Ramdez plot into the whole—to name only the most glaring. Nevertheless, I want to argue here that it is the alembic in which Spark discovers both the method and the mode that make her fiction unique and indelible.

Archeology

One might start rehabilitating the novel by pushing its unexpected *archeological* value, recuperating for its readers a now vanished way of life. It describes a world—post-partition Palestine centered on a divided holy city—that vanished utterly two years after the book appeared. In this sense it can be read as a sort of Proustian project before the fact. Of course Proust knew his world was ending even as he finished writing the *Recherche*. Spark could not have known that the city she so carefully recorded would so swiftly vanish. In fact, its final pages seem to suggest these divisions are permanently in place. Nevertheless, the effect is the same. In Spark's pages we encounter a seemingly solid system of expectations and protocols, of hostilities and allowances, that must appear to twenty-first century readers as remote, indeed as implausible, as the subtle cadencing of a vanished *faubourg*.

And unlike Proust's Paris, post-1967 Jerusalem gives this archeological project a particular and poignant urgency. As the noted architectural historian Simone Ricca painfully details in *Reinventing Jerusalem* (2007), not just the old way of life but the city itself swiftly disappeared after the 1967 War. With the defeat of the Arabs, a complex, compartmentalized, contested history rapidly gave way to ethnic cleansing and gentrification in pursuit of a totalizing, homogeneous heritage. Thus, within a few years of the war, most of the overcrowded, shabby Jewish Quarter had been demolished (35), along with the entire Moroccan quarter (43). Soon thereafter every trace of the "Palestinian heritage" had been "erased, both from the physical map and from the map of memory" (43). Yet we find this erasure at least partially reversed in the careful mapping that shapes Spark's fiction. In a curious way, then, one that is rich with Sparkish irony, readers of *Mandelbaum Gate* owe a considerable debt to Spark—despite herself—for her endeavors as Mrs. Tolstoy.

Nevertheless, I want to argue that reading the novel archeo-logically, or even just historically, misses its most compelling claim to renewed notice. _Mandelbaum Gate_ constructs itself elaborately and deliberately as a different sort of fiction, an apocalyptic, not a historical, novel. Indeed, as an apocalypse (future-drawn), rather than being antihistorical it is fundamentally antihistoricist (past-obsessed). The novel explicitly breaks itself into two parts, divided by Barbara Vaughan's decision to pass through the Gate and initiate the pilgrimage. At that point the novel radically changes. Its principal figures, in the first part confused, impotent, meandering, become, in the novel's preferred term "passionate," daring, erotically charged and active, impulsive, violent and effective. They disappear from history; where they are, what they do, slip into mystery. And within that mystery they find opening toward them a fundamentally differ-ent and liberating order of space and time, of understanding and of agency. One of the reasons, I would argue, that the novel has been so frequently misread, or perhaps under-read, is that this strongly indicated break does not figure significantly in accounts which see the pre-pilgrimage, the pilgrimage, and the post-pilgrimage as es-sentially homogenous.

History and Apocalypse

Part One situates its characters in a dreary world frustrating on all sides and in all ideologies, Muslim, Christian, Jewish, all alike consumed by "the laborious construction of ruins . . . the principal means by which the forbears of the whole human race, stretching back into history, had passed the time of day" (104). Devious, mendacious Abdul Ramdez escapes this omnipresent aridity, but he manages his evasion only through sly and conscious manipulation of alcohol-fueled fantasy, what the novel calls Abdul's Orange Groves. Part Two, "The Passionate Pilgrims," virtually flings its principal characters, Barbara, Freddy and Suzi, out of laborious, ruinous history into apocalypse, a break Spark both names and interprets with her repeated focus on the lines from Revelation (3:16): "I find thee neither cold nor hot; cold or hot. I would thou wert one or the other. Being what thou art, lukewarm, neither cold nor hot, thou wilt make me vomit me out of my mouth." Those lines not only recur continually in the opening section of the book (17, 46, 54, 90) but finally come to function as a virtual open sesame, catapulting the characters into a form of metahistory. It is their shared agreement on the centrality of that warning and their contempt for the ethos of the lukewarm that pushes Barbara and Freddy over the brink into revelatory release.

In their apocalypse-shaped pilgrimage the pair, abetted by Suzi, enjoys a vertiginous, merry discharge of any "sense of tomorrow"

(105). They find themselves "outside the context of worry" (256), in a literally astonishing, albeit temporary, cornucopia of plentitude. Where history enforces endless postponement of fulfillment, apocalypse allows them "to expect the unexpected" (180), and to find in the unexpected an almost overwhelming "beauty and insight and delight" (304). In history one must search for meaning; in the apocalyptic— apocalypse literally meaning uncovering—answers "simply [come]," as Freddy observes of his unmasking the spies, "immediately then and there" (230). One doesn't have to puzzle through. "I simply knew it," he can crow. In apocalypse, desire and the means to fulfill desire come immediately and easily to hand. Indeed the means often offers itself before the desire is felt. Gay Freddy sleeps happily and successfully with amorous Suzi. Even dour Ricky is gladly deflowered by old Ramdez the rutting bull. Time and space have flowered so bountifully they constitute for all "a respite from responsibility for [the] self" (255).

And not only does Spark, within her novel, posit apocalypse as the preferred alternative to her characters' earlier immersion in history; I want further to argue that the novel also poses apocalypse as an alternative model for late-modern storytelling. This gives *Mandelbaum Gate*, whatever its shortcomings, one of Muriel Spark's most enduring claims to critical interest. In this bold swerve she suggests intriguing possibilities for a road not taken at the point where an exhausted modernism was being overtaken by emerging postmodernism. If others had taken this route, they might have produced contrarian accounts of both alternatives, modernist absurdism and postmodern solecism. *Mandelbaum Gate*, historically a novel of what was and now isn't, thus also becomes narratively a novel of what might have been but wasn't.

Modes of Apocalypse

My understanding of apocalypse derives from figures not usually found in contemporary criticism, major theologians Rowan Williams, John Zizioulas, and N. T. Wright. As suggested by the ecumenical range of these figures—two Anglican, the other Eastern Orthodox—my argument takes seriously Spark's investment in theology, but it also contests the standard line of criticism that reads her as a staunch and indeed doctrinaire Roman Catholic. Although her early fiction does ground itself in her then-recent conversion to the Roman communion, by the mid-1960s she was working hard and successfully to separate from any sort of conventional orthodoxy, emerging instead, like the oxymoronic Barbara Vaughn, "a Gentile Jewess, a private-judging Catholic, a shy adventuress" (194). My reading does not stress biography; but it should be noted in passing that _Mandelbaum Gate_ marks a clear and energetic stage in that exercise of "private judging." I am convinced that reading Spark through an exclusively Roman Catholic lens induces a sort of myopia. Correcting that lens through other Christian perspectives allows us to see more accurately the full field in which her imagination plays merrily back and forth between affirmation, sometimes, and subversion, often. It helps us to see that whatever she came to affirm during her process of conversion to the Roman church, the one thing that remained bedrock, rooted in her most fundamental identity as a Scotswoman, was her skepticism. If then there's any one term we might risk using to sum up a spirit so protean, it has got to be that word least likely to apply to "good" Catholics, antinomian.

Subverting all orthodoxies, and the authorities that draw upon and reinforce them, _Mandelbaum Gate_ constructs itself from a wide range of witty, often surprising substitutions that align, overlap, and reinforce each other in an almost infinite series of refusals and revisions. The most obvious and significant of these substitutions involves the way in which Part Two, the comic, frequently almost farcical pilgrimage, replaces the fragmented, tortuous, unhappy Part One, repetitive life stuck in and around Jerusalem. But even a short list of the most intriguing substitutions would also have to include

- The keynote opening scene in which Freddy substitutes verse for a polite bread and butter note; this verse is also, as Freddy makes clear (5), a substitute for the conversation he as a guest failed to provide;
- Crucially, Barbara is substituted for Kyra, the Ramdez servant, so that she can make it safely through the pilgrimage;
- Barbara then substitutes herself for one of the Ramdez bar girls in order to remain concealed in Jericho, and at the conclusion she substitutes for the nun whose clothes she has stolen in order to pass back through the Mandelbaum Gate;
- The narrative of pilgrimage is replaced by illness and extended convalescence in Jericho, while the pilgrimage itself substitutes for that summer's focus of attention, the Eichmann trial;
- The espionage plot involving the pipes depends on mock pipes, with different dimensions, being substituted for the real thing;
- Suzi substitutes for her brother Abdul, the real object of Freddy's erotic attention, while Freddy is a substitute for

> Alexandros, Suzi's official lover, and Joe Ramdez substitutes for Barbara as the object of Ricky's passion;
> * Freddy substitutes the lines from Horace in place of Joan Gardiner's secret message, and then he substitutes for the Horace his own translation of the lines;
> * The murder of Freddy's mother by her servant substitutes for the bloodshed that is expected in the violent Holy Land;
> * Ricky, thinking she will destroy any chance of Harry Clegg marrying Barbara, substitutes the forged baptismal certificate for the real one, thus unwittingly enabling the marriage to take place; and
> * most grandly, at an archetypal or allegorical level, Jacob substitutes himself for Esau at Beersheba (22), securing his blind father's blessing.

My favorite substitution of all, however, turns on the witty way in which Spark plays with the archetypal figure of the Scarlet Woman (Revelation: 17). Suffering from scarlet fever, but also pretending to be one of the Ramdez whores, Barbara becomes both literally and metonymically a scarlet woman. But from the beginning the Scarlet Woman of the Apocalypse was read as a figure for Rome, the enemy of the just. And Barbara is of course the figure for Rome in the novel, the convert to Roman Catholicism, waiting on a letter from Rome to approve of the marriage she plans. The spin of substitutions seems at this point almost to exceed the power to name: the virtuous woman substitutes for the whore, as disease substitutes for fervor, as Rome replaces—well, Rome.

These substitutions and others like them encourage and support a reading that sees substitution not only as a structuring principle within the novel but also as a key way in which the novel imagines itself: as a something novel (adjective, no caps) that substitutes itself for THE NOVEL (noun, all caps), as the novel had come paradigmatically to be defined by mid-twentieth-century argument and practice, whether in its more traditional form as realism, or its newer, experimental, absurdist form, the *nouveau roman* or antinovel.

That is indeed the point toward which most of its contemporary readers continually returned—though, predictably, they registered Spark's departures from the norm as failure, not replacement. As Hynes succinctly summarizes the critical consensus (and this not from Spark's detractors but from scholars who had chosen to make her their subject): "the basic objections are that novels are inherently realistic and Muriel Spark therefore cannot be taken quite seriously as a novelist" (7). Thus in *Mandelbaum Gate* even critics favorably disposed to Spark's work, such as Frederick Karl, found "the plot too convoluted, the characters underdeveloped, and the facts of history . . . slighted" (cited in Hynes, "Introduction" 5). Criticism could condone departure from the mimetic, but only if its purpose is to emphasize fiction's recognition of itself as fabrication, renouncing as absurd, indeed mocking, any claim to offer something like truth. But even for those intrigued by Spark's experiments in narrative, absurdism seemed incompatible with her religion. Thus, typically, Richard Mayne, writing shortly after the novel appeared, laments that "assertiveness [. . .] isn't the only mark of the narrator's presence. Her other main quality [. . .] is a mother-knows-best certainty [. . .] a matter of moral absolutism which can't be finally separated from the fact that Muriel Spark is a Roman Catholic novelist" (49). And even Patrick Swinden's extremely subtle, admiring 1973 essay on the novel, which starts by suggesting parallels between Spark and Robbe-Grillet, reluctantly concludes that Spark goes beyond pattern-making to produce "something which arises out of plot but which has a higher status than plot," something which "provokes a correspondence between plots and those real and subsistent truths of which they are held to be the fictional analogues" (71). This sort of correspondence, Swinden admits, is more likely to attract a Catholic than a non-Catholic reader of the book.

Frank Kermode, perhaps Spark's most perceptive and admiring critic, certainly her most talented critic, makes this "correspondence" the key to his claim for the novel's meaning and importance. *Mandelbaum Gate*, Kermode insists, shows what is still possible for the novel after the antinovel; it is, in effect, a triumphant instance of the anti-antinovel. As Kermode notes, "Her novels quite deliberately raise difficult questions about the status of fiction," and she is "even somewhat arrogant about the extent of the novelist's power" (179). But her brilliantly experimental ingenuity is only one side of Kermode's equation. The other side praises the very quality to which other critics object: her insistence that "a genuine though limited relation exists between the forms of fiction and the forms of the world, between the novelist's creation and God's" (179). All the "many aspects of the 'kind of truth' that fictions provide," Kermode insists, she binds up "into one volume" (186). Spark's methods make her, he claims, despite or because of her modernity, Dante's avatar, depending on how you feel about Dante: "Pending the true Transfiguration, which is of eternity, she decides that something of the sort is known in time, since memory, and history, bring health, and this recollection of the *données* of God's plot enables us to do as we must: 'what is to be borne is to be praised'" (182).

Of course, that's just plain wrong—about this novel's plot; about God's plot I don't claim to know. In *Mandelbaum Gate*, health is not achieved, it is arbitrarily given, taken away, and restored. Mysteriously, Barbara is suddenly stricken with scarlet fever, but in a version of the disease so unaccountably mild that it causes merely temporary discomfort and then lenient, prolonged, and productive debility, its symptoms eased by the mysterious physician who draws the Christian figure of the fish, the IXTHOUS, in the sand as he strengthens her for the rigors of the long postponed tour of the Holy Land (342). (Because I have actually had scarlet fever, this incident pushes hard against even my most willing suspension of disbelief.) If health, physical or mental, is enjoyed here, it is experienced only after and as long as one has escaped from history. In the same way, as Freddy's story insists, you have something like health only when you burn history—specifically, his family's letters—and flush them down the toilet. Those who demand that he remember, like his vicious mother and her pathetic servant Benny, are those who destroy. In the parallel plot, Ricky's attempt to use the birth certificate, surely one of the most powerful documents of memory, to ruin Barbara's affair is foiled only when she inanely corrects it, displacing history with invention. The novel makes this point over and over again as its characters first experience the burdens of history and memory and then flee from them into the apocalyptic liberating pilgrimage.

Kermode (mis)reads Spark as a modernist Dante for two reasons that interpenetrate and reinforce each other. *Mandelbaum Gate* appeared at roughly the same moment when Kermode had given the lectures (1960-61) that he published as his much noticed study of time in the novel, *The Sense of an Ending*. His argument there distinguishes among three notions of time: chronos (diurnal time), kairos (God's time), and aevum (time as the imagination plots it). As the language suggests, this is a thoroughly Scholastic trio, based in an Aristotelian and neo-Aristotelian hierarchy of progressively more complex forms, connected through analogy. Unsurprisingly, and crucial to Kermode's claims for the novel's status, is the analogy between the experience of kairos and the experience of aevum. We can know God in his works because they are his reflection, and since humankind is his supreme reflection, we can know God best when humans do their most God-like thing, that is, create. It is this system of correspondence through creation that Kermode finds working through Spark's novel in an exemplary way, though he does not use his special vocabulary to make his point (probably because the study was originally published as a review in *The Atlantic*).

That's the first of the two reasons why Kermode (mis)reads Spark as a modernist Dante, one that points back to Kermode's own work. The second, the one that points toward Spark, derives from his unexamined tendency, and the tendency of virtually everyone who remarks on Spark's Catholicism, to equate Catholicism with Scholasticism. (It helps arguments like Kermode's that the same point is made quite regularly, though not infallibly, by the Papacy.) Kermode assumes a syllogism that runs something like this: since he is a Catholic and Muriel Spark is a Catholic, and since he thinks like a standard Catholic in neo-Scholastic categories, with Dante as the supreme artist of that discourse, so must she. But Muriel Spark is at great pains, in much of her work, and certainly in *Mandelbaum Gate*, to underscore her identity as a "private judging" Catholic (194), who not only relentlessly mocks traditional sorts of Catholic credulity but whose novel actively supports illicit sex, both recreational and commercial, and who sides with her heroine's decision to marry her lover with or without the Church's permission. She is not a Catholic novelist and this is not a Catholic novel in the sense in which those terms could apply to a range of her contemporaries from Graham Greene and Evelyn Waugh to Georges Bernanos and Shusaku Endo. In Spark's work, extramarital sex is not necessarily sin. Redemption does not require the renunciation of the self. Damnation does not loom over every moral quandary. And official Church teaching is rarely if ever the most reliable guide to life. And in no way is she more private judging than in her adherence to the, as it were, rival school to Scholasticism, the theological road less taken, but not therefore heretical—the road not of Knowing but of Unknowing.

Unknowing

Throughout her work and career Muriel Spark alludes to her debt to the text and the tradition of the medieval mystical treatise *The Cloud of Unknowing*. In this novel, the allusion surfaces literally as Freddy begins to reconstruct his experience within the apocalyptic pilgrimage: "the events were to come back to Freddy . . . like a cloud of unknowing, heavy with the molecules of accumulated impressions. . . . It had seemed to transfigure his life" (163). For Barbara also the two weeks in Jericho "passed like an amorphous cloud of cosmic matter" (321). In those weeks she lives out the experience of Unknowing: "She did not think, now, of unpicking knots, for there was some definite purpose in the air about her, liberated as she was. . . . Knots were not necessarily created to be untied. Questions were things that sufficed in their still beauty, answering themselves" (337).

Unknowing is the less usual theological practice distinguished as *apophatic* (Greek: to deny) from the more usual *kataphatic* (Greek: to affirm). The kataphatic affirms that, because humankind is made in God's image, human reason can understand, though imperfectly, the divine—and also the divine plan for creation. The apophatic insists that God's ineffable otherness makes the divine unknowable to the intellect; nevertheless, "our soul . . . is wholly enabled to comprehend by love the whole of him who is incomprehensible to every created knowing power" (Griffin 17). The kataphatic mind ascends to the divine. The apophatic soul receives the imprint of God's grace. Kermode identifies Catholicism with the kataphatic, supremely expressed philosophically in Scholasticism and aesthetically in Dante's *Commedia*, and, he argues, redeployed by Spark in contemporary terms. But Catholicism also contains the apophatic line, stretching back to both Hebrew and Platonic sources, including in addition to the anonymous *Cloud* such notables as Meister Eckhart and John of the Cross. And it is with that apophatic, unknowing, transfigurative, and apocalyptic line that Muriel Spark—in passages like "Questions were things that sufficed in their still beauty, answering themselves"—most significantly identifies her own work and interests.

Because apophasis prohibits "*any* thematizing of divine presence, any ultimate return to an analogy between God and the subject" (Williams 25-26), it subverts every return to, reliance on, or celebration of the argument from analogy underlying Kermode's (mis)reading. Unknowing knows there's no way a novelist's pattern can claim to echo or copy or imitate the divine plan, simply because the divine plan is ineffable. As the novel's Part Two makes clear, plans, all plans, even in the most ordinary areas of activity, are a sort of folly, depending as they do on informed assumptions of predictability. The novel's pilgrimage is so giddy precisely because it overtakes the pilgrims. Nothing happens to or for them as planned on the far side of the Gate. Sprung from both politics and their individual pasts, the pilgrims encounter what feels like sheer happenstance and good fortune (what Spark would call *grace*), not remotely like design. It is simply that "something has happened . . . which is not what would have been anticipated, and which seems to provide evidence for the active presence of an authority, a power, at work, not invading the created order as an alien force, but rather enabling it to be more truly itself"—to cite Wright's account, not of the novel, but of the fulfillment of prophecy (188). And here it may be helpful to remember that Spark herself made no plans; she wrote until a novel worked itself through, and often found herself surprised when she realized today had surprisingly become the final day and the book was done.

For Barbara and Freddy, to experience unknowing is to be *transfigured*, not emptied. Unknowing is never mere negation. "[H]eavy with the molecules of accumulated impressions" (Griffin 163), the cloud is, as described by the author of *The Cloud*, "amorphous" but also full of "cosmic matter" (Griffin 321). We can get a particularly rich sense of what that "matter" might be from Rowan Williams's nuanced treatment of the apophatic. In a chapter titled "Hegel and the Gods of Postmodernity," he offers a philosophical reading of Unknowing that seems to resonate remarkably with what Spark is doing in *Mandelbaum Gate*. His reading is particularly intriguing because, boldly, he avoids iconic figures of Christian theology. Instead he grounds his argument for the enduring and contemporary importance of the apophatic in Derrida and, as his title suggests, even more significantly in Hegel, figures he takes to be indispensable to any genuinely contemporary theology.

Hegel begins with "the sheer historical vulnerability of the human" (Williams 32). Humans long to, and need to, know, and yet are so situated that they are forced constantly to "look warily at systematic claims to overcome the plural and conflictual character of our speech and the world" (33). The systematic (the kataphatic) is always in some sense the catastrophic, the attempt to bridge the never to-be-closed gap between sign and referent endlessly deferred, never to succeed. And this suspicion of system, and of anyone who claims with authority to represent, coincides also with a crucial and recurring feature in Spark's fiction. Her novels (*pace* Kermode) regularly insist that one cannot claim to know the real, any real, and most particularly God's will or plan. All attempts to claim or, worse, impose magisterial knowledge are always dangerously risible in her fiction, often associated with duplicitous, narcissistic or power-seeking savants, therapists, journalists and clergy, the guardians in their different ways of history and of books. One has only to mention Jean Brodie for the point to become mordantly pellucid.

But for Hegel, unlike Derrida, beyond the problematic of speech and its attempt to construct a world, there awaits an *actuality*, "toward which all acts of understanding (all negotiations) intrinsically move" (Williams 29). Of course, Hegel acknowledges, this goal or *telos* to which reflection is directed is "not *representable* (not present) in the structure of any given historical consciousness or set of consciousnesses, not *a* meaning which a speaker or writer could articulate as a piece of communicable information" (29). But more than this his argument insists we "challenge the all-sufficiency of simple identity and simple difference" (29). We have to move beyond the dual phantasmata of a confidently positive knowledge and outright rejection of the possibility of knowledge, seeking to remain open to the traces of actuality. This attentive openness Williams identifies as the essence of Unknowing, a nuanced and modest discourse, patient with contradiction, welcoming the surprise of the actual in play. Williams might indeed be describing Spark's passionate pilgrims as he paraphrases what he takes to be the core of Hegel's thought: "What is strange to reason moves around in the field of cognition: we can indeed abstract to the trace of a perpetual shadow . . . but this shadow *can only 'appear'* in the historical process of making (communicable, communal) sense, in the following of discourse" (30).

The novel's Hegelian Apocalypse—with what is strange indeed to reason moving around in the pilgrims' field of cognition, communal and communicable because of its situation in discourse—contravenes the Fundamentalist Rapture that is the form of apocalypse Americans know best. Yes, as it begins on the Sabbath night of August 12, Spark appears to mobilize the traditional imagery of end time and judgment: "It was nearly half past five, and a great sunset had begun to blaze across the hills of Jerusalem, darkening the valley of Gehenna that ran beneath [Freddy] to join the valley of Jehosophat in the East" (157). At this point St. John the Divine seems to morph into John Bunyan: "He [Freddy] stood there, on the stony path on the ridge of the Hill of Evil Counsel which rose behind him to the summit of Haceldama, the Potter's Field." But, as is typical for Spark, it's all a ruse, an in-joke. This isn't going to be the end of time. The pilgrims are not about to be caught up into the empyrean. The world is not coming to an end. Just the reverse: they are about to find themselves mysteriously informed and empowered through the "lenient remifications" (281) of a whorehouse/pesthouse, as the world, their part of it at least, becomes merrily renewed. The time-bound do not escape into eternity. Instead, the actual now breaks into the diurnal, redeeming and redirecting both discourse and process. Pre-pilgrimage (in a passage Kermode takes to be normative Spark) a stalemated Barbara finds her mind "impatient to escape from its constitution and reach its point somewhere else. But that is in eternity at the point of transfiguration. In the meantime what is to be borne is to be praised" (30). But this sort of Roman Catholic double-whammy— sublimation and transference—Spark leads us to consider not virtue but malaise, Barbara's numbed, stale, and other-worldly script from which apocalypse in the novel's second half releases her.

Spark's antirapturous notion of apocalypse echoes, and I suspect may well be indebted to, Albert Schweitzer's enormously influential 1906 *Quest for the Historical Jesus*, reissued in 1954 in the wake of his 1952 Nobel Prize. (We need to know a lot more than we do about the complex skein of theological influences on Spark during and immediately after the period of her conversion. I doubt she herself read Schweitzer, but I have little doubt those around her did, those who preached retreats, reviewed books, gave sermons, and the like.) For theologians moving along what N. T. Wright calls the *Schweitzerstrasse*, the gospels are about time, specifically about the kingdom of God breaking into the present. Their model of apocalypse is *horizontal,* spreading out across space in time, not *vertical,* rising above time and space into eternity. Horizontal apocalypse urges not what Dominic Crossan calls "the darkening scenario of an imminent end of the world" (238), but its reverse: "a radical subversion of the present world order" (Wright 57). Not the end of the world, that is, but the disruption, at least, of the way of the world. Not the end of time, but the end of the present.

I suspect it's the subversive drive in horizontal apocalypse that anchors its appeal for Spark. From "The Seraph of the Zambesi" onward—the kinetic, elusive angel igniting the tawdry, banal Nativity pageant—her most characteristic, memorable writing celebrates subversion and the subversive, undercutting every orthodoxy, every claim to authority, every canon and icon, particularly those of the self-proclaimed sort. She has no interest in what Crossan refers to as the *sapiential*: historically authorized teaching rooted in the past. Compared with the urgency and the potential of the present, historicism, no matter how well-intentioned, she treats as both intellectually suspect and spiritually irrelevant. Certainly that seems the judgment that drives the novel's relentless satire on those credulous pilgrims who long to locate not only every event in the Gospels but even those "events" that have no place in Scripture, like the Milk Grotto "where for some reason [Mary] happened to be nursing the infant Jesus, in consequence of which the walls of the grotto turned white" (240). When the actual pilgrimage occurs, then, it appears almost as afterthought squeezed into a brief summary passage. Rather then making the past available, apocalypse opens a renewed present in which the trio of characters communally take action, transforming simultaneously both self and other. Apocalypse thus figured offers neither escape to a future nor return to a past. It opens instead present and pressing liberation "from a sterile and reductive adhesion to a fixed perception of a fixed state of affairs" (Williams 30). It repudiates powerfully everything that might be summed up in the apocalyptic *Schweitzerstrasse*'s dark offset, the *Eichmannstrasse*: the history of our time.

The Trial

Readers may miss the novel's apocalyptic thrust because, as the novel concludes, time continues. For the three pilgrims life goes on, in Athens and London (368), Jordan and Jerusalem: all "the places of history" that have become "familiar" (369) to them and to the reader. Of course, they are changed, changed utterly, in their deepest affections and identities, liberated from those bullies, Ma Hamilton, Joe Ramdez, and Ricky, and from the lives those bullies determined. "It's marvelous," Barbara exclaims when she learns she can be married canonically (367). And her pilgrimage partners might also as easily exclaim in the same thrilled way. But can it be apocalypse they have experienced if they turn from it back to narrative?

Sure, because horizontal apocalypse must assume that life goes on; breakthrough is not breakdown. Horizontal apocalypse abrogates not time but history, history as Spark sees it, "progress, enlightenment, and industry, as it had been from time immemorial . . . a society with a sense of tomorrow" (105), that is, "the laborious construction of ruins . . . golden ruins, piled on the foundations of earlier ruins" (104). In question is History as it is epitomized in the novel's account of the Eichmann trial, the novel's pivot.

Eichmann's trial carries such resonance in our common cultural syntax that Spark's readers seem generally challenged to grasp her peculiar take on it. Joseph Hynes claims that the "Eichmann trial occupies a modest position in her intent" (6). Fredrick Karl thinks the trial is there only to point out "Israeli efficiency," though its role in the novel as a whole "never really becomes clear" (42). Kermode allows it a more significant function: "Barbara here [at the trial] decides, as it were, in passing, that she has to see the holy places on the Jordan side. They [i.e., the holy places] are basic to *her* kind of meaning, as to [. . .] Spark's" (185). But he gets that meaning dead wrong, a point the narrative reinforces with delicious irony when its pilgrimage displaces holy places in favor of a bordello, a way-station for spies and scarlet women, including its scarlet-fevered protagonist. Barbara sees at the trial not merely an antithesis to the holy. Nor is it just Hannah Arendt's banality of evil that, appalled, she glimpses. (Of course Arendt's famous banality of evil, so badly clichéd now, was virtually brand-new when Spark was writing *Mandelbaum Gate.* Chronologically, Barbara attends the trial before Arendt wrote, before the trial had been, indelibly, read.[1]) Listening to the trial's tedious processes Barbara does indeed hear banality, but a quite different banality from that of evil, a banality even larger, if that's possible, than the banality of evil; it's the banality of organized life, the banality of socially shaped and typified time, the banality, in a word, of history.

In this novel the trial is only peripherally about the Holocaust, only marginally about Eichmann. The scene of the trial is about the trial itself, the trial as a fundamental and revelatory, quasi-liturgical, ritual. It is not being used, as figures like Hannah Arendt use it, to frame Eichmann as evil's alternative to civilization, or the corruption of civilization, or even the collapse of civilization. Eichmann's trial here exposes the truth of civilization itself, stripped to its core. "It was a highly religious trial," revealing "the complex theology in which not his own [Eichmann's] actions, not even Hitler's, were the theme of his defense, but the honour of the Supreme Being, the system, and its least tributary, Bureau IV—B—4" (212-13). This is not, Saul Ephraim warns, "the most interesting part of the trial" (210), because it lacks affect, drama, characters. But its importance rests in its very lack of interest, its _systematic_ repetitiveness, its samenesses, "its dead mechanical tick."

Those terms don't describe the criminality of the Third Reich, or rather they don't only describe the Third Reich. As the day wears on, Barbara comes to see, and we see through her eyes, that it is in fact the trial that is on trial. Well-intentioned, justified, nevertheless the trial can not help but become the mirror-image of Eichmann's deadly railroad timetables. It's the trial itself, and not simply what is on trial, that for Barbara produces the revelation, which—she will later understand—"rolled away the stone that revealed an empty hole in the earth, that led to a bottomless pit" (344). The Holocaust shows itself in this ironic anti-Easter as the metastasis of the disease that is history, the disease that is _system_, any system, every system, the disease reproduced from era to era that classifies, that groups, that reduces the individual to the integer. (In other terms: knowing, the kataphatic.) That's the hell at the bottom of the hole that is time: the way, violently or prudentially, all power, every authority, political, intellectual, religious, inevitably strips away individuality and difference, insisting each being finally count itself fungible. Life lukewarm, in the apocalyptic phrase that recurs throughout the book, neither hot nor cold, neither alive nor dead, merely historical.

Rejecting history, Spark through Barbara rejects the "nightmare" that is "being in general"—to adapt John Zizioulas's comment on Emmanuel Levinas (48). Being in general "enslaves us in sameness." Against it one must struggle toward a "freedom for otherness . . . expressed whenever the human being refuses to be identified as part of a class, or group, or even a category or stereotype of natural or moral qualities" (40). It is precisely this state of "otherness" that Spark registers as apocalyptic, the all-subsuming substitution that "create[s] a world other than the given one . . . in the radically ontological sense of the emergency of new identities" (48). It is crucial, then, that one not only resist being the criminal but also resist being the just judge. Resistance of this sort moves beyond _mere_ morality to the fundamental dynamic of ontology. "If free, the human being . . . aspires to achieve through otherness . . . not simply difference but uniqueness" (3). Such uniqueness is exactly what Barbara experiences in that crucial moment when she, rejecting the trial, determines to go through the Gate.

Passing literally and figuratively through the Gate that enforces boundaries, Barbara now finds herself suffused with a shocking sense of psychic wholeness: "For the first time since her arrival in the Middle East she felt all of a piece; Gentile and Jewess, Vaughan and Aaronson [. . .] flowering in the full irrational norm of the stock she also derived from: unself-questioning, hierarchists, anarchistic imperialists, blood-sporting zoophiles, skeptical believers—the whole paradoxical lark" (194). She finally feels herself liberated from all the divisive, confining, delimiting, historicist categories of the knowing social text. In phrases that seem to resonate for both character and creator, "She [. . .] for the first time in this Holy Land, felt all of a piece, a Gentile Jewess, a private-judging Catholic, a shy adventuress." Knowing gives way to unknowing, offering in Rowan Williams's paraphrase of Hegel, "a structured wholeness nuanced enough to contain what appeared to be contradictories" (29-30).

All of a piece and unique, Barbara finally accesses the agency that has eluded her throughout the first half of the narrative. Not only does she elude all efforts to trace her as she glides back and forth in her pilgrimage, she also, effortlessly, manages to solves the espionage mystery that has baffled both Israeli and British intelligence, in the process bringing down an entire nest of spies. And at the same time, her supporters, Freddy and Suzi, apparently simply by proximity to her energy field, enact comparable, intertwined narratives of erotic and domestic liberation.

But Spark does not treat this release only as a matter *for* character. She also—and more significantly for the purposes of this argument—represents it as a matter *of* narrative form. The trial seems for Barbara to come "from the pages of a long *anti-roman*" (212). "What are we waiting for," a judge asks, and Barbara hears herself answering "We're waiting for Godot" (213). Gradually the whole long day comes to resemble "one of the new irrational films which people can't understand the point of, but continue to see" (210). And, in fact, I think I know the film she means. It is Michelangelo Antonioni's *L'Avventura* (1960-61), the plot of which *Mandelbaum Gate* uncannily—I'd say deliberately—echoes (and which of course Barbara could easily and recently have seen). In Antonioni's film, as in Spark's novel, a frustrated woman, trapped in a fruitless relationship, travels to an exotic location. Midway into the story, suddenly and mysteriously she disappears, undercutting both conventional narrative structure and rational explication. After that disappearance, however, the two stories differ radically. We never again see Antonioni's missing protagonist. The search for her, the film's second half, is blind, barren, repeatedly full of betrayals, and ultimately doomed. Her pursuers famously finish staring out over a screen divided between an empty sea and a blank wall. *L'Avventura* shows all the key markers of what Frederic Jameson calls second modernism (200), briefly characterized below. As Jameson's account helps clarify, rejecting films (and fictions) like Antonioni's, Spark is also rejecting the key aesthetic practice of her day, the aesthetic that insists life can be neither hot nor cold, pushing out, like her heroine, into a mode insistently contrary to prevailing orthodoxies.

The Gate as Gag

In his remarkable analysis of the passage from midcentury realism to postmodernism, "The Existence of Italy" (1992), Fredric Jameson defines "second modernism" as the successor, fifty years later, to the high modernism that emerged before and around World War I, supremely realized by "masters" such as Stravinski, Picasso, Proust, and Joyce. Second modernism, neither completely modern nor yet postmodern, came to dominate serious work across genres in the period immediately following World War II, the time of *noir*, of the antiroman, of the "art" film, the kind of work epitomized, as Barbara notes, by the plays of Samuel Beckett. As masterfully summarized by Jameson, second modernism is plotless, ironic, autonomous (antigeneric, anticonventional), stylistically self-conscious, elitist in subject matter and/or in audience appeal, insistently reducing all experience to anomie and ennui (200-1). Or as Barbara summarizes it, thinking about "the new French writers" she teaches to "the sixth form": "repetition, boredom, despair, going nowhere, for nothing . . . enclosed in a tight, unbreakable statement of the times at hand" (210).

Of course, *Mandelbaum Gate*, so much the novel of a specific place at a specific moment, is of its time. And it is, in the way of most modernist texts, whether first or second, ironic, antigeneric, or anti-conventional. But the novel wears its moment with a difference. It—and all of Spark's fiction that follows from it—is resolutely not plotless, though its plots are far from straightforward. It mocks elites; think of the Cartwrights and their puppet theaters. And it insists that apocalypse can transform individual lives into something meaningful, effective, exciting, and above all merry. It is, then, deeply, deliberately idiosyncratic, regularly dismissed in its time as frivolous—in other words, entirely, to coin a term, *sui generic.* I propose to name this genre by appropriating an element Jameson identifies as a recurring modernist feature: the *gag.*

Modernism, Jameson argues, regularly brandishes an apparently autonomous sentence, or sentence-like episode; in film the comparable figure is the auteur's characteristic image or emblem. These autonomous elements "document their right and their capacity to exist all by themselves," gratuitous, their only justification the pleasure they offer (205-6). Though Jameson is interested in the gag only as a sort of textual free-floater, I want to use gag to describe what becomes the characteristic feature not only for the second half of *Mandelbaum Gate* but for all of Spark's fiction after that turning point—after Spark herself passes through this "gate" of formal and thematic innovation. And I mean gag not only in its contemporary sense as joke or funny story, but even more significantly as something that silences, stifles, restrains. This is a key yoking when we recall that gag appears to move from the latter sense to the former as a term for the actor's ad-libbed interpolation within a scripted performance, no bad emblem for Spark's resistant disruption of modernism's script.

The second half of *Mandelbaum Gate* reads as an extended, virtually uninterrupted series of gags, from Barbara's mock-Gothic abduction from the convent (180) to the wonderful, bizarre joke in which she crosses back across the Gate in a habit stolen from a hapless nun: "'Poor woman, she was only two minutes having a shower-bath, and then she comes out of the cubicle and all her things gone.' [. . .] 'Not a mortal stitch to put on'" (363). But this gaglike quality of the novel also adumbrates what will become the new form for Spark's subsequent fiction. From this point, and through the remainder of her career, the apocalyptic will routinely stifle the plausible, the unpredictable will overrule the prosaic. In the place of modernism's fierce insistence on all that constrains the free play of individuality (Jameson 167), Spark will insist on the counter-discovery of plenitude, surprise, sheer pleasure. From *Mandelbaum Gate* on she will find a seemingly infinite variety of ways apocalyptically to recapture fiction's fundamental capacity to invent.

Early in her career, the unfailingly astute John Updike recognized Spark as a major new voice in contemporary fiction. In a review originally published in *The New Yorker* in 1961, Updike commented on what he took to be Spark's "dispassionate elevation above the human scene." He also placed Spark on one side of the enduring divide between "English fiction [. . .] since Chaucer" and "our novels"—"American" stories like those of "Ishmael and Huck [. . .] adrift on vessels whose course they cannot control" (68). Though Updike admired much in Spark's work—"its greater gaiety and ease of contrivance, its [. . .] superior finish, and its flattering air of speaking to the reader who [. . .] may be spared the obvious"—he came down finally on the American side. American writing plumbed for him a deeper truth: namely, that all elevated, dispassionate claims to "knowledgeability" inevitably falter before a "human experience [. . .] mired in [. . .] solipsism."

Apt though that appraisal was, within a very few years Updike would have seen a new and different Spark, still undermining solipsism but now also deriding knowing, substituting for both the kind of sustained gag she described in her American Academy of Arts and Letters Address of 1971. There she insists that "Ridicule is the only honorable weapon we have left" (35), arguing for "a less impulsive generosity, a less indignant representation of social justice, and a more deliberate cunning, a more derisive undermining of what is wrong" (35*)*. Neither knowingly elevated above the human condition nor willing to concede the inevitability of solipsism, Muriel Spark, cunning, derisive, had become, ten years after the Updike piece, a joyous contrarian, a subversive who refuses self-righteousness, a writer engaged, not enraged.

And it is through *The Mandelbaum Gate* that the way to this new writing, indeed to this new writer, emerges, tautly and tartly responsive to the oppressions, the evasions, and the openings of her time.

Note

1. As Bryan Cheyette notes ("Writing" 109), Spark based her account of the trial in the novel on transcripts that she made while attending the proceedings in Jerusalem.

Works Cited

Cheyette, Bryan. "Writing against Conversion: Muriel Spark the Gentile Jewess." *Theorizing Muriel Spark: Gender, Race, Deconstruction*. Ed. Martin McQuillan. Basingstoke, UK: Palgrave, 2002. 95-112.

Crossan, J. Dominic. *The Historical Jesus: The Life of an Mediterranean Jewish Peasant.* San Francisco: Harper Collins, 1991.

Griffin, Emilie. Ed. *The Cloud of Unknowing.* San Francisco: HarperCollins, 1981.

Hynes, Joseph. Ed. *Critical Essays on Muriel Spark.* New York: G. K. Hall & Co., 1992.

———. "Introduction." Hynes 1-18.

Jameson, Frederic. *Signatures of the Visible.* New York: Routledge, 1992.

Karl, Frederick R. "On Muriel Spark's Fiction to 1968." Hynes 41-43.

Kermode, Frank. "The Novel as Jerusalem: Muriel Spark's *Mandelbaum Gate.*" Hynes 179-86.

Mayne, Richard. "Fiery Particle—On Muriel Spark." Hynes 47-54.

Ricca, Simone. *Reinventing Jerusalem: Israel's Reconstruction of the Jewish Quarter After 1967.* London: I. B. Tauris, 2007.

Spark, Muriel. "The Desegregation of Art." Hynes 33-37.

————. *The Mandelbaum Gate*. New York: Alfred A. Knopf, 1965.
Swinden, Patrick. "Spark's Plots." Hynes 65-73.
Updike, John. "Picked-Up Pieces." *The New Yorker*. 9 and 16 February 2009.
Williams, Rowan. *Wrestling with Angels: Conversations in Modern Theology*. Grand Rapids, MI: W. B. Erdmans, 2007.
Wright, N.T. *Jesus and the Victory of God*. Minneapolis: Fortress, 1996.
Zizioulas, John D. *Communion and Otherness: Further Studies in Personhood and the Church*. London: T & T Clark, 2006.

CHAPTER 8

"HER LIPS ARE SLIGHTLY PARTED": THE INEFFABILITY OF EROTIC SOCIALITY IN MURIEL SPARK'S *THE DRIVER'S SEAT*

Jonathan Kemp

There is no better way to know death than to link it with some licentious image.
—Marquis de Sade, qtd. in Bataille, *Eroticism*

Eroticism, it may be said, is assenting to life up to the point of death.
—Georges Bataille, *Eroticism*

What is at stake here is the priority of rendering oneself vulnerable to the risk of the stranger.
—William Haver, *The Body of This Death: Historicity and Sociality in the Time of AIDS*

In Muriel Spark's short novel *The Driver's Seat*—described on the cover as "a metaphysical shocker"—we are presented with the story of a thirty-four-year-old woman, Lise, who, in the throes of a nervous breakdown, disengaged and prone to manic laughter, flies abroad and orchestrates her own brutal murder at the hands of a man who has just emerged from an asylum after six years of treatment for sexually assaulting women. The fact that her murder is foreshadowed at the start of chapter three led Spark to call the book a "Whydunnit?" rather than a "Whodunnit?" This echoes Lise's own description of a book she carries prominently throughout the story and finally gives to a hotel porter, telling him it's a "whydunnit in q-sharp major" (101).

The style of Spark's prose in this novel is lean and taciturn: we are given very little on which to base any speculation as to Lise's motives, certainly no psychological explanations of her actions are offered in any straightforward manner. Everything is described externally, as if it were being viewed through a camera lens. This narrative device is an example of what we might call subjectivity without psychology, actions and speech offered without any explicit recourse to the inner workings of the mind. The familiar novelistic device of an omniscient narrator with insight into character motivation is replaced by a sequence of snapshots that offer external description without access to the internal state of Lise's psyche. In this respect the narration is almost cinematic in its attention to surface detail and action. The narrator/witness is no wiser as to why Lise does what she does than is the reader. It is, in a very real sense, superficial, all surface, but self-consciously and stylistically so for reasons that will be offered. No attempt is made, in other words, to explain the purpose of the events reported or to speculate on their causes. To put it yet another way, unspeakability and its effects have become part of what the novel might be suggesting, its theme.

In this essay I offer a queer reading of *The Driver's Seat* that focuses on the symbolic meaning of Lise's murder as a kind of existential comportment that gestures toward the ineffability of the death drive's compulsion to transcend the isolating fact of death through the continuity offered by lust. A gesture, that is, toward the unsayability of self-erasure as a limit-experience on which sociality as such is predicated. Developed in dialogue with theorists ranging from Luce Irigiray, Julia Kristeva, Gilles Deleuze and Felix Guattari, and David M. Halperin, my reading can be called queer not because it argues for a homoerotic or same-sex desire at work within the text, but because it is pitched against the norm, buckling commonsense notions of the self by excavating all psychology; queer, that is, in that it offers no essence to the self, but rather posits the self as some form of discursive residue devoid of meaning or interpretable content. Queer in the sense offered by William Haver, as a loss or lack of authority: "Here, at the site of a pure interruption, at which we never arrive because it is never outside the here and now, there can be no authority" ("Queer" 292). Spark's use of the present tense refuses to escape the here and now and as such sustains the text's interruption, its disruptive, queer energy.

Lise's Parted Lips

I suggest the novel can be read—through the motif of Lise's parted lips and the metaphor of the book—as a presentation of the unpresentable in Jean-François Lyotard's sense; that is, as the inexpressibility of the violent erasure of the self that constitutes the social and/or political. The name Haver gives to this moment or phenomenon, this "thought of that which it is ultimately impossible to think" is "the body of this death." He writes, "Impossibly, but necessarily, the body of this death is at once singular and multiple. In both its singularity and its multiplicity, but above all in the essentially erotic conjunction of its singularity and multiplicity, the body of this death is an impossible object for any apperception, any phenomeno-logical apprehension, any auto-affectivity, any specular capture" (*The Body* xi).

In other words, there is a certain ineffability to the body of this death, a certain unsayability, or unspeakability, something that might not only define its nature (if nature is capable, as a word or concept, of ever naming something truly wild) but also install a resistance to definition within that very move; for it "is the occasion for any possible representation whatever." According to Haver, the body of this death nevertheless eludes capture by any form or system of representation, such as language or thinking. The closest we can come, perhaps, to defining the body of this death is to describe it as "the ultimately unspeakable radical historicity and sociality of erotic existentiality" (xi).

One of the aims of this essay is to elucidate further what is at stake in understanding the social and the political, which requires an engagement with an erotic limit that "exceeds the figure of the particular in any dialectic" (xi). Unpacking this impossible, yet necessary, singular-multiplicity as it appears in Spark's novel, I will explore how this limit contours representation while at the same time resisting it, how it is an unspoken—indeed, unspeakable—predicate of sociality per se. In other words, the socio-political is that unspeakability.

This reading focuses on two tropes or leitmotifs in Spark's novel: first, the book that Lise carries conspicuously with her before handing it to the hotel clerk on finally finding her man, her "type," the one who will murder her (Richard); and, second, as already mentioned, the image of Lise's mouth, lips slightly parted, that recurs throughout the novel. Taken together, these tropes, I will suggest, speak the unspeakability, represent the unrepresentability, of what the novel is about, that is, what it cannot say but can only gesture toward. This cannot be said, furthermore, not because the words do not exist or because there is not time enough to say it—although both these reasons are, in a very real sense, true —but because that unsayability itself is what structures the fact that we can say anything at all. In effect, it is a discourse about discourse, a language about language, and it contours the social at the same time as it disappears within it. That is, this unsayability, as a socio-political erotic comes out of language and disappears into, moves away from it, eludes it in informing what it might mean to be human. That is why language, or language's failure, is so central here, and that is why Lise's parted lips are such a telling metaphor for it. They represent the unsayable at the same time as they signify the erotic. They recall, inevitably, the other lips, the labia, whose multiplicity, according to Luce Irigaray, refuses and challenges the singular logic of the phallus and whose liminality opposes phallogocentrism, the master discourse that venerates instrumental reason and invests in the consolatory powers of the rational. But whereas Irigaray makes much of the fact that the labia are always touching, creating an erotic circuit, Lise's lips are always parting, suggesting neither reason nor its opposite (whatever that might be).

Language and/of the Body

Indeed, Spark's prose style in *The Driver's Seat* could not be further from the flowing, elusive, excessive style most often associated with *écriture féminine*, but even this sparse, clipped writing exceeds the void or absence that constitutes its center. It is a deliberate avoidance of the linguistic games and excesses of modernism, yet at the same time indebted to modernism's breakthroughs—in particular, its use of the present tense and prolepsis. Resisting the internal monologues of Woolf and Joyce, however, Spark's prose opts instead for the external fractures and guessing games of the antinovelists such as Robbe-Grillet and Sarraute.

There is, nevertheless, a trope centered on multiple languages or tongues at work in the novel: Lise speaks four languages, and her murder will be reported in four languages. She cries for help in four languages when Bill tries to rape her and commands Richard to murder her in four languages. These four languages are, in other words, employed in very different circumstances, instantiating multiple uses. But if language is incapable, at times, of any meaningful communication, it matters not at all how many languages you speak or comprehend. The ineffable resists or eludes all language systems, including the visual or nonverbal. As Elaine Scarry comments: "Physical pain does not simply resist language but actively destroys it, bringing about an immediate reversion to a state anterior to language, to the sounds and cries a human being makes before language is learned" (4). But it is not simply that pain might be the opposite of language, or the cessation of language, or even the active destruction of it—more than this, what Spark's novel seems to offer is a stylistic comment on, or movement toward, thinking the unthinkable. She gives the unbidden thought a voice. In this sense, it is not so much the content of the novel that offers up such a reading but the way that it is written. As Martin McQuillan notes: "As in the case of the *nouveau roman*, Spark's concern is with the forms of thinking sustained by the mode of writing, in order to constitute a political engagement, and not the realm of novelistic content" (13). Archly playful and emotionally disengaged, Spark's prose plays willfully with time. After starting practically midsentence during a scene Lise is having with a shop assistant over a stain-resistant dress, the narrative "rewinds" to the recent events leading up to Lise's eruption of rage: "I won't be insulted!" (9). At the start of chapter three Lise's death is announced in the future perfect tense, a prolepsis that Joseph Hynes reads as "a refashioning of the ancient encounter between foreknowledge and predestination" (80). More than that, however, it is a stylistic device that foregrounds the construction of the story.

Given that the act of writing emerges within *The Driver's Seat*'s temporal games, it is perhaps significant that, throughout the novel, Lise carries a book and constantly draws attention to it.[1] She purchases it at the airport before boarding her flight. She has a brief conversation with another woman, who is looking for books in English with pastel colored covers to match the shades of her home's interior decoration. Lise comments that the books on display are "all very bright-coloured" before selecting one for herself "with bright green lettering on a white background with the author's name printed to look like blue lightning streaks. In the middle of the cover are depicted a brown boy and girl wearing only garlands of sunflowers." Lise then proceeds to hold the book up against her coat, "giggling merrily, and looking up to the woman as if to see if her purchase is admired," but the woman complains "'Those colours are too bright for me. I don't see anything'"—as if the garishness had momentarily blinded her (22). Given that we have already been told that Lise's coat is striped white and red and her dress is yellow, mauve, orange, and blue, this kaleidoscope of color could indeed momentarily blind the woman. Lise is out to be as conspicuous as possible, and she carries the book before her at several points in the novel as a way of drawing attention to herself. During lunch with Mrs. Feike the book is moved by the waiter and Lise returns it to its prominent position. Lise's outfit is laughed at continuously and she is stared at by strangers because her clothes stand out—on one occasion she is asked if she is going to join a circus, and on another a woman in the street comments: "Dressed for the carnival!" (69). In the scene where Lise buys the dress and coat, she ignores the sales assistant's suggestion that they not be worn together, declaring, on the contrary, that they go very well together. Bizarrely, Lise refers to the colors as very natural: "absolutely right for me" (11). If her desire is to be memorable, then there is a very specific logic at work here, a carnivalesque logic that throws into radical doubt all we think we know. There is a certain abjection at work in the construction of the carnival: Lise's carnival outfit is aimed at making her stand out from the herd, a gesture that also marks her as different and therefore in a liminal position within the social body, constituting an ambiguous opening in the text. As Kristeva points out, "abjection is above all ambiguity" (*Powers* 9).

In this novel, Spark uses clear language to construct a tale riddled with ambiguities. The fact that the novel refuses to offer up any neat meaning for Lise's actions constitutes one of its boldest moves, for it constructs a dynamic of interpretation within the narrative itself. Devoid of an omniscient narrator's commentary, in a very real sense, one constructs this novel through the act of reading: an act of reading that is profoundly deconstructive or dislocatory. Spark's use of the present tense "emphasizes the narrator's detachment as each moment is carefully picked out without comment [offering] no enlightenment" (Sproxton 137). Any commentary is provided by the reader. Or, as Judith Roof puts it, "narrating does not align the story with any definite understanding and thus exposes narrative's failure of insight" (52). I am not concerned here, however, with categorizing the novel as anti-postmodernist or pro-postmodernist, but rather with exploring further what might be achieved by resisting such a move via an appeal to the body's erotic sociality; like Spark's text, the body is a mode of practice that will always resist any easy categorization. In other words, Spark's novel can be said to indict language with a failure to represent the ways in which a certain risk—both erotic and, in a very real sense, deadly—qualifies any relationship we might name the social. Put yet another way, what we call representation is the institutionalization of an experience at once both overwhelmingly complex and astonishingly simple: the experience of the social that, at least potentially, is always already erotic and deadly or destructive of the individual. Accordingly, my next section explores how murder might be understood in this context of the unspeakable as a radical constituent of all language.

Death as the Failure of Language

Spark's novel certainly confirms Sigmund Freud's conclusion in "Beyond the Pleasure Principle" that "the pleasure principle seems actually to serve the death instincts" (268). Something Freud doesn't remark on, however, is how death is always already social, as is pleasure. In the act of murder, the two are very clearly and violently brought together. In volume 2 of *The Accursed Share*, Georges Bataille, writing on the prohibition against murder, claims that the origin of our "loathing of decay" is the "loathing of nothingness . . . which is not physical since it is not shared by animals" (79). Animals feel no conscience when they kill; they have no disgust to overcome. There is, then, a certain animality, a certain becoming-animal at the heart of the impulse to murder. Bataille then links the horror of murder with the disgust we tend to have for excrement. When we murder, we produce a corpse that is analogous to shit. There is, in other words, something profoundly excremental, Bataille maintains, about the act of murder. "Life," he writes, "is a product of putrefaction, and it depends on both death and the dungheap" (80).

By restoring us to the "power of nature," which is read as a "*repulsive* sign" of the universal ferment of life" (80), the act of murder retains its status as a taboo through this association of corpse and/ as excrement. In *Eroticism*, Bataille associates life and death in the limit-experience that the latter provides, a limit-experience that defies linguistic expression, such that: "In the end the articulate man confesses his own impotence" (276). That is, language fails in the face of the ineffability of erotic sociality. Language is impotent. Or, as Spark's narrator puts it, "As the knife descends to her [Lise's] throat she screams, evidently perceiving how final is finality" (106–07). That scream is language's failure. After instructing Richard on precisely how she wishes to be murdered, Lise is forced to concede to his will as he ignores her instructions: "'I don't want any sex,' she shouts. 'You can have it afterwards. Tie my feet and kill, that's all. They will come and sweep it up in the morning.' All the same, he plunges into her, with the knife poised high. 'Kill me,' she says, and repeats it in four languages" (106). After organizing her demise and planning it so precisely, in the final moment her will is thwarted and the sex she has resisted throughout the novel is forced on her. After fending off sexual advances from Bill and Carlo (the mechanic she meets after the student demonstration when she takes cover in a garage), Lise puts herself in a position with Richard where she is defenseless and her own will is subsumed to his. This scene brings to mind Angela Carter's comment in *The Sadeian Woman* that "Flesh has specific orifices to contain the prick that penetrates it but meat's relation to the knife is more random and a thrust anywhere will do" (138).

Richard had thought Lise was afraid of sex, but in a conversation prior to the murder she admits that "'It's all right at the time and it's all right before . . . but the problem is afterwards. That is, if you aren't just an animal. Most of the time, afterwards is pretty sad'" (Spark 103). As Alan Bold remarks, "This shock ending is ironical in the extreme. Lise's dream of manipulating the precise manner of her death is destroyed by her murderer's refusal to accept her every instruction. By choosing, by exercising his free will against her authority, he diminishes her dream, transforms it into a nightmare" (94).

The central relationship in this novel is, after all, that between murderer and murderee, and how the one finds the other; how Lise tracks down the man she instinctively knows harbors the desire to kill a woman is the main narrative thread. Her conspicuousness is therefore doubly significant—not only does it mark her out as different from everyone else, from all the other women in their "dingy" clothes (Spark 21), but it is also the signal to her murderer. She tells Mrs. Fiedke, "The one I'm looking for will recognize me right away for the woman I am" (65); indeed he does, for Richard, her murderer, her "type," recognizes Lise immediately when they are seated next to one another on the plane. So terrified is he that he moves seats, only to encounter her again in the hotel lobby later that night when she instructs him to go with her to the parkland where he kills her. Although he puts up some resistance, he acquiesces up to the point when he thwarts her will by raping her before, not after, her death. When asked by the police after his arrest what had frightened him about Lise on the plane, he replies, "I don't know." He tells them: "She spoke in many languages but she was telling me to kill her all the time," suggesting some kind of psychic transmission from murderee to murderer that the latter finds it impossible to ignore or resist. The police, on the other hand, are closed off to everything, encased in "the upholsters and epaulets and all those trappings devised to protect them from the indecent exposure of fear and pity, pity and fear" (107). These concluding words of the novel echo Aristotle's definition of tragedy in *Poetics,* but given the fact that the police are protected against exposure to these two emotions that constitute the tragic, pity and fear, can it be called a tragedy?

Becoming-Animal

In *Anti-Oedipus*, Deleuze and Guattari develop a radical theory of subjectivity that posits the subject as a residue of the processes of coding and overcoding by which the flows and multiplicities of the social body are mapped and restrained. They call the chaotic unravelling of these restraints decoding. They argue that in advanced societies such as ours, decoding and coding are almost indistinguishable processes. That is, the high levels of complexity found in modern life necessitate an understanding of the subject as always already fractured, or "schizo." In short, fragmentation at the level of the ego is the inevitable outcome of modern overcoding. Because of this fragmented overcoding, their form of "schizo-analysis" regards the psychotic as having something fundamentally profound to say about the nature of the processes of overcoding by which the body is repressed.

Deleuze and Guattari argue that this privatization, or overcoding, both consolidates the public self and at the same time holds in check the self's desires. Furthermore, this process takes as its model the sublimation of anality. According to this model, learning when to shit and when not to shit are coterminous with learning what to say and what not to say; both are a form of discipline, one corporeal, the other discursive. Bodily regulation of flows and discursive decorum go hand in hand. The animality we are metamorphizes into something we call "human" as this acquisition of language occurs, but it never disappears: it breaks through the limits of language all the time. Becoming-animal is to move away from language as the ego fragments and dissolves: "Her lips are slightly parted and her nostrils and eyes, too, are a fragment more open than usual; she is a stag scenting the breeze, moving step by step . . . she seems . . . to search for a certain air-current, a glimpse and an intimation" (72–73).

What Deleuze and Guattari term "becoming-animal" is essential to the appearance of the body without organs (BwO). This BwO constitutes a different organization of the body, a *dis*organization consisting of several strata where "behind each stratum, encasted in it, there is always another stratum." The BwO is a multiplicity; it constitutes a challenge to the conformity to which bodies are exposed, the command that "You will be organized, you will be an organism, you will articulate your body—otherwise you're just depraved" (*Thousand* 159). Eroticism dissolves the organization of the body's intensities; depravity is corporeal disorganization. The conflict established between the imperious demands of the self and the need to conform to social regulations can be seen in the character of Richard, who after his years of treatment is confronted with a woman who wants him to murder her, who picks up on his deepest desire and recognizes in it the complement to her own: organization versus depravity.

Like Deleuze and Guattari, Kristeva also argues that "language acquisition implies the suppression of anality" (*Revolution* 152). In *Revolution in Poetic Language*, Kristeva asserts that this suppressed anality, and the jouissance it harbors, nevertheless find their way into the symbolic order and do so, moreover, by breaking language much as the roots of a tree might rupture the neat uniformity of paving stones. Poetic formations of language such as those found in Mallarmé and Joyce, serve to disturb the symbolic through their eruption of semiotic flows. Anality, Kristeva argues, both agitates the subject's body and subverts the symbolic function: "The jouissance of destruction (or, if you will, of the 'death drive'), which the text manifests through language, passes through an unburying of repressed, sublimated anality" (150). This jouissance of destruction—which also goes by the names "semiotic" and "genotext" —is none other than the heterogeneous flows of the body. Given that the notion of the abject developed by Kristeva names the process by which the human subject constitutes itself through ejecting the things it does not contain, how are we to understand murder, as outlined by Bataille, as an act intimately bound up with the disgust of excrement?

The things we eject from the psyche in constituting our subjectivity are characterized as waste and include the experience of sensuality or jouissance that attends the process of abjection. The reduction of anxiety that comes from the removal of those things considered horrific or abject come at a price: all sensuality, all "open" corporeality must also be reduced. As such closure is not possible, for what Kristeva calls the semiotic lodges the body/bodily within the symbolic, outlawed by the protocols of representation, though by no means any less real. The unsayable, in other words, always attends this act of annihilation/production of waste.

Narrative Noncommitment

It is Lise's reasoning that is the unsayable in Spark's novel. At one point in the narrative, the narrator breaks off and declares: "Who knows her thoughts? Who can tell?" (50). A page earlier, a similar question arises: "Lise is lifting the corners of her carefully packed things, as if in absent-minded accompaniment to some thought, who knows what?"(49). Furthermore, it emerges that on most of the occasions that Lise actually speaks, she is telling lies. Are we to assume that what lies unsaid/unsayable is close to the truth? By offering subjectivity without psychology, Spark refuses to answer that question.

As Joseph Hynes argues: "The effect of such narrative noncommitment is of course to suggest that this is the universal human condition and not merely Lise's here-and-now" (86). Her lips part, as if she is about to speak, but the thought is not given a voice, it slips away from speech. The parting lips signify here not only desire but the unsayability of desire. The ambiguity of Lise's reasoning—we are given fragments or clues to piece together, not an obvious trajectory of facts—lies beneath the ambiguity of the text. Is Spark arguing for the existence of the death drive? Is she accusing modern culture of being a suicide cult? Is she defending the right to desire your own slaughter? Assuming she is saying something more profound than sex and death are somehow connected, I would like to read this short novel as one that "denies itself the solace of good forms," that "puts forward the unpresentable in presentation itself" (Lyotard 81).

There are thirteen instances when we are told that Lise's lips are parted, and in a novel of only 107 pages, that means, on average, she is parting her lips once every ten pages. Furthermore, this parting of the lips occurs in one "whose lips are usually pressed together with the daily disapprovals of the accountants' office where she has worked continually, except for the months of illness, since she was eighteen, that is to say, for sixteen years and some months" (Spark 9). Elsewhere, the narrator informs us "her lips are a straight line" (18); they are linked to textuality and silence, both the line of text and its erasure or inability to stand for something. Her lips provide both a word or statement's emphasis and its erasure. When Lise's colleagues insist that she take a holiday, she looks at them "one by one, with her lips straight as a line which could cancel them all out completely" (10).

The fact that this trope of the parted lips appears three times at the very opening of the novel would indicate that we are to make something of this—that it is significant (though of what we are never told). Spark is drawing attention to Lise's parted lips. It is not usual behavior for Lise: we are told that her lips are usually closed. She parts them, as if she is about to speak, but thinks better of it. From the unknown title and contents of the book Lise carries to the unspoken thoughts of all the novel's characters, unspeakability is expressed not only though the novel's form but also its content. Unspeakability becomes, in other words, a recognizable trope throughout the novel. But rather than being a lack, this unspeakability is a kind of plenitude. An example of this plenitude is found when Mrs. Fiedke asks how Lise will know this man, her "type": "Will you feel a presence? Is that how you'll know?" she asks. "'Not really a presence,' Lise says. 'The lack of an absence, that's what it is'" (71). That, for Lise at least, there can be a distinction between "presence" and "lack of absence" is exemplary of that unspeakability. But what form is that unspeakability taking on here? How does it conjure and connect with the erotic?

If Irigaray's touching lips create a self-sufficient libidinal economy, Lise's parted lips would seem to suggest something approaching the opposite, what I am calling erotic sociality. Lise's parted lips convey not merely unspeakability, but are also, importantly, a sign to the other, a gesture of what Bataille calls continuity, that erasure of the self that occurs not only through pleasure but also through pain.

Lise's parted lips would seem to signify, in other words, a form of erotic comportment. They are a signifier of that compulsion toward the other that grounds sociality within an "originary ontological promiscuity" (Haver, *The Body* 192). This erotic sociality is constituted by a space devoid of language, lacking expression not because we have yet to find the methods with which to express it, but because its inexpressibility is what remains when language meets a limit, or when the body collides with its material inescapability. Furthermore, and crucial for this reading of Spark's novel, a certain anonymity is required for this inexpressibility to reveal itself —what Haver calls "the priority of a rendering oneself vulnerable to the risk of the stranger over any structure of intersubjective recognition in the quite literal multiplicity of 'the body'" (*The Body* xiv), a priority that is the grounding for any sociality, any ethico-political being, whatsoever.

How else are we to understand Lise's claim to Richard that young women are murdered because "'they look for it'" (Spark 104)? Perhaps Spark left enough clues in the form of her "post-modern poesis" (McQuillan 11) to read it as a ridiculous satire? How else to read the novel but as a satirical comment on what Spark calls—in an essay written the same year as *The Driver's Seat*—the "desegregation of art"? In that essay, Spark advocates "the arts of satire and of ridicule. And I see no other living art form for the future. Ridicule is the only honourable weapon we have left" (qtd. in McQuillan 13). Furthermore, she argues that, "we should all be conditioned and educated to regard violence in any form as something to be ruthlessly mocked" (13). The novel does, after all, violently parody both the girl-seeks-boy holiday romance and the Whodunnit thriller. Its style is arch and disengaged, and the world it presents "is filled with creatures whose mindlessness is just short of Lise's disaster" (Richmond 117). If it is "a study, in a way, of self-destruction," as Spark herself has remarked (qtd. in Richmond 111), then Lise's is not the only self that destructs. Rather, it is the impossible multiplicity of the social body itself that disintegrates or dislocates at that moment when full continuity and full discontinuity, both life and death, unite in the pleasurable and murderous erasure of the self.

Determining the Queerness of the Text

In this respect, we can see *The Driver's Seat* as exemplifying Leo Bersani's notion of the queer as something antisocial, or against the social, or as something that is, as Lee Edelman has suggested, opposed to futurity. If, as David M. Halperin claims, "'queer' does not name some natural kind or refer to some determinate object," but is "an identity without an essence," then Spark's novel is indeed

queer, and its refusal to traffic in commonsense notions of character
psychology is a major factor in determining the text's queerness (62).
Spark refuses, or challenges, what constitutes a sense of self: "The
self is a new strategic possibility, finally, not because it is the seat of
our personality but because it is *the point of entry of the personal
into history*, because it is the place where the personal encounters
its own history—both past and future" (106).

When Lise meets Bill at his hotel in the late evening, before
finding Richard, Bill tells her: "I was nearly giving you up. . . I was
just about to go out and look for another girl. I'm queer for girls. It
has to be a girl" (92). How else are we to understand, as queer, a
man's heterosexual desire? To be "queer for girls" is an oxymoron
that renders the notion of a normal self problematic. Likewise, Mrs.
Fiedke's comment, "Look at the noise" (56) queers the senses, queers
sense, and queers logic beyond recognition. These examples make
"strange, queer or even cruel what we had thought to be the world;"
this queer experience forces thought to "confront its own essential,
and enabling, insufficiency" (Haver, *Queer 291*). The novel could be
said to scramble meaning and refuse easy interpretation by disrupt-
ing both identity and representation. It disturbs our understanding
of the modern subject by suggesting that we need to account for the
queer interplay of pain and pleasure, death and the social, in order
to have a fuller understanding of what is at stake in talking about
the socio-political or ethical subject. For there is, ultimately, no one,
no self, that could be said to be in the driver's seat.

Note

1. Lise writes "Papa" and "Olga" on the packages she buys, names that
    are either, in the first case, too generic to carry much meaning or, in
    the second, do not name any character in the novel (Spark 85). Writ-
    ing, in this instance, has ceased to offer meaning. Furthermore, she
    writes in lipstick, drawing a connection between speech and writing
    that scrambles meaning, drawing attention once again to her parted
    lips. If those names are significant—if they signify at all— within the
    novel we are not privy to that meaning. Writing with lipstick, with
    something aimed at drawing attention to the lips, brings together
    speech and writing, overlays the two concepts without suggesting
    how meaning might be carried by the signifiers *Papa* and *Olga*.

Works Cited

Bataille, Georges. *Eroticism*. Trans. Mary Dalwood. London: Marion Bo-
yars, 1987.

———. *The Accursed Share: An Essay on General Economy*. Trans. Robert
Hurley. Vols. 2 and 3. New York: Zone, 1991.

Bersani, Leo. *Homos*. Cambridge: Harvard UP, 1995.

Bold, Alan. *Muriel Spark*. London: Methuen, 1986.

Carter, Angela. *The Sadeian Woman*. London: Virago, 1979.

Deleuze, Gilles, and Felix Guattari. *Anti-Oedipus: Capitalism and Schizophrenia*. Trans. Robert Hurley, Mark Seem, and Helen R. Lane.
Minneapolis: U of Minnesota P, 1983.

———. *A Thousand Plateaus: Capitalism & Schizophrenia*. Trans. Brian
Massumi. London: Athlone, 1992.

Edelman, Lee. *No Future: Queer Theory and the Death Drive*. Durham:
Duke UP, 2004.

Freud, Sigmund. In "Beyond the Pleasure Principle." *The Essentials of
Psycho-analysis*. Trans. James Strachey. Ed. Anna Freud. Harmondsworth: Penguin, 1991. 218–68.

Halperin, David M. *Saint Foucault: Towards a Gay Hagiography*. Oxford:
Oxford UP, 1995.

Haver, William. *The Body of this Death: Historicity and Sociality in the
Time of AIDS*. Stanford: Stanford UP, 1996.

———. "Queer Research: or how to practise invention to the brink of in-
telligibility." *The Eight Technologies of Otherness*. Ed. Sue Golding.
New York: Routledge, 1997. 277–92.

Hynes, Joseph. *The Art of the Real: Muriel Spark's Novels*. New York:
Fairleigh Dickinson UP, 1988.

Irigaray, Luce. *This Sex Which Is Not One*. Trans. Catherine Porter and
Carolyn Burke. Ithaca: Cornell UP, 1985.

Kristeva, Julia. *Powers of Horror: An Essay on Abjection*. Trans. Leon S.
Roudiez. Ithaca: Columbia UP, 1982.

———. *Revolution in Poetic Language*. Trans. Leon S. Roudiez. Ithaca:
Columbia UP, 1984.

Lyotard, Jean-François. *The Postmodern Condition: A Report on Knowledge*. Trans. Geoff Bennington and Brian Massumi. Manchester:
Manchester UP, 1992.

McQuillan, Martin. "'I Don't Know Anything about Freud': Muriel Spark
meets Contemporary Criticism." *Theorizing Muriel Spark: Gender,
Race, Deconstruction*. Ed. Martin McQuillan. London: Palgrave,
2002. 1–35.

Richmond, Velma Bourgeois. *Muriel Spark*. New York: Frederick Ungar,
1984.

Roof, Judith. "The Future Perfect's Perfect Future: Spark's and Duras's
Narrative Drive." *Theorizing Muriel Spark: Gender, Race, Deconstruction*. Ed. Martin McQuillan. London: Palgrave, 2002. 49–66.

Scarry, Elaine. *The Body in Pain: The Making and Unmaking of the World*.
Oxford: Oxford UP, 1985.

Spark, Muriel. *The Driver's Seat*. Harmondsworth, UK: Penguin, 1970.

Sproxton, Judy. *The Women of Muriel Spark*. London: Constable, 1992.

CHAPTER 9

"LOOK FOR ONE THING AND

YOU FIND ANOTHER": THE

VOICE AND DEDUCTION IN

MURIEL SPARK'S *MEMENTO MORI*

Allan Pero

And mortified from every side
The voice of memory comes crying.
> —Muriel Spark, "The Ballad of the
> Fanfarlo," *Collected Poems I*

They are the messengers who run
Onstage to us who try to doubt them,
Fetching our fate to hand.
> —Muriel Spark, "The Messengers,"
> *Collected Poems I*

In attempting to rethink a common misperception about Muriel Spark's texts, I want to pay attention to a persistent but neglected problem that is more often overheard than heard by critics: the voice. By overheard, I mean that the voice is acknowledged as an ambient noise or trope that lurks only in the background of a particular text's content. My approach will be to foreground the voice as a conceptual and theoretical difficulty that requires a more inflected response. For example, in her third novel, *Memento Mori*, we are made privy to a strange series of telephone calls in which an unidentified speaker offers an aggregate of elderly people a piece of advice: "Remember you must die" (2). As several critics, Joseph Hynes among them, have observed, the novel is driven by the characters' different reac-

187

tions to the injunction of this mysterious voice (97). But this text is not the only one that exploits the literary and conceptual possibilities of the sonic. Indeed, Spark's work abounds with people who hear or overhear uncanny sounds and voices: the clacking typewriter in *The Comforters*, the long-dead neighbors who disturb Miss Carson in "The Party Through the Wall," the voice of Roy, Dame Lettice's wandering nephew, in the radio play "The Interview," the murdered narrator of "The Portobello Road," and the bizarre repetition of the overheard phrase in the story "Quest for Lavishes Ghast." However, *Memento Mori* brings into greater relief the fact that Spark is not merely deploying supernatural or metafictional devices in a witty and accomplished way. Her novel places a kind of sonic pressure on the difference between speech and the voice. What is that difference? Speech is, of course, the communication of words with the instrument of the voice. But what is the voice? In Lacanian terms, as Mladen Dolar explains, the voice is a much more difficult object to place since it is a symptom of what is left over from speech, an uncanny object that speech cannot completely master. In other words, the voice as symptom, as a thing without a body, is that which exceeds speech or that which exceeds speech's capacity to make sound meaningful (Dolar 15). The problem of voice as a thing without a body, as an enigmatic object of desire is, I contend, what drives the mystery of the plot. If this is the case, then we must assume a different critical attitude to the plot of Spark's novel than has been adopted by past commentators on the text.

Before I turn to exploring the implications of this different critical perspective, I want to outline briefly how the novel is usually read. What strikes me as problematic about most critical reactions to *Memento Mori* is that it is read from the perspective of its ending and not from its beginning, which, as Nicholas Royle reminds us, opens the novel "*in media res*" (190). That is to say, one should not read the text retroactively as a novel about the supernatural or seductive power of Death.[1] Instead, as I suggest below, the text emerges as an entrancing, significant break from the traditional detective story or the hardboiled detective novel through its meditation on the voice without object. Although Joseph Hynes (136–37) quite rightly shows that Spark is engaged in a novelistic critique of the detective genre (especially in his reading of *The Comforters*), he does not consider how Spark is prodding the genre in a more late modernist direction through its parodic attitude to deductive psychology. In the novel that follows, we assume initially that we are meant to pursue the characters' reactions as clues to the identity of the voice, who is, by hilariously maddening turns, described as sinister and civil, young and old, male and female, and even more variously as a government official, a man of the Orient, and a Teddy-boy (147–48, 152). If we recall that the narrative thrust derives from the characters' reactions to these memento mori, we will also remember something else: we expect, for two-thirds of the novel, to be granted a satisfactory reason for these calls. In other words, there is a culprit whose actions will be exposed and explained by a rational or irrational motive.

What we have forgotten is that we expect the different responses to the mysterious calls to form some kind of choral harmony that will decipher the apparently pure contingency of their appearances. In many ways, the novel follows the desire of the different suspects—some hoping for financial gain, others for psychological power over other characters. Desire, criminal or otherwise, is then called on to explain the presence of the voice. It would seem that if we are sufficiently let in on the secrets of Mabel Pettigrew, Tempest Sidebottome, Eric and Godfrey Colston, or Guy Leet, we will eventually be led to the body behind the voice. Disciplined by the tropes that govern the mystery novel, we begin reading paranoically, as it were, hectically searching for conspiracy and confirmation of our suspicions with each turn of the plot. Of course, the coherence of any conspiracy theory we might generate or toss aside with each new revelation is finally thrown into abeyance. Under these circumstances we are complicit in what D. A. Miller has called the "radical *entanglement* between the nature of the novel and the police" (2). The nature of this entanglement emerges in the different modes of surveillance that govern both the novel and policing; in the detective novel, surveillance is granted a special and extraordinary position. The surveillance is merely a necessary component of finding the killer or thief. But Miller's point in bringing the two genres together is that, in the so-called ordinary novel, the characters and their motives are just as determined by external forces as the characters that populate detective fiction, but by more subtle and naturalized forms of surveillance.

However, this does not mean that the lack of a final solution to the narrative perforce makes the search for a tidy conclusion redundant. Rather, we should consider how the form that surveillance takes helps to construct both the characters and the readers. As I will show, Spark's novel is suggesting that we follow the logic of the *nouveau roman* in that the telephonic voice functions as the constitutive element of surveillance that produces the communal identity of the characters. If we read the novel as a mystery, what intercedes to frustrate our desire for its explanation? I think that an ironic relation to the sign of the clue, that is, the mysterious voice, is crucial to thinking through how the search itself is a meditation on the problem of remembering that we must die. In relying on a Lacanian conception of the voice as symptom, I will contend that we must pay closer attention to the voice as excess and to the gap between speech and the voice, because they are the most important clues in working through how Spark's novel critiques the deductive (and seductive) logic that governs the mystery novel.

"My Embarrassing Vancourier":
The Possible Solution and the Impossible Voice

Nicholas Royle, in a witty and playful essay, unforgettably called "Memento Mori," asks a perfectly reasonable question: "how can you remember what has not happened and indeed never will be something that you could verify as having happened to you? As if it would be possible to say: Look, I have died! It's a good job I remembered" (197). His meditation on the problem of warning and reminder that inheres in the phrase "memento mori" assumes, in order for his deconstructive reading to do its unworking, that in attending to the advice to remember to die, one must be able to "verify" its having been accomplished. Here he places the emphasis on the paradox of verifying what one is not around to verify. But I would place the emphasis elsewhere: rather than the structure of one's relation to death itself, what is key is the chasm between warning and reminder, a gap produced by the presence of the voice. This gap forms the very substance of the novel's mystery. The necessity of the memento mori lurks precisely in the impossibility of its verification; that is, one must remember in advance to die in order for it to be accomplished. Like the voice, death exceeds our ability to fashion meaning out of it as an event. If our own deaths are beyond our comprehension, if, in psychoanalytic terms, we cannot consciously or unconsciously know our mortality, then what is the purpose of the advice to remember we must die? It is not, in other words, our task to remember our deaths; our task is to remember that Death is the other who, absurdly, grants us a lifetime guarantee to our having loved and lost, desired and failed—to our having existed. In another sense, the voice on the telephone insists on the gap between the repetitive, reminding nature of desire and the warning, the death that will finally close the gap that desire produces.

By way of explanation, let us turn to Spark's amusing parody of the scene of summing up, in which the detective gathers the various characters together for the purpose of clearing up the mystery. In this case, everyone arrives at the detective's house for a lovely tea. Henry Mortimer, the retired Chief Inspector, is not the brilliant amateur detective we find in Poe or Conan Doyle, nor is he the hardboiled freelancing agent we encounter in Chandler or Hammett. However, he is of a philosophical turn of mind and does have a Watsonian partner, his wife, who is sympathetic and watchful of his talent, in which the outside world is less and less interested. More important, he is set apart from the police, who are put in the "embarrassing" position of being unable to discover the offender (*Memento* 142). The clues with which Mortimer grapples are, as I have already noted, that the voice always says the same thing, and that the voice is always different: each victim hears a different voice, which fascinates over and above the meaning of its speech. This difference is the excess, the irrational element, that makes the presence of the voice all the more mysterious; the voices appear to be intensely personal in the experience of each recipient, yet as Roland Barthes reminds us in his own work on the voice, even in the consistency of their message they express nothing of the speakers (182). Mortimer, of course, is called on to fashion a sense of unity out of this confusion by producing, in a nice twist, the moment of *habeas corpus*. In this manner, Spark inverts the prompt and usual appearance of the body as the mystery's trigger.

As Slavoj Žižek explains in his reading of the mystery novel's different inflections, the detective is often presented with a "false solution," through which he or she is expected to reveal the true solution (113). In *Memento Mori*, what is the false solution or pattern that governs the strange phone calls? It is the fact that everyone who receives the call is more than seventy years of age, or that—as Alec Warner, the assiduous gerontologist (and the figure of ordinary surveillance in the text) would put it—each of them is "one of us" (93). Spark is quite careful to subvert any other obvious pattern or connection, since we are suddenly introduced to several new characters at the Mortimers' tea. As seasoned readers, we know that a character with whom we are unacquainted cannot be the criminal. That is to say, it simply isn't sporting to drag a new character in so late in the game to assume, arbitrarily, the mantle of guilt. The pattern is thus all we have to go on, but we must remain on our guard; it is a false solution. Otherwise, we are put into the position of taking the false solution for the real one. The logic of this misprision is that we take the calls for granted and offer rationalizations such as "Well, they're all quite elderly; what do they expect?" But if we refuse to accept the imposed normalcy of the pattern, and the attendant ageism implicit to the conclusion, what truth emerges? We must recognize that the false solution is a deception that is meant to throw us off the trail. In terms of reading the novel, we must assume that the pattern is itself a message meant to deceive us. But the deception is not simply an obstacle in the path of truth; its very intention must be incorporated into the case file. That is to say, as Žižek explains, a psychoanalytic approach demands that the deception must be taken into account with the other facts in order for the truth to reveal itself (115).

The retroactive meaning Mortimer ascribes to the events is achieved not by attaching a body to the voice, but by focusing instead on the body of the message. He offers a short rehearsal of the savor that the knowledge of one's death can give to life, that death should instead be thought of as "ever-present" and that it "ought not to take one by surprise" (150). Despite all attempts made by the police to track down the source of the calls, they are revealed to be untraceable. But it is precisely the absence of a trace that leads Mortimer to his conclusion. The senselessness of the phone calls is endowed with meaning: death gives spice to life. The problem is that the meaning ascribed to them does not explain *why* they happen. In this gesture, Mortimer is radically undermining the traditional role of the detective by refusing to fully narrate and explain the traumatic shocks produced by the phone calls. The trauma of the voice on the phone, then, is still not accounted for by Mortimer's theory of the crime. Privately, he believes that the voice on the phone belongs to Death itself, but he resists telling them the name of the culprit because it would disrupt the victims' unique and highly emotional reaction to the calls.

In this way, the gap or white noise in the music of reality is not quite filled in with intelligible, harmonious sound. That the impossible has happened (Death on the phone for you, dear) remains just that: an impossible but necessary truth. The final explanation, then, is that the caller is "whoever we think he is ourselves" (152). Here, Spark cleverly provides us with a logic that is the obverse of Agatha Christie's *Murder on the Orient Express.* In Christie's novel everyone did it, while in Spark's novel, anyone did it. What is the point of this obversion? It is to bring the truth to the fore that the deception intended to hide—that the advanced age of the victims is a false lure? What Mortimer's explanation does is attempt another kind of murder. By symbolizing the event, Mortimer produces death by letter—the letter, which as we know, killeth. By implicitly asking us to think Death the culprit, we (and several of the characters, including Janet Sidebottome and Miss Lottinville) are happily able to incorporate this possibility into a religious or philosophical insight about the paradoxical value that the annihilating power of Death gives to life's pleasures, to the immortality of the spirit beyond the ephemerality of the body, or to the moral structure that the finality of Death provides. Indeed, several thought-provoking and sensitive readings of the text have meditated on these very questions.[2]

But my question is: are we not comforted a little too easily by such insights? Or, more to the point, are we not too easily swayed by Mortimer's opinion? It seems that, in accepting Mortimer's narrative, we are ourselves disavowing or avoiding the gap or debt generated by the appearance of the voice. In being granted access to the secret of the crime, we are lured into accepting this explanation as the true one. However, in accepting the notion that the voice on the phone belongs to Death, we are attempting to escape the truth of the chilling desire or thrill produced not by the message, but by the voice without trace or body. After all, would we repair so quickly to the consolations of philosophy or religion if we received such calls? Would our fascination with insisting on finding a body for the voice not be whetted by Mortimer's solution? What the novel has left open, then, is a question that the narrative must perforce continue to investigate.

A Telling Mortgage:
The Voice, Death, and Symbolic Debt

Instead of removing the possibility that one or more of the people at the final gathering is responsible for cancelling the symbolic debt produced by the incursions of the voice, Mortimer attempts to place the voice's reminders as a form of credit to the soul. The debt remains, but we have not yet reached our credit limit. Since the culprit is not singled out, we (and the characters) are deprived of the satisfaction of having our account (the possibility of having done it) settled. What Žižek calls the "inner truth" of our repressed desire to kill is not exonerated by the deductive facts surrounding the culprit's guilt (117–18). In this context, it is not insignificant that Martin Heidegger refers to death as a settling of accounts. In separating the authentic and inauthentic attitudes of *Dasein* to its own death, he falls back on economics to explicate the distinction (286). By exploring the anxiety that surrounds the truth of death, Heidegger ironically transforms our very being, *Dasein* itself, into a product that has been bought on tick. Before meeting the Grim Repo Man, *Dasein* must make sure it can cover its debt. But, as is so often the case with an easy payment schedule, by the time *Dasein* has made the final payment, death has already rendered being worthless. Moreover, because Mortimer is himself ensnared in the circuit of debt (he too receives the calls), he cannot offer symbolic payment of the debt; in his solution, Mortimer can only extend everyone's credit.

It is also crucial that the detective is the only person who hears a female voice on the telephone. Again, Spark is waxing ironic with the hardboiled detective genre. Rather than provide the spectacle of a final confrontation between the detective and the femme fatale, in which the hero rejects the feminine embodiment of mortal threat by killing her or sending her to prison, Spark's novel offers a "gentle-spoken and respectful" woman whom Mortimer will patiently wait to embrace (153). What are the implications? His refusal to betray his ethical relation to the problem of memento mori is mediated by his decision not to assume that the calls are simply a malicious game; in tacitly accepting her calls, Mortimer does not disavow his own debt in order to project it on the femme fatale. As a result, he leaves open the ethical possibility of accepting the terms of his own debt to his desire, a stance that is philosophically consistent with his theory of the crime.

In this sense, the novel's critical stance to the hardboiled detective genre is consonant with Dame Lettie's wrongheaded accusation (shamelessly articulated by Alec Warner) that Mortimer himself is the culprit. In an ironic variation on Robbe-Grillet's *The Erasers*, we are invited to suspect that the detective is, in all likelihood, the criminal. Since Spark's novel was published six years after Robbe-Grillet's, we are put in the uncomfortable position of giving some credence to Dame Lettie's theory, but only insofar as detective novels traditionally set out red herrings through which we are led to the identity of the real culprit. That is, if we are not to be misled by the lure of the false solution, then we are credulous about Dame Lettie's theory of the crime only to the extent that, in the refractive logic of the clue, it will lead to a kind of resolution by association. Here Mortimer's actions suggest that he is a composite of two avatars of the detective figure. If the brilliant amateur avoids being implicated in the crime by exchanging the name of the culprit for a fee—and the hardboiled detective is always already caught up in the web of deceit and murder—then Mortimer is, by demanding no payment and keeping open the ethical aperture opened up by the memento mori, necessarily turning the aggression of the crime on himself. This impulse toward accusation is part and parcel of the genre's usual (though not universal) uneasiness with symbolic debt. Since the detective will not exonerate the group by naming the culprit, then it is fitting that he would mistakenly receive credit for committing the crime.

It Insists: Hysteria and the Desire of the Object Voice

The credit extended by and to the detective in turn extends to the narrative, since, as I have already said, the summing up occurs but two-thirds through the novel. Although some characters say they are prepared to one day pay the price of their desire, others are, of course, unhappy with the implicit guilt attached to their desire. Another possibility repeatedly presents itself as an explanation:

mass hysteria. It would seem to be invoked to be dismissed, but it warrants some attention. Mortimer himself acknowledges that mass hysteria cannot be summarily ruled out, since no possibility can be eliminated. This admission does not, of course, mean it is the true solution, but it does point to how several characters, among them Godfrey and Dame Lettie, relate to the voice. As Sigmund Freud's work suggests, the importance that several of the characters ascribe to the calls is evidence of an identification with the position of victim through the appearance of the voice as symptom. By identifying with the symptom, the hysterical victim basks in the reflected glory that being a recipient of the memento mori produces (Freud 136–37). But the fact some characters must take messages for other people from the voice rules out the diagnosis of mass hysteria. As a group, however, they react as slaves to the voice as a version of what Hegel calls "the absolute master": Death (194). But the hysterical reaction to the voice suggests something more complex. If Death is the master, then why would he (or she) require that we remember to die? Why does Death need this form of recognition? In this articulation of desire, the memento mori produces a lack or gap that reveals the voice's mastery is not absolute; the voice, like anyone else, apparently experiences desire. As Jean Taylor, Charmian's retired maid, remarks, "If you don't remember Death, Death reminds you to do so" (175). But even the tidiness of her epigram is sullied by the fact that several people, among them Charmian, have already remembered their obligation to die. In other words, they do not need a reminder. So the burden of the question remains: if I already remember that I must die, then what does the voice want? What does the voice want from *me*?

For example, Dame Lettie, in commiserating with Jean Taylor over her annoyance with the calls, becomes quite frosty at Jean's suggestion that she might follow the advice of the voice on the phone, snapping, "I do not wish to be advised how to think" (39). The diverse reactions of people like Dame Lettie (and we can include Godfrey and Mabel in this list) are, in a psychoanalytic sense, hysterical but cannot be subsumed under the rubric of mass hysteria. Jacques Lacan's reading of what he refers to as the hysteric's discourse is that the master is not simply rejected by the hysteric, but is found crucially wanting. That is to say, the hysteric wants a master, but a master who is under her/his control (*Seminar* 129). Furthermore, Dame Lettie's desire to climb the rungs of power in her search for a master, from law enforcers to lawmakers, is another index of her hysterical relation to the master's failed performance of mastery. As her remark attests—although Dame Lettie is hysterically resisting the voice's claim to power, hectically and repeatedly pointing out his

impertinence—she cannot simply ignore or even, as Mortimer suggests, find solace in the calls. Like the hysteric, she finds the master
wanting, yet certainly does not find him boring.

With this problematic of mastery in mind, we can now turn
more fully toward the concept of the voice as excess, as an enigmatic
object of desire. Instead of thinking about how the voice reminds
her that she is in fact still alive, Dame Lettie hysterically reduces the
aperture of her desire to one object: uncovering the meaning that will
presumably be yielded by knowing the voice's origin. Her increasing
anxiety about the source of the voice is predicated on a logic similar
to what Lacan calls "the agency of the Letter," or the repetition of
the signifier "Remember you must die" that continues to *insist*—
traumatically hectoring and reminding her—despite her attempts to
confer stable meaning on it (*Écrits* 428–29). Dame Lettie begins a wild
investigation by using her last will and testament as a criminologist
would a fingerprint or a bloodstain; by threatening to cut different
people out of her will, she hopes to at last expose and uncover the
culprit. Like Hamlet, she hopes in the letter of her will to catch the
conscience, not necessarily of a king, but certainly that of a killer. In
her refusal to remember the master's injunction, to do the work of
dying, she naturally assumes there must be someone out there to do
it for her. As we have seen, one of her prime suspects was Mortimer,
whom she had engaged to find a body to attach to the voice. But
his refusal to yield to her desire, his failure as a master to find the
culprit produces paranoid fantasies that a gang is responsible, and
that there is a conspiracy afoot that has corrupted even the police
themselves. In a nice irony, she and the police stand deadlocked in
mutual accusation. While she thinks them corrupt, they think that
the calls are "hallucinations" produced by the victims (205). This
development should, she believes, prompt (however impotently) "a
question in the House" of Commons (178).

A House Calls: Hearing the Uncanny Voice

What is the resolution to this deadlock? Dame Lettie's stubborn
denial prods her to have her home telephone disconnected; such is the
hysterical logic of a particular relationship to telecommunications—if
I did not receive the message of the voice's desire, then I am not
responsible for answering it. In this way, she unwittingly becomes an
exemplar of having failed to see the truth behind Marshall McLuhan's
dictum "the medium is the message" (7). In removing the medium,
Dame Lettie thinks she is cutting off the message's disturbing content.
But the presence of the medium has already effected a change in the
conditions that now absolutely shape her life. An effect of this change

is produced by the hysteric's fascination with governing the master. Obviously she wants a master, one who can adequately perform mastery to her satisfaction. In attempting to control the content of the message, Dame Lettie imagines that she has shifted the balance of power. The problem with her assumption is that it disavows that the message has been transferred to another, more intimate, medium: the house itself. Having terrified and bullied her maid into quitting, she is left alone to listen:

> She listened to the wireless till half-past nine. Then she turned it off and went into the hall where she stood for about five minutes, listening. Eventually, various sounds took place, coming successively from the kitchen quarters, the dining-room on her right, and upstairs. . . . Finally she climbed slowly up to bed, stopping every few steps to regain her breath and to listen. . . . She fell asleep at last. She woke suddenly with the noise in her ears, and after all, was amazed by the reality of this. (178–79)

One of the striking elements of this passage is that it draws our attention to another aspect of the terror and anxiety that some of the calls have provoked—the problem of listening. To what is she listening? Common sense would say that she's listening for her murderer, for the body she imagines is attached to the voice on the telephone. But Dame Lettie, enraptured by the Siren call of the voice, has long abandoned the safe shores of common sense. As the passage clearly demonstrates, she is hearing something quite different. She is listening for the answer to the "question in the House"—the voice's desire is still a question for her (154). The question in the house has rendered her home uncanny or unhomely.

What the passage also explores is the voice as an object of fascination. Having silenced the content of the message, she is nevertheless left with the voice. If she cannot or will not hear the words of the message, then she is left with another problem of interpretation, of reading not the words spoken, but the desire of the voice (Copjec 189). If the voice is the leftover or remainder of articulative speech, then it cannot be readily heard or understood as a sonorous object. It implies that the voice as object, in psychoanalytic terms, is a registration of a void or nothing, "an antimony between ear and voice" insofar as it exceeds conscious hearing or understanding (J.-A. Miller 139). What Dame Lettie is listening for, then, is the unconscious desire of the voice, over and above conscious speech. She is caught in the snare of repetition; she repeatedly listens for the voice, for its desire, in the hope of being able to answer it and thus hopes to escape its seductive, yet elusive song. Although Fotini

Apostolou quite aptly draws our attention to the seductive power of Death in the text, I want to push her argument further. The seduction is even more mysterious than that of Death; it is a fascination with the unconscious knowledge the voice has to offer but, tantalizingly, does not necessarily provide. This is one of the reasons why the voice is no longer on Dame Lettie's telephone. Although the medium of the instrument itself would seem to have replaced the body of the Other, its presence produces another uncanny effect. It further eliminates the distance between people, deepening the illusion that already marks our relation to the voice on the telephone. The speaker is strangely more real, more fascinating than he or she is in person. (An example of this phenomenon from mundane reality is our apparently unquenchable desire for surveillance, that we give and receive calls about being in a grocery store, on a subway train, or other fascinating tidbits. In this sense, the desire toyed with in calls like these cannot be produced by or reduced to the content of the message).

If the voice on the phone seems to command her from a distance, she attempts to subvert this power by removing its instrument, but succeeds only in producing a siege mentality. In removing the telephone, Dame Lettie has not produced a barrier; she has actually further collapsed the distance between herself and the object voice. But the primary difficulty with her stratagem is that she is confronted by the limits of that power. She may have collapsed the distance, but she has not, as media promises, seized power "over distance as such" (Weber 114). The more invisible the source of the voice is, the closer it seems to be (Dolar 66–67). In this manner, Dame Lettie unconsciously wishes to listen repeatedly to the void opened up by the unhomely voice, by a lack unmediated by speech.

Her Master's Voice: Death and Desire in *Memento Mori* and *The Driver's Seat*

Before I turn to the final sentence of the passage quoted above, I want to make a necessary detour by offering a comparison between Dame Lettie's death and the heroine of another Spark novel, *The Driver's Seat*. The novel is about a woman named Lise, whom, we discover in the opening of the third chapter, will be dead by morning. More surprisingly, we come to realize that she will be the *conducteuse* of her own execution. Unlike Dame Lettie, Lise is searching for "the lack of an absence" (*Driver's Seat* 105). That is to say, she is an inversion of Dame Lettie, but in a specific sense. While Dame Lettie is ambivalently content to listen over and over for the uncanny presence of the object voice, Lise wishes to occupy the very absence that the voice opens up. Both women are, in different ways, attempting to master Death: Dame Lettie by attempting to defer the disappearance of the voice and transform it for her immortal enjoyment into a species of "desert island disc," and Lise by coldly attempting to occupy the place of Death. The schism between voice and ear surfaces in Lise's repeated instructions to her killer. He is caught up in the fascination not of her instructions (which he repeatedly disavows wanting to follow), but in the uncanny parallel between her spoken desire and his unconscious desire. His is not the confusion of "What does the other want from me?" Rather, it is a confrontation with the voice of memory that calls him to his (and Lise's) fate: "How did the other know my desire?" In four different languages, she orders him to kill her; in these repetitions, the killer's memory of his desire to kill is jogged (117). What the relationship between them reveals is that each must be a servant of two masters. He is the agent of Death, given its instrument and commanded by Lise, the femme fatale *manquée*. In effect, Lise is hysterically repeating different versions of "Remember, I must die!" But it is the very repetition that reveals her to be just as much shaped by desire as her killer; her dependency on him shows that she is not the master of death. As Maurice Blanchot contends in *The Space of Literature*, suicide is a means of avoiding the truth of Death's mastery. The suicide does not master death, but instead attempts to eliminate it as possibility, as a future (104). Judith Roof, in her reading of *The Driver's Seat*, takes pains to demonstrate that, like Lise, the narrative itself is shaped not by mastery, but by "a questing that attempts to match the known with an unknown, an effect with a cause" (52). Lise, then, does not assume the place of Death, only the place of the cadaver. This is why her last conscious thought cannot be reported, but only assumed. Having collapsed the distance between present and future, Lise can herself only surmise, and not enjoy, "how final is finality" (117).

By contrast, Dame Lettie's attempt to defer death is ended when she is confronted with a body that would seem to be attached to the voice. The roar of "the noise in her ears" suggests that the voice is actually inside and outside at the same time (*Memento* 183). The noise is "in her," but its source simultaneously appears to be another body, which now stands over her and beats her to death. Just as Lise must confront "the finality" of death, that she has eliminated the future that a natural death would provide, Dame Lettie is "amazed by the reality" that the voice does not belong to the body that crushes her skull. And is this not a definition of the uncanniness of the mysterious voice? That the expected, in its senseless repetition, ironically produces the unexpected? She hears a voice of satiated desire in the hall, not the murderer in her bedroom, say "That's enough, let's go" (178). I would argue that what makes the reality so "amazing" is not simply the surprise of the event, but that she is confronted one last time by the distinction between the voice that fascinates and the body who kills. In listening so intently for one thing, she has tragically and absurdly heard another.

Again, the conventions of the detective novel are quickly called on to subvert any supernatural explanation of her murder. We discover that her self-imposed isolation had become the stuff of gossip and had left her vulnerable to burglary and attack. But there is a remainder of her battle with the voice that has prompted more detective work. Her persistent attempts to master the voice through the written word, evinced in the twenty-two versions of her will, have required that the police interview and eliminate from suspicion the list of beneficiaries in order to substantiate their charge of murder. After so much of the narrative has explored different avenues of resolving the mystery of the phone calls, the gap opened up by the voice is revealed to have a necessary function. That is to say, it must now be structurally shored up in order to return to the kind of normality that separates the detective novel from its workaday counterpart. If Dame Lettie has, in her anxiety, come too close to the voice, then the law must work to return the voice to a proper distance. Why? It is precisely because the voice cannot be identified that the police now have no choice but to maintain the gap between everyday reality and the un-canny presence of the voice by insisting that there is "no connexion" between the calls and Dame Lettie's murder (208). The voice, as an object of desire, is thus revealed to be absolutely essential to the production of articulative speech; it is an index of the gap in reality—desire itself—that is necessary for reality to be constituted by us. This moment offers one final gesture in re-imagining and reshaping the distinctions between the novel and detective fiction. In opening up the problem of the voice, Spark asks us to remember that desire itself is a mystery governed by a deceptively simple premise: "you look for one thing, and you find" an other (212).

The Listener's Reward

So it came as a surprise to the listener-in,
And later, to recall, a diversion,
To find them versed in symbols, but alas, tuning in
Each to the wrong wavelength to a foreign station.
    —"Communication," *All the Poems of Muriel Spark*

Muriel Spark's work often invokes the gap between expectation and desire, between reality and fantasy, or between fact and fiction. As I have suggested above, *Memento Mori* is specifically concerned with the gap between speech and the voice. As the novel in its deft and playful treatment of detective fiction shows, the voice is not simply the medium of linguistic communication. It is an enigmatic object of desire that resists symbolization or explanation. Not only does the novel persistently refuse to attach the voice to a definable body or object, it also cunningly works to demonstrate that ascribing the voice to Death is itself simply a means of avoiding the uncanny anxiety and fascination provoked by its mysterious presence. In this sense, my reading does not attempt to undermine the importance of Death in the novel, but instead points to the very gaps and contradictions that the voice as object introduces to forestall its absolute conflation with Death. Our fascination with the voice is, in part, produced by its independence from articulative speech; this independence opens up a space—desire itself—that makes our relation to an Other possible. Moreover, meditating on this space in Spark's work suggests how we, as critics "versed in symbols," might approach the supernatural and metafictional tropes that populate her fiction, plays, and poetry. One of the tasks her texts ask us to perform is to think through the psychological and affective dimensions of listening to (versus just hearing or noting) the "foreign station" called the object voice.

Notes

1. See "On *Memento Mori*" (109) and *Seduction and Death* (93).

2. See Ruth Whittaker, *The Faith and Fiction of Muriel Spark* (53–58) and Jennifer Lynn Randisi, *On Her Way Rejoicing: The Fiction of Muriel Spark* (91–92).

Works Cited

Apostolou, Fotini E. *Seduction and Death in Muriel Spark's Fiction*. London: Greenwood, 2001.

Barthes, Roland. "The Grain of the Voice." *Image Music Text*. Trans. Stephen Heath. London: Fontana, 1977. 179–89.

Blanchot, Maurice. *The Space of Literature*. Trans. Ann Smock. Lincoln: U of Nebraska P, 1989.

Copjec, Joan. *Read My Desire: Lacan Against the Historicists*. Cambridge: MIT P, 1995.

Dolar, Mladen. *A Voice and Nothing More*. Cambridge: MIT P, 2006.

Freud, Sigmund. *Civilization, Society, and Religion: Group Psychology, Civilization and Its Discontents, and Other Works*. Trans. James Strachey. The Penguin Freud Library. Ed. Albert Dickson. Toronto: Penguin, 1991.

Hynes, Joseph. *The Art of the Real: Murial Spark's Novels*. Rutherford, NJ: Associated UP, 1988.

Lacan, Jacques. *Écrits*. Trans. Bruce Fink. New York: Norton, 2006.

———. *The Seminar of Jacques Lacan: Book XVII: The Other Side of Psychoanalysis*. Trans. Russell Grigg. New York: Norton, 2007.

McLuhan, Marshall. *Understanding Media: The Extensions of Man*. Ed. W. Terrence Gordon. Corte Madera: Gingko, 2003.

Miller, D. A. *The Novel and the Police*. Berkeley: U of California P, 1988.

Miller, Jacques-Alain. "Jacques Lacan and the Voice." *The Later Lacan: An Introduction*. Ed. Véronique Voruz and Bogdan Wolf. Albany: State U of New York P, 2007. 137–47.

Randisi, Jennifer Lynn. *On Her Way Rejoicing: The Fiction of Muriel Spark*. Washington: Catholic U of America P, 1991.

Roof, Judith. "The Future Perfect's Future: Spark's and Duras's Narrative Drive." *Theorizing Muriel Spark: Gender, Race, Deconstruction*. Ed. Martin McQuillan. New York: Palgrave, 2002. 49–66.

Royle, Nicholas. "Memento Mori." *Theorizing Muriel Spark: Gender, Race, Deconstruction*. Ed. Martin McQuillan. New York: Palgrave, 2002. 189–203.

Spark, Muriel. *All the Poems of Muriel Spark*. New York: New Directions, 2004.

———. *Collected Poems I*. London: Macmillan, 1967.

———. *The Driver's Seat*. New York: Knopf, 1970.

———. *Memento Mori*. Harmondsworth: Penguin, 1973.

Weber, Samuel. *Mass Mediauras: Form, Technics, Media*. Ed. Alan Cholodenko. Stanford: Stanford UP, 1996.

Whittaker, Ruth. *The Faith and Fiction of Muriel Spark*. London: Macmillan, 1982.

Žižek, Slavoj. "Two Ways to Avoid the Real of Our Desire." *Psychoanalytic Literary Criticism*. Ed. Maud Ellmann. New York: Longman, 1994. 105–27.

CHAPTER 10

MATTERS OF CARE AND CONTROL: SURVEILLANCE, OMNISCIENCE, AND NARRATIVE POWER IN *THE ABBESS OF CREWE* AND *LOITERING WITH INTENT*

Lewis MacLeod

Early in *Loitering with Intent*, Fleur Talbot expresses a "need to know the utmost" (26), a need that troubles many of Muriel Spark's characters with variously comic and tragic consequences. Although Fleur tends to be regarded as a positive presence in the novel, urges to excess knowledge (and its links to power) are usually disparaged by Spark and her critics. According to Ruth Whittaker, such impulses tend to belong to "manipulators of various kinds: blackmailers, teachers, film-makers, poseurs and con men" (168). Judy Sproxton calls the desire to know everything the "antithesis of Christianity" (147), while Ian Gregson thinks it demonstrates "how unwilling human beings are to accept merely human status [and] how ready they are to aspire to God-like judgment and control" (106)—how eager they are to "dominate others" (108).

So, while Dorothea Walker insists that Fleur is a "moral mythmaker" (75), mythmaking is elsewhere seen as both immoral and dangerous. Decades ago, David Lodge figured Spark's achievement in terms of an original manipulation of omniscience, a manipulation, he argues, that is closely linked to Spark's Catholicism. Spark doesn't accept Sartre's position that a limited, human perspective is the (only) perspective from which "good" fiction can be delivered, but her assertion of the legitimacy of omniscience is layered and, I'd

203

like to argue, often contradictory. For Spark, omniscience remains a narratologically and ethically viable possibility; it's just that some efforts at omniscient understanding are "at God's side" (Walker 75), while others do the work of evil.

What I want to suggest is that Spark's engagement with the poetics and politics of excess knowledge goes beyond a simple celebration and/or condemnation of the basic concept of omniscience; instead, she attempts to differentiate between different manifestations of the information gathering enterprise. Crudely, Spark is at pains to differentiate between "spying on" and "watching over" individuals. The former belongs to decidedly worldly blackmailers and con men, the latter to divine care and eternal order. Some mythmakers are moral, some satanic.

This, at least, is the critical orthodoxy surrounding Spark's fiction. Here, I would like to contest this divide and demonstrate the several similarities between Fleur's apparently moral urge to omniscience and the more obviously immoral (or perhaps amoral) urges of Sir Quentin in *Loitering with Intent* and Alexandra in *The Abbess of Crewe*. Specifically, I approach these novels in terms of contemporary theories of surveillance and narrative in an effort to show how different modes of information gathering and information processing might work to illuminate various aspects of Spark's (and her characters') storytelling strategies. I use Michel Foucault's notion of the panopticon and the various theories of observation, power, and discipline that flow from it as a starting point to read my way through the various plots and procedures that constitute these two novels.

The Abbess of Crewe and Panoptic Power: On Seeing and Being Seen

In *Surveillance Society*, David Lyon claims Foucault's panopticon is "caught in the opposing gravitational fields of Christianity and the Enlightenment" (18). The panopticon, as a term if not a concept, begins in Jeremy Bentham's prisons, structures that, according to Foucault, involve polarized notions of visibility and privacy divided in terms of the power of the state. For Foucault, "each individual subjected to discipline was totally seen without ever seeing, whilst the agents of discipline see everything without being seen" (*Discipline* 202). The prison guards in the tower see and know every action of the prisoners, but the prisoners see neither each other (they are divided by walls) nor their observers, who are elevated and hidden behind blinds and dark glass. The subordinated subject, then, knows nothing of the wider system in which s/he is situated, while those in a position of dominance are at once outside the system and privy to its most intimate workings. This, quite clearly, is surveillance as a mode of discipline and power.

Lyon positions the panopticon between Christianity and the Enlightenment because both, for different reasons, make claims to be all-encompassing, all-knowing modes of detached understanding. For Christians, God knows everything and sees everything even though he works in mysterious ways. When the nuns in *The Abbess of Crewe* pray, for example, they profess "to hate [their] own will" (9) because they (in word at least) accept the extreme limitation of their powers of perception relative to the massive scope of God's will and understanding. For the Enlightenment Humanist, all-encompassing knowledge is possible without divine transcendence; the apparent chaos of the natural world is simply order and symmetry lying in dormancy, an intricate system awaiting the application of human reason and rationality (and the suspension of superstition and emotion) to unlock it. As Zygmunt Bauman puts it, for the Enlightenment thinker, "the 'messiness' of the human world is but a temporary and reparable state, sooner or later to be replaced by . . . orderly and systemic rule" (*Postmodern Ethics* 13).

Not surprisingly, both Christian and Enlightenment thinking are preoccupied with the metaphorical relationship between vision and knowing. For the Christian, Jesus is the way, the truth, and the light. For the Humanist, the "light" of the Enlightenment is the source of power and mastery. Both figure blindness/darkness as the opposite of their project.[1] For Lyon, the "Enlightenment elevation of vision" lies at the root of the panoptic impulse and underscores contemporary privileging of both "eye-witness" testimony and its automated companion, closed-circuit television ("Search" 4). It is also, of course, at the root of the Christian impulse toward the confessional, a process by which the confessor makes visible and/or audible the hidden aspects of his/her conscience/consciousness. For Foucault, "confession [is] one of the West's most highly valued techniques for producing truth." This is so emphatically the case that Foucault argues that "Western man [is] the confessing animal" (*Sexuality* 59). Despite their differences, then, both secular humanism and Christian religious observation operate in terms of some imperative of disclosure, either voluntarily or involuntary, and both take the project of universal knowledge to be both viable and ethical.

The point here is that, although "the idea of omniscient visibility lies behind . . . many surveillance schemes" ("Search" 5), "watching" takes a variety of forms. Many contemporary theories of surveillance now stress the importance of other modes of "dataveillance" and the degree to which "watching may be metaphorical (the work-timing machines in the factory, the office files, and the city plan) as well as physical" ("Search" 9). In *The Abbess of Crewe*, for example, audio recordings are more important to Alexandra than her videotapes, but she still figures sound as a mode of "watchfulness" (24) and her recording equipment functions in manifestly mystical terms; the bugs and wiretaps are "fearfully and wonderfully beyond the reach of humane vocabulary" (23). Charting her own delicate course between the worldly and Christian implications of surveillance, Alexandra considers her tapes a matter of "security" and herself as the "only arbiter of what [security] consists of" (3). She not only sees, but more importantly seeks to *judge* all, and in this regard she becomes embroiled in what Gary Genosko and Scott Thompson call the "fantasm of completeness" that troubles disciplinary surveillance projects (133). She seeks to know and tame the world in some encyclopedic, comprehensive sense and to use this understanding to shape and govern her cloistered world. Her process of observation is always implicitly a project of construction, not just in terms of the accumulation of data (the degree to which observation involves *making* tapes), but, more significantly, in terms of her effort to construct herself and her position of power inside the convent. As Alexandra's preoccupation with Felicity indicates, Alexandra must simultaneously follow and create her destiny. Here, watching is most definitely not waiting. In Christopher Dandeker's terms, it's a matter of "'visible coercion' [being] supplanted by detailed disciplinary practices and the sustained observation and monitoring of conduct" (25). It is an "attempt to monitor and/or supervise objects or persons" in pursuit of "an explicitly stated goal" (38).

Here, we confront what Lyon calls the "two faces" of surveillance, a dichotomy he describes in this way:

> I may ask you to "watch over" my child to ensure that she does not stray into the street and risk getting hit by a car. In this case, I have protection primarily in mind so that the child is shown care in a context where she can flourish. Or I may ask you to "watch over" the same child to ensure that she does not get up to mischief. Now I am appealing to . . . criteria . . . to do with direction, proscription [and] control. The same process, surveillance—watching over— both enables and constrains, involves care and control. (*Surveillance Society* 3)

This difference, I suggest, underscores the current critical division implied between Spark's two views of omniscience. The degree to which God's omniscience influences fallible human will is viewed as a matter of care; the degree to which Alexandra observes in an effort to gain power for herself is viewed as matter of control.

Still, despite this key difference, both God's and Alexandra's modes of surveillance have important procedural similarities, insofar as both derive authority through corporeal absence. Alexandra's disciplinary position in the system of surveillance necessitates her simultaneous dependence on surrogates to do her bidding. Repeatedly, Alexandra insists on positioning herself in the "region of unknowing" (65), even as she seeks omniscience from an anonymous hideaway. So, even as "surveillance strategies [operate] as a means of making visible that which is being lost from sight," the "rise of surveillance has everything to do with disappearing bodies" ("Search" 15). What is made visible are the misdeeds of the subjects of discipline; what disappears are the bodies of the regulators of discipline. For Alexandra, as with Foucault's prison guards, disappearing amounts to an assertion of power.[2]

And, while Alexandra withdraws from sight, Mildred and Walburga experience their situatedness in the surveillance project in such a pronounced way as to cease to experience it at all:

> So very much elsewhere in the establishment do the walls have ears that neither Mildred nor Walburga is now conscious of them as they were when the mechanisms were first installed. It is like being told, and all the time knowing, that the Eyes of God are upon us; it means everything and therefore nothing. The two nuns speak as freely as the Jesuits who suspect no eavesdropping device more innocuous than God to be making a chronicle of their present privacy. (58)

The ubiquitousness of the panoptic presence is such that it becomes naturalized, and what was once awkwardly intrusive becomes a simple matter of fact.[3] For Lyon and other panoptic (and postpanoptic) thinkers, the "hiddenness or mutuality of vision" functions as a stratifying system of power ("Search" 8). So, although Mildred and Walburga are agents of discipline in the context of the convent as a whole, they are ultimately subjects of Alexandra's discipline insofar as they are "seen without seeing" in the discourse Alexandra controls. Without mutuality of vision, Mildred and Walburga are no better off than the Jesuits and the rest of the nuns.

At different points in the novel, the narrator differentiates between the observed and the observing in revealing ways, recognizing that the regular nuns are at once the objects of an international media circus and themselves on permanent media blackout. The absolute absence of mutual observation makes them simultaneously subject to television crews that are going "about like a [satanic] raging lion seeking whom they may devour," and without access to "a wireless or a television set [through which] they would be learning the latest developments in Crewe Abbey scandal" (88, 8).

A media circus, of course, is also a "surveillance carnival" in some kind of odd Bakhtinian sense. It disrupts relations between the mighty and the lowly, insofar as the media presence is at once a raging lion and a helpless supplicant, desperately seeking sightlines it can never quite achieve.[4] Reporters and photographers are both insignificant ("What does it matter, another reporter trying to find his way into the convent or another photographer as it might be?" [5]) and the source of a bizarre kind of power. In coming into the open, these observers abandon the panoptic power of anonymity, but, in claiming this confrontational space, they also produce a kind of carnivalesque suspension of conventional hierarchies. Media reporters, unlike prison guards, accept their subordinate positions insofar as they admit their desire for a particular revered object ("the story"); yet, at the same time they make the revered object the subject of positioning and processing by its apparent subordinates. The paparazzi (a term unknown when the novel first appeared and unavoidable in contemporary Western life) may find their existence only in a parasitic way, yet their watching is also a boundary-breaking, system-disrupting mode of observation. In many ways, *The Abbess of Crewe* hinges on two distinct modes of surveillance in contest with each other. The question is, can Alexandra's mode of seeing and knowing withstand the media's parallel attempt to see, know, and situate her?[5]

Loitering with Intent and Narrative Practice: On Privacy and Self-Disclosure

This struggle to determine who gets to watch and tell, and who must be seen and situated, also typifies Fleur's struggle with Sir Quentin in *Loitering with Intent*, but *Loitering* figures *The Abbess of Crewe*'s preoccupation with surveillance in ways that are much more specifically interested in narrative procedure, in the ways narratives are produced and received. In the later novel, privacy becomes a central preoccupation as characters struggle to maintain some kind of private sphere that might establish what Georges Duby calls a "zone of immunity," a space outside the situating, omniscient impulses of the public sphere (vii). The desire to maintain privacy is, of course, at the centre of many objections to surveillance procedures because any surrender of privacy tends to be considered as a surrender of personal control. The private, according to Lyon, marks "the threshold [over which] the individual [has] a large measure of control" (*Surveillance* 20) and exists in contradistinction to a wider sphere of relative powerlessness. Edwina, for example, frustrates her son's efforts to position and silence her and claims: "I can do what I like in my own flat . . . can receive or not receive according to my own likes" (*Loitering* 33). Here, Edwina explicitly asserts her authority over the signals she receives and sends within the limited sphere of the flat, establishing not just a mutuality of vision, but her own countervailing ability to situate and silence Quentin. Inside the flat, she reminds him, "I pay the rent. Your home is in the country" (190). Quentin eventually retreats to the country to escape Fleur's unsettling gaze, a gaze his mother's authority condones and makes possible.[6] Fleur's getaway with Wally is similarly unsettled because Fleur observes signals Wally wants to keep in the private sphere: "what annoyed him most was my seeing the evidence of a previous week-end for two" (199). This isn't spying, of course, but Wally's sense of being seen and exposed is unmistakable and signals the demise of their relationship.

Perhaps most significantly (and most obviously), Fleur is at pains to disrupt Sir Quentin's panoptic impulses. Although they begin their relationship collaborating in the inherently confessional project of producing autobiographies, Fleur, unlike Quentin, eventually insists that a "zone of immunity" ought still to be observed. Indeed, Fleur seems to make immunity a necessary condition for friendship. Rather than imagining friendship as a matter of deep intimacy, she thinks of it in terms of the preservation of private space. Of Solly (one of Spark's most universally sympathetic characters), she says: "he had some other private life [that] wasn't the sort of thing one would want to find out . . . there was always something about Solly into which no real friend of his could intrude" (143). Later, when she reveals her private intuitions about Quentin to Wally, she immediately recognizes her frankness as a stumbling block between them: "I regretted having spoken my thoughts" (156). In these cases real friendship is a matter of suspending her pervasive "need to know the utmost," of observing less, not more, of escaping observation in order to preserve friendly relations.

The necessity of a zone of immunity is not at all clear to the members of the Autobiographical Association, and Fleur repeatedly warns Dottie against expressing any "true revelation" (66) of herself. Sir Quentin, she claims, is "destroying [people] with his needling after frankness," and frankness here is synonymous with the desire for omniscience (116). Too late, the Baronne Clotilde du Loiret recognizes Quentin as a threat to her "private life." "I . . . object to being prayed over" she says (111), because Quentin's prayerful "watching over" is a matter of worldly manipulation, not divine protection. In the terms outlined above, it is a matter of control, not care.

Still, not all mediated self-disclosure is problematic. While most theories of surveillance emphasize its coercive tendencies, emerging arguments within the discourse sometimes figure "surveillance [as] a desirable opportunity for self-display," as a matter "self-expression" rather than "self-repression" ("Search" 15). In her discussion of home webcams, Hille Koskela argues that "exposing oneself can be connected to identity formation" and that some modes of detached observation work in such a way as to turn "'overseers' . . . into 'viewers'" (172, 176). For Koskela, the collapse of a clearly-bounded private sphere and the loss and/or abdication of the zone of immunity can amount to an opportunity for establishing, not erasing, identity. In *The Abbess of Crewe*, for example, Felicity offers her image and her "insufferable charisma" to the T.V. cameras as a challenge to Alexandra's authority (13), just as Alexandra herself later achieves "complete success" (111) in front of the camera when "audiences [goggle] with awe at [the] lovely lady" (112). In each case, self-presentation becomes a mode of power, a way of contesting the representations other forces have used to construct and situate them.

In *Loitering with Intent*, the members of the Autobiographical Association clearly see their memoirs as a means of forwarding these kinds of idealized self-images. Their contributions are marked with a "transparent craving . . . to appear likeable" (31), and their self-constructions appear to Fleur as efforts toward "a constancy and steadiness . . . they evidently [wish] to possess" (41). For members of the association, the self-orchestrated confession of autobiography is conceived as a way of asserting a kind of authority they lack in real life. The narrative framework is figured as a means of self-transformation, and, although Quentin sometimes likes to foreground the "delicate purpose" and "top secret" nature of the memoirs (16), the type of disclosure and monitoring the memoirs entail is often figured in terms of surveillance's more admired sibling: fame. For both the members of the Autobiographical Association and devotees of the home webcam, privacy, as an impediment to frankness, is voluntarily discarded by those with the ambition to be seen in a new, not-quite-real light.[7]

The problem, of course, is that a proliferation of life-details does not a life-story make. Koskela's webcammers broadcast their lives more or less directly to the world, without what she calls "'official' observers" working as intermediaries (176). The members of the Autobiographical Association, in contrast, hand their information over to Fleur (and later Quentin) for further processing. When Fleur agrees to work for the association, Quentin imagines the organizing and processing of the facts of each member's life to be a low-level, clerical matter. He tells Fleur that she "should easily be able to rectify any lack or lapse in form, syntax, style, characterization, invention, local colour, description, dialogue, construction and other trivialities" (24). These matters, of course, are anything but trivial. They amount to the entire framework into which the facts of each life are to be placed. Quentin imagines the facts will somehow speak for themselves, but the facts always speak through some type of processing system, and these systems are vitally important in both surveillance and narrative theory.

Summarizing Maria Los's study of the ethical implications of surveillance, Lyon argues that surveillance displaces morality "and undermines any notion of truth by preferring . . . the data image to the lived reality of the personal narrative" ("Search" 13). Under the conditions of ubiquitous surveillance, the fetishization of data obscures truth and morality because it neglects the narrative dimension that shapes the data itself.[8] In *The Power of the Story*, Michael Hanne argues a similar position from a narratological perspective when he claims storytelling is "the radar-like mechanism we use to constantly scan the world around us, [the mechanism] by which we give order to, and claim to find order in, the data of experience. If we cannot narrate the world in this everyday manner, we are unable to exercise even the slightest degree of control, or power, in relation to the world" (8). Consequently, the apparently trivial matter of subcontracting the shaping of data into story amounts to nothing less than surrendering the ability to "narrate the world" and accepting, instead, a subordinate position in somebody else's narrative. In terms of Lyon's surveillance theory, surrendering the framework of one's narrative is to be under somebody else's control, not in somebody else's care.

Having surrendered the data of their lives to Fleur, the members of the Autobiographical Association become characters in her narrative framework rather than autonomous self-narrating subjects. Though they are not quick to recognize it, they are no longer in the privileged position Cellini imagines when he claims "all men . . . should write the tale of their life with their own hand" (125). Instead, they repeatedly encounter the difficulties of writing the tale of their lives through somebody else's hand. Fleur's tendency to listen without talking is, of course, an audio version of the panoptic effort to see without being seen; the result of a desire to gather information without informing on oneself. This is the position of power, and although the members briefly protest that Fleur's revisions to their lives are "rather extravagant" (37), they eventually accept her versions over their own. They do so, it seems, because her constructions of them make narrative, not factual, sense.[9] That is, they are compelling *stories*, not historical truths, and they operate according to a narrative economy that values an intriguing scenario that will appeal to readers over the tedium of what really happened. For Fleur, "the facts" are simply the data from which she constructs an autonomous (or semi-autonomous) story world. What results are fictionalized life stories that supplant lived experience. At one point Mrs. Wilks specifically praises the "stark realism" of Fleur's fabrications (43), and Sir Eric is forced to engage in a public debate about his own childhood experiences because his readers all value narrative truth over historical fact. As Fleur later observes, she is "an artist, not a reporter" (152). She *creates* worlds; she does not document the real one. In this regard, Walker claims, "the novelist is at God's side" (75).

"Everything Happens to an Artist": On the Implications of Creating People

I am not contesting Fleur's world-making power, though I do not think she quite deserves the moral approbation Walker and others bestow on her. Yet, even if we accept Fleur's position at God's side, it seems clear (as her repeated invocation of her mid-twentieth-century position makes plain) that she is at God's side at a particular point in history. Importantly, Fleur's manipulations of the truth are possible because she and her characters are situated in "modern times" (37)—times in which premodern truth claims no longer have any clear purchase. The time-space Sir Quentin calls "modern times" is, in fact, something quite like the postmodern times outlined by Zygmunt Bauman in *Postmodernity and Its Discontents* when he describes the transition from a singular theory of Truth to a pluralistic theory of truths (116).[10] For Bauman, the day-to-day life of the postmodern world is marked by an "underpowered institutionalization of differences" that makes notions of both truth and durable identities untenable (123). Under the conditions of postmodernity, Bauman argues, "the givenness [and] obviousness . . . of every man's or woman's place in the chain of being" is destroyed with the result that "the 'real world' acquires in ever greater measure the traits traditionally reserved for the fictional world of art" (122, 123). In *Loitering with Intent*, this underpowered institutionalization of difference takes the form of both an undervaluation of historical fact (through the free manipulation of the autobiographies) and an overvaluation of fictional signals (through the apparent manifestations of *Warrender Chase* in the "real world" of Spark's novel). As Sir Eric loses ontological purchase and becomes a fictional character, the events of Fleur's novel seem to gain ontological purchase and influence "real world" events.

The increased influence of the fictional over the nonfictional mode is, again, a matter of distinguishing between data and the data processing of narrative construction. Although Fleur's artistic process involves "loitering with intent" insofar as she is involved in a silent process of observation and surveillance to gather copy for her "novel in larva" (14), she, unlike the members of the Autobiographical Association, understands the distinction between narratable and non-narratable events. She understands that stories, even autobiographical ones, must be interesting first, historically accurate second (or third, or fourth). While Sir Quentin pushes for ever-increasing frankness (for the proliferation of data), Fleur figures the urge-to-completeness, the impulse toward data, as the major hurdle to be overcome in her dealings with the autobiographies. In this regard she adheres to Hanne's position that narrative power resides precisely in its tendency to "discard massive quantities of material which we deem to be unimportant" and to insist instead on "the few items we regard as significant" (8).[11] Nicholas Rescher claims that "in the real objective reality of nature and of history there is no selection: not by importance, not by merit, not by purpose" with the result that "reality is totally unfocused." Under these conditions, "the truth" means little when it is not processed in narrative terms. Narrative, he claims, is not "an optimal instrument for depicting reality as nature encompasses it," but it is "singularly well fitted" to the production of *meaningful* (as opposed to actual) story worlds (36).[12]

For Fleur, the problem of writing memoirs stems from an overload of insignificant data and the consequent marginalization of the few signals that are important. She remarks on "how much easier it is with characters in a novel than in real life. In a novel the author invents characters and arranges them in a convenient order. Now that I come to write biographically I have to tell whatever actually happened and whoever naturally turns up. The story of a life is a very informal party; there are no rules of precedence and hospitality, no invitations" (59). In narrative, if not surveillance terms, the truth of "whoever turns up" is less convincing than the truth of selective focus because selective focus makes the narrative world limited and therefore knowable. In *Heterocosmica*, Luomír Dolezel makes the limited, incomplete nature of fictional worlds central to their effectiveness . Because the fictional world is not overloaded with useless detail, he argues, it is knowable in ways the real world can never be.[13] Fleur claims she could have "realized" the members of the association with "fun and games" (116) but that, under the influence of Quentin, their unfocused frankness destroys them as both "real" people and as characters in a narrative.

Ultimately, Fleur figures experience itself as a matter of surveillance and narrative processing: those who are capable of observing and narrating the world have experiences; those who don't, don't.

"When people say that nothing happens in their lives I believe them," she says, "But you must understand that everything happens to an artist" (116). "Everything" happens to an artist because chance experiences are observed and processed in some "shadowy way" (151), then "redeemed" into viable narrative forms (116). Fleur's awareness of herself as an artist (as someone who gets to experience everything) is "a conviction so strong that [she] never [thinks] of doubting it" (26). As such, she thinks of it not so much as a talent or a career, but as an elevated mode of being. Shaw claims that "'vocation' is not too strong a word" to describe Fleur's view of herself as an artist (56); I would argue it's not nearly strong enough. Fleur takes her God-like position as creator very much to heart and tends to assume the intellectual, even ontological, inferiority of those around her. In this regard, I think, she is very much like all the rest of Spark's demonic mythmakers who aspire to God's power and vision. In very many ways, Fleur's various conflicts in the novel are centered on challenges to her world-making abilities. More than once, she reacts to a stressful situation with a stylistic critique designed to differentiate herself (as artist) from her (lower level) adversary.[14] Her continued frustration with Dottie involves Dottie's refusal to follow Fleur's various dictums and dictates. "You have to follow my instinct," Fleur tells Dottie, "I have to work it out through my own creativity" (66).[15] The message here, quite clearly, is that non-artists ought to be watched over by the artist. What is less clear, to me at least, is whether the artist is caring for, or attempting to control, those s/he observes.

Fleur's experiences with the publisher Revisson Doe make all of this even more plain. Their confrontation is similarly predicated on both stylistic choices (she notes his careful transitions between "I" and "we") and grounded in the assumption that, by her very nature, she, not he, belongs in the position of power. His suggestion that "an author is a publisher's raw material" (135) is not at all unlike her view that "everything happens" to an artist; yet she is infuriated by his effort to position her as subject to his processes. Although she figures others as "the straws from which I have made my bricks" (196), she objects to being somebody else's straw. She thinks the notion that there are limits to her powers of observation to be "a silly proposition" (40) and claims that "there are very few predicaments in a writer's life where it would be the slightest use explaining the in's and out's to a priest" (171). She does so despite her religious convictions and because she cannot imagine any authority (even divinely anointed authority) beyond herself.

Bluntly, I really don't think there's much behind the pervasive critical notion that Fleur's claims to vision and power are fundamentally different from the other overarching omniscient impulses we find throughout Spark's oeuvre. Sheryl Stephenson imagines Fleur's talents to be "moral, reflective and creative" and devoid of the "authoritarian tendencies" of other would-be narrators (80, 79), but to me Fleur's project seems every bit as egocentric (if not as destructive) as everybody else's. She fits much better in the group of "corrupt egotists" (Shaw 68) than she does in the group of normal, everyday people. Fotini Apostolou argues that "everyone is free to play with the text . . . in *Loitering with Intent*" (2), yet it is clear that most people don't get to play at all. Getting toyed around with is not at all the same thing. The only people who get to play are the novel's two aspiring omniscients: Fleur and Quentin. Fleur's struggle with Quentin for narrative mastery has clear ontological implications, but (while I don't wish to redeem Quentin's behavior) both combatants are capable of playing dirty in their efforts to gain and/or maintain authority. When Quentin is in ascendance, she feels her lack of ontological purchase and begins to imagine herself as a poorly written character, a "grey figment" (94) in somebody else's narrative, but she routinely figures others as similarly malleable, half-developed entities. As many characters in Spark's fiction find out, this is not a fun position to be in, but it is worth remembering that Fleur is alerted to the possibility that Quentin has stolen her text while she herself is contemplating stealing somebody else's. The trigger that alerts Fleur that Dottie has stolen her novel occurs while she is reading Cellini and pondering her own mode of plagiarism: "one could take endless enchanting poems out of this book simply by flicking over the pages, back and forth, and extracting for oneself a paragraph here [and] a paragraph there" (126).

To me, this seriously compromises her moral outrage about the fact Quentin has stolen "not only the physical copies [of *Warrender Chase*], but the very words, phrases, [and] ideas" (145). Despite her apparent worries about Quentin's treatment of his followers, she is always more concerned with his expropriation of her text (the source of her authority as artist) than she is about the fate of real people. After she reads the scraps of Quentin's diary outlining his manipulations of the association members, "what infuriates [her] most" are the excerpts "straight out of *Warrender Chase*" (186). This seems to suggest that Fleur's desire to "know the utmost" is ultimately a matter of power and control over the text, not the care and comfort of others, and it begs questions about how "self-evident and luminous" Fleur really imagines everybody else to be (96). Certainly, she suggests a sense of ontological superiority and dominance in her claim that she "could have invented" everybody in the association and in her sense that Quentin is "unreal," while her character, Warrender Chase, is the "real man on whom I had based Sir Quentin" (105, 181). Walker is undoubtedly right to argue that, in Spark's work, "the line between fiction and reality becomes fine indeed" (72), but it is clear to me that Fleur expects to be in control of that line and that she resents all suggestions that she is not.

Conclusion: Of Ascetic Priests and Errant Abbesses

In his discussion of "Truth, Fiction, and Uncertainty" in *Postmodernity and Its Discontents*, Bauman cites Nietzsche's idea that truth is often regarded as the territory of "ascetic priests" who have proven themselves "fit for . . . intercourse with something Wholly Other" (113). The "wholly other" is absolute truth, and the ascetic priests amount to the various types of truth-theorists produced in the philosophical tradition. Bauman argues that in the postmodern period of multiple truths, strong truth claims are no longer possible in the same way they were in the past. Instead, he suggests, we experience a nearly complete inversion of Plato's desire to cast the poets out of the Republic and arrive instead at a point at which "artistic fiction turns into the shelter . . . or . . . the factory of truth" (124). I would like to conclude by suggesting that both *The Abbess of Crewe* and *Loitering with Intent* accept the notion of fiction as a factory of (lower case, multiple) truth(s), while simultaneously maintaining the significance of "ascetic priests"—figures who imagine themselves to be the keepers of the gateway between truth and falsity. Both Alexandra and Fleur operate along the boundary between fiction and nonfiction, and Spark's version of fictional truth upholds many of the hierarchical power structures we tend to associate with the strong truth claims of the past.

In *Fictional Worlds*, Thomas Pavel claims that "societies that believe in myths [unfold] at two different levels: the profane reality, characterized by ontological paucity and precariousness, contrasts with a mythical level [that is] ontologically self-sufficient, containing a privileged space and a cyclical time" (77). Both Fleur and Alexandra are involved in complex manipulations of the distinctions between fictional, factual, and mythical discourses exploiting the variable truth-claims associated with each mode of discourse, sometimes to assert power, sometimes to escape blame. Alexandra, for example, repeatedly claims to "have entered the sphere . . . of mythology" as a means of escaping profane reality and accessing authority (*Abbess* 12), while Fleur objects to Quentin because he is "stealing [her] myth" (*Loitering* 139), usurping her claim to ontological self-sufficiency. In both of these constructions, myth figures as a "zone of immunity," as a way of asserting autonomy, evading imposition, and maintaining power. Under the umbrella of mythology, Alexandra feels safe from earthly investigation. Without her myth, Fleur feels she is at Quentin's mercy. In each case, mythology works to devalue actuality and escape the possibility of observation. Mythological status is a way of seeing without being seen.

Pavel's "ontologically self-sufficient" level of myth, of course, is simultaneously the home of Newman's "self-evident and luminous" entities. Alexandra and Fleur imagine themselves to belong to this mythic order and variously show contempt and impatience whenever the profane makes demands. Accused by Dottie of being "out of [her] element in our world" and by Wally of being "somewhere else" when they are out together (107, 200), Fleur makes a half-hearted attempt to concentrate "on the actuality of the occasion" of her lovemaking, but finds such presence to be "far, far worse" than the mythical displacement she generally enjoys (204). Similarly, Alexandra's defense of her surveillance regime rests on her ability to transcend the literal and enter a mythic plane. "The facts of the matter are with us no longer," she claims. "We can't be excommunicated without the facts" (16). Her parallel claim that she has "entered the Age of the Holy Ghost" (5) can be read as a rejection of the corporeality of God-Made-Man and as a retreat in to the least understood, least accessible position in the trinity. Elsewhere so interested in gathering data, Alexandra seeks shelter in myth's stability and its imperviousness to factual inquiry. Just as Fleur rejects "the facts" of autobiography, Alexandra claims "history doesn't work" and instead maintains that myth will always exist outside the grasp (and, more importantly, the jurisdiction) of real life (12). The police force's reluctance to deal with ecclesiastical crimes in terms of English law makes this plain. At several different points in the novel, Alexandra employs her characteristic strategy of turning a solvable "problem" into an unfathomable "paradox" as a means of reinforcing her position at the gateway between the profane and the mythic.

Importantly, this gate swings both ways for the priests who control it. Although Fleur often claims an enormous amount of reality for her story-world(s), she sometimes attempts to empty her work of any ontological purchase whatsoever. Although she claims "*Warrender Chase* [is] action just as much as when I was arguing with Dottie over Leslie" (59), she occasionally argues for the thoroughgoing unreality of her project. When she is annoyed by questions about what her characters are really like, she claims that her characters don't exist at all, that they are "only words" (72), "only some hundreds of words, some punctuation, sentences, paragraphs, marks on the page" (83). Alexandra does the same sort of thing, first when she pretends to be performing in "the drama *The Abbess of Crewe*" (22), and later when she really begins to refigure her story in terms of the self-consciously fictional "film and stage offers" she intends to pursue (113). For Fleur and Alexandra, the fictional mode of "pretend" is a zone of immunity as well, and this dramatizes the absolute lack of mutuality of vision that exists between the ascetic priests and their subordinates. Both Fleur and Alexandra seek a monopoly on what counts as truth. In Bauman's terms, they reduce truth to its "disputational use," using the "rhetoric of power" to create, erase, and transcend experience as they see fit (12).

Despite Spark's expressed belief in eternal and absolute truth, both *The Abbess of Crewe* and *Loitering with Intent* seem to foreground the slippage of truth and the degree to which truth can be manufactured by those who profess to observe and know all. Societies that believe in myths may unfold on two different levels (the profane and the mythic), but, Pavel claims, they also generally tend to differentiate between "at least three kinds of statements: factual statements, which cover everyday life, true statements, referring to gods and heroes, and fictions, which include stories other than myths (fables, funny moral stories)" (41). To a very significant degree, both Alexandra's and Fleur's powers rest in their ability to exploit the different implications associated with these three levels of discourse.

Obviously, Pavel's neat distinctions are routinely problematized in Spark's fiction where the factual, the fictional, and the mythic often seek to invade each other's territory and use each other's tools. Yet the claim that there are no longer reliable distinctions between factual, fictional, and mythic discourses does not lead to the conclusion that all the world has become fictionalized, just that Spark's novels (and her characters) often make appeals across the borderlands of these historically distinct discourses. Although the nonfactual often seems to supplant the factual in Spark's work, we do not have one all-encompassing fictional mode of discourse (what Marie-Laure Ryan calls a "panfictional" mode of discourse), but rather multiple modes that make appeals to each other's truth claims. For example, when Fleur claims that "without a mythology, a novel is nothing" (139), she simultaneously appeals to the mythic level (which Pavel figures as "the very paradigm of truth" [76]) and to the level of light entertainment (such as funny stories or fun and games). Similarly, when Alexandra imagines she has graduated from mythology to become an "object of art, the end of which is pleasure" (113), she treats fictional pleasure as hierarchically superior to mythic truth. In these cases, the characters recognize that a story with an "undecidable reference world" (Ryan 172)—one that at different times operates as a factual, a fictional, and a mythic discourse—allows for fictional utterances to make the authoritative claims of myth while simultaneously avoiding any need for nonfictional justification through the historical record.

Once the facts are no longer verifiable or solid, Fleur and Alexandra figure their various statements as either mythic or fictional according to their own interests. In this way, they claim all the advantages of truth, none of the responsibilities of proof.

Ryan ultimately argues that, historically speaking, "the decline of myth was compensated by the rise of the novel, that the novel inherited many of the mythic properties/functions left unclaimed after the decline of traditional mythic structures." Data-gathering, storytelling artists like Alexandra and Fleur, then, get to "play pretend" while simultaneously making the kinds of mythic truth-claims usually associated with ascetic priests. "The unchallengeable but . . . figural truth of myth," Ryan argues, provides "an alternative to both the literal claim-to-truth of nonfiction and the make-believe truth of fiction" (182). It offers a way to speak authoritatively without appealing to facts. In the surveillance terms I've been using, it amounts to an "unchallengeable" perspective, a way of situating without ever being situated. As ascetic priests of the mid-twentieth-century, Alexandra and Fleur claim the power to observe others and dictate what counts as truth because they understand that the apparent collapse of strong truth-claims offer them unprecedented world-creating powers. Controlling the intersections of nonfiction, fiction, and myth, Fleur and Alexandra see and know *everything*. For them, truth has not disappeared into a panfictional context, it has just been reduced and then redeployed to fit their needs. In *The Abbess of Crewe* and *Loitering with Intent,* truth is still very much around, and each woman's power depends upon both the concept of truth and on some special claim at privileged access to it. In these novels, truth still exists; it's just lost its self-sufficiency and had to seek shelter in the employment of the ascetic priests.

Repeatedly, Alexandra cites Pound's "In Durance" to claim that she is "homesick after [her] own kind" (59, 106). I hope to have demonstrated that Fleur *is* one of Alexandra's own kind, that both are ascetic priests with access to the "wholly other" realms of fiction and myth, that both feel separated from, and superior to, other people by virtue of their ability to survey, process, and produce the world (or worlds). At some other point in history, they might simply have been storytellers, fiction-makers, or professional tellers of lies. Under the conditions of postmodernity, however, they work as mythmakers because truth can no longer make the strong claims it once did. Situated at the historical moment when surveillance practices proliferate just as faith in absolute truth dissipates, Spark's characters exploit the indeterminate, liminal ground between data and narrative, fact and myth, to produce their power. "Banished from reality," Bauman claims, "truths may only hope to find their exilic 'second home' in the house of art" (126). Both Alexandra and Fleur live in the house of art, and, as masters of that domain, they watch over their various subjects, marshalling them all into their own peculiar, overarching designs: "Who doesn't yearn to be part of a myth?" (*Abbess* 12).

Notes

1. To a lesser degree, they also figure deafness (and/or the overwhelming noise that makes designation impossible) as a subordinated binary. In either case, they figure their system as the root of clarity and order, their opposites as emptiness, fear, disorder, etc.

2. As I will argue in more detail later, Fleur's observational practices are similarly predicated on the notion of seeing without being seen. Her attempt to "be her own truth-teller" is closely linked to the fact that she is "reluctant to put herself on display" (Shaw 61).

3. As Lyon and others note, such normalizing of excessive supervision is the lynchpin of reality TV. Saturated by monitoring systems, reality TV personalities are imagined to behave normally in the abnormal context of intrusive recording devices. Such programming also, of course, tends to set aside some kind of confessional through which the personality can make visible aspects of his/her make-up/reasoning process that the "regular" cameras cannot pick up.

4. This is not to suggest that the media do not eventually get the photos and stories they seek, but only to note that the circus only exists in a state of incompleteness. Once the story/image has been secured to some kind of general satisfaction, the story dies and the circus disperses.

5. For more on *The Abbess of Crewe* and media presence, see Barbara Keyser's essay, "Muriel Spark, Watergate and the Mass Media."

6. In terms of feminist discourses to do with the gaze, Edwina's figurative stare down with Quentin can be read as an example of "a woman who 'looks a return' at a man [and] threatens to immobilize him." For Beth Newman, returning the gaze is an act of resistance that reminds the (male) viewer that he (unlike Alexandra and Foucault's prison guards) is not anonymous and has himself been located and situated. The male gaze is disrupted by "the knowledge that the other sees and therefore resists being reduced to an appropriable object" (Newman 451).

7. Quentin's own preoccupation with fame is, of course, manifested in his neurotic interest in how people are described (or overlooked) by *Who's Who*.

8. *Memento Mori*'s Alec Warner's continued frustrations also dramatize the problems associated with an overdeveloped faith in data at the expense of a selective processing system.

9. Sproxton imagines this in terms of the "lack of inner standards" (41) of the members of the association, though, as indicated above, I think it is more productive to imagine it in terms of the information-gathering and processing methods that typify both surveillance and narrative construction.

10. This is, of course, exactly the world Spark herself describes in her interview with Frank Kermode when she speaks of fiction producing "a kind of truth" (80).

11. Jean-François Lyotard makes a similar claim when he argues that "narrative . . . is a mechanism . . . for forgetting" (xii). Alexandra takes this idea to extreme measures when she begins to construct her case for the Vatican. Although her control room is full of "spools, spools and spools" of data, she understands that her fate lies in the art of selective deletion (71).

12. While I am aware that Whittaker and others imagine Spark's engagement with postmodernity to be a matter of using "twentieth-century technology . . . to deal with eternal truths" (Whittaker 158), I find each novel's sense of ontological instability to be much stronger than its sense of divine order.

13. As Bauman puts it, "The assumptions I need to accept in order to agree that the marriage of Scarlett and Rhett [took] place are few and conveniently simple. . . . The reasons for which I trust historians who tell me that Napoleon died in 1821 are by comparison much more complex and cumbersome" (*Postmodernity and Its Discontents* 119–20). In Rescher's more pithy terms, "reality is to fiction as chess is to tic-tac-toe" (35).

14. I am thinking specifically about her attack on Leslie (through Dottie): "eliminate that dreadful recurrent phrase. . . . 'With regard to'" (106), and her response to Quentin's suggestion that she has been trying to get herself into Edwina's will: "The noun 'promise' is not generally followed by the verb 'effected'" (117).

15. Although Fleur intends her advice to be helpful, her didactic assumption of superiority is very similar to Alexandra's characteristic hubris. When Winnifrede dares to claim the power to observe and think for herself (to be an agent, not an object of surveillance), Alexandra says: "If you believe your own ears more than you believe us, Winnifrede. . . . It may be you have lost your religious vocation, and we shall all quite understand if you decide to return to the world" (70–71). In each case, the self-appointed agent of omniscience disciplines her inferior through an invocation of her access to some higher plane of understanding (creativity for Fleur, religious vocation for Alexandra).

Works Cited

Apostolou, Fotini. "Textasy: The Seduction of the Text in Muriel Spark's Work." *Critical Survey* 13.1 (2001): 94–112.

Bauman, Zygmunt. *Postmodernity and Its Discontents*. New York: New York UP, 1997.

——. *Postmodern Ethics*. Cambridge: Blackwell, 1993.

Dandeker, Christopher. *Surveillance, Power, Modernity: Bureaucracy and Discipline From 1700 to the Present Day*. Cambridge, UK: Polity, 1990.

Doležel, Lubomír. *Heterocosmica: Fiction and Possible Worlds*. Baltimore: Johns Hopkins UP, 1998.

Duby, Georges. "Foreword." *A History of Private Life*. Ed. Paul Veyne. Cambridge: Harvard UP, 1987. vii–xi.

Foucault, Michel. *Discipline and Punish: The Birth of the Prison*. London: Penguin, 1979.

——. *The History of Sexuality: Vol. 1. An Introduction*. 1976. Trans. Robert Hurley. New York: Pantheon, 1978.

Genosko, Gary and Scott Thompson. "Tense Theory: The Temporalities of Surveillance." Lyon, *Theorizing* 123–38.

Gregson, Ian. *Character and Satire in Postwar Fiction*. New York: Continuum, 2006.

Hanne, Michael. *The Power of the Story: Fictional and Political Change*. Providence: Berghahn, 1994.

Kermode, Frank. "The House of Fiction: Interview with Seven English Novelists." *Partisan Review* 30 (1963): 61–82.

Keyser, Barbara. "Muriel Spark, Watergate, and the Mass Media." *Arizona Quarterly*. 32.2 (1976): 146–53.

Koskela, Hille. "'The Other Side of Surveillance': Webcams, Power, and Agency." Lyon, *Theorizing* 163–81.

Lodge, David. *The Novelist at the Crossroads*. Ithaca: Cornell UP, 1971.

Lyon, David. "The Search for Surveillance Theories." Lyon, *Theorizing* 3–20.

——, ed. *Theorizing Surveillance: The Panopticon and Beyond*. Uffculme, Devon, UK: Willan, 2006.

——. *Surveillance Society*. Buckingham, UK: Open UP, 2001.

Lyotard, Jean-François. *The Postmodern Condition*. Trans. G. Bennington and B. Massumi. Minneapolis: U of Minnesota P, 1984.

Newman, Beth. "'The Situation of the Looker-On': Gender, Narration, and Gaze in *Wuthering Heights*." *Feminisms*. Eds. Robyn R. Warhol and Diane Price Herndl. New Brunswick: Rutgers UP, 1997. 449–66.

Pavel, Thomas G. *Fictional Worlds*. Cambridge: Harvard UP, 1986.

Rescher, Nicholas. "Questions about the Nature of Fiction." *Fiction Updated: Theories of Fictionality, Narratology, and Poetics*. Eds. Calin-Andrei Mihailescu and Walid Hamarneh. Toronto: U of Toronto P, 1996. 30–38.

Ryan, Marie-Laure. "Postmodernism and the Doctrine of Panfictionality." *Narrative* 5 (1997): 165–87.

Shaw, Valerie. "Fun and Games with Life Stories." *Muriel Spark: An Odd Capacity for Vision*. Ed. Alan Bold. Totowa, NJ: Barnes and Noble, 1984. 44–69.

Spark, Muriel. *The Abbess of Crewe.* New York: Viking, 1974.

———. *Loitering with Intent.* 1981. New York: New Directions, 2001.

———. *Memento Mori.* 1959. New York: New Directions Books, 2001.

Sproxton, Judy. *The Women of Muriel Spark.* London: Constable, 1992.

Stephenson, Sheryl. "'Poetry Deleted,' Parody Added: Watergate, Spark's Style and Bakhtin's Stylistics." *ARIEL* 24.4 (1993): 71–85.

Walker, Dorothea. *Muriel Spark.* Boston: GK Hall, 1988.

Whittaker, Ruth. "'Angels Dining at the Ritz': The Faith and Fiction of Muriel Spark." *The Contemporary English Novel.* Eds. Malcolm Bradbury and David Palmer. London: Edward Arnold, 1979. 157–79

APPENDIX

A BIBLIOGRAPHY OF RECENT

CRITICISM ON MURIEL SPARK

Allison Fisher (with the assistance of Shannon Thomas)

This selected bibliography lists critical studies of Muriel Spark's literary work not included in the 2002 volume *Theorizing Muriel Spark*, edited by Martin McQuillan and published by Palgrave Macmillan. Mc-Quillan's text provides a very full bibliography; the present bibliography serves as an update some eight years later while also identifying several studies that do not appear in McQuillan's list. The bibliography attempts to suggest the scope and diversity of recent scholarship on Spark as well as provide a resource for future research.

Journal Articles, Interviews, and Book Chapters

Alonso, Pilar. "The Macrostructural Function of Recurrence in Complex Narrative Discourse." *Aspects of Discourse Analysis*. Eds. Pilar Alonso, María Jesús Sánchez, John Hyde, and Christopher Moran. Salamanca: Ediciones Universidad de Salamanca, 2002. 45–77. Uses Spark's work as a case study.

Aly, Abdel-Moneim. "The Theme of Exile in the African Short Stories of Muriel Spark." *Scottish Studies Review* 2.2 (2001): 94–104.

Anastas, Benjamin. "Rejoice, Stupid: The Novels of Muriel Spark." *Book-Forum* 9.3 (2002): 26–27.

Apostolou, Fotini. "Seduction, Simulacra and the Feminine: Spectacles and Images in Muriel Spark's *The Public Image*." *Journal of Gender Studies* 9 (2000): 281–97.

———. "Textasy: The Seduction of the Text in Muriel Spark's Work." *Critical Survey* 13.1 (2001): 94–112.

225

Brown, Peter Robert. "'There's Something about Mary': Narrative and Ethics in *The Prime of Miss Jean Brodie*." *Journal of Narrative Theory* 36 (2006): 228–53.

Cheyette, Bryan. "Diasporas of the Mind: British-Jewish Writing beyond Multiculturalism." *Diaspora and Multiculturalism: Common Traditions and New Developments*. Ed. Monika Fludernik. Amsterdam: Rodopi, 2003. 45–82.

———. "Muriel Spark's *The Prime of Miss Jean Brodie*." *A Companion to the British and Irish Novel, 1945–2000*. Ed. Brian W. Shaffer. Malden, MA: Blackwell, 2005. 367–75.

Christianson, Aileen. "Muriel Spark and Candia McWilliam: Continuities." *Contemporary Scottish Women Writers*. Eds. Aileen Christianson and Alison Lumsden. Edinburgh: Edinburgh UP, 2000. 95–110.

Collins, Angus P. "'Listening to the Silence': Sound and Religious Belief in Muriel Spark's *A Far Cry from Kensington*." *Logos* 4.3 (2001): 143–58.

Devoize, Jeanne. "Muriel Spark b. 1918." *Journal of the Short Story in English* 41 (2003): 243–54.

Glavin, John. "Muriel Spark: Beginning Again." *British Women Writing Fiction*. Ed. Abby H. P. Werlock. Tuscaloosa: U of Alabama P, 2000. 293–313.

Gregson, Ian. "Muriel Spark's Caricatural Effects." *Essays in Criticism* 55.1 (2005): 1–16.

———. "Muriel Spark's Puppets of Thwarted Authority." *Character and Satire in Postwar Fiction*. New York: Continuum, 2006. 99–109.

Horner, Avril, and Sue Zlosnik. "'Releasing Spirit from Matter': Comic Alchemy in Spark's *The Ballad of Peckham Rye*, Updike's *The Witches of Eastwick* and Mantel's *Fludd*." *Gothic Studies* 2.1 (2000): 136–47.

Kort, Wesley A. "Taking Exception: Muriel Spark and the Spiritual Disciplines of Personal Space." *Place and Space in Modern Fiction*. Gainesville: UP of Florida, 2004. 128–45.

Krupnick, Mark. "Religion and the Modern Novel." *Commonweal* 127.9 (2000): 11–14.

Labay-Morère, Julie. "'Voices at Play' in Muriel Spark's *The Comforters* and Evelyn Waugh's *The Ordeal of Gilbert Pinfold*." *Etudes Britanniques Contemporaines* 30 (2006): 83–93.

Mackay, Marina. "Muriel Spark (1918–)." *Multicultural Writers since 1945: An A-to-Z Guide*. Eds. Alba Amoia and Bettina L. Knapp. Westport, CT: Greenwood, 2004. 478–81.

March, Cristie. "Undue Influence in Muriel Spark's *The Prime of Miss Jean Brodie* (1961)." *Women in Literature: Reading through the Lens of Gender*. Eds. Jerilyn Fisher, Ellen S. Silber, and David Sadker. Westport, CT: Greenwood, 2003. 240–42.

McIlvanney, Liam. "The Politics of Narrative in the Post-War Scottish Novel." *On Modern British Fiction*. Ed. Zachary Leader. Oxford: Oxford UP, 2002. 181–208.

Mengham, Rod. "The Cold War Way of Death: Muriel Spark's *Memento Mori*." *British Fiction after Modernism: The Novel at Mid-Century*. Eds. Marina MacKay and Lyndsey Stonebridge. New York: Palgrave, 2007. 157–65.

Miller, Gavin. "National Confessions: Queer Theory Meets Scottish Literature." *Scottish Studies Review* 6.2 (2005): 60–71.

Nakagami, Reiko. "Truthful Lies and Fantasy Realism: Irish Murdoch's
Under the Net and Muriel Spark's *The Comforters.*" *Hitotsubashi
Journal of Arts and Sciences* 45.1 (2004): 11–19.

Ranger, Graham. "Elaborated Upon with Due Art: Reading to Type in
Muriel Spark's *The Driver's Seat.*" *Impersonality and Emotion in
Twentieth-Century British Literature.* Eds. Christine Reynier and
Jean-Michel Ganteau. Montpellier, France: Université Montpellier
III, 2005. 183–93.

Ross, Michael L. "Roman Catholic Carnival: Muriel Spark's Passage to
Jerusalem." *Race Riots: Comedy and Ethnicity in Modern British
Fiction.* Montreal: McGill-Queen's UP, 2006. 137–59.

Sawada, Chikako. "Muriel Spark's *The Finishing School* and Postmodern
Endings." *Studies in English Literature* 48 (2007): 1–20.

Spark, Muriel. "Interview with Dame Muriel Spark." By James Brooker.
Women's Studies 33 (2004): 1035–46.

———. "An Interview with Dame Muriel Spark." By Robert Hosmer. *Salmagundi* 146–147 (2005): 127–58.

Stannard, Martin. "Nativities: Muriel Spark, Baudelaire, and the Quest
for Religious Faith." *Review of English Studies* 55.218 (2004):
91–105.

Stark, Lynne. "Agnes Owens's Fiction: Untold Stories." *Contemporary
Scottish Women Writers.* Eds. Aileen Christianson and Alison Lumsden. Edinburgh: Edinburgh UP, 2000. 111–16. Relates Owens's
fiction to Spark's oeuvre.

Stead, Alistair. "'Drastic Reductions': Partial Disclosures and Displaced
Authorities in Muriel Spark's *The Driver's Seat.*" *Re-Constructing the
Book: Literary Texts in Transmission.* Ed. Maureen Bell. Aldershot:
Ashgate, 2001. 158–69.

Stonebridge, Lyndsey. "Hearing Them Speak: Voices in Wilfred Bion, Muriel Spark and Penelope Fitzgerald." *Textual Practice* 19.4 (2005):
445–65.

Suh, Judy. "The Familiar Attractions of Fascism in Muriel Spark's *The
Prime of Miss Jean Brodie.*" *Journal of Modern Literature* 30.2
(2007): 86–102.

Swindell, Anthony. "Latecomers: Four Novelists Rewrite the Novel." *Bibli-
cal Interpretation: A Journal of Contemporary Approaches* 15.4–5
(2007): 395–404.

Vara, Maria. "The Victim and Her Plots: The Function of the Overpower-
ing Victim in Muriel Spark's *The Driver's Seat.*" *Gramma* 9 (2001):
139–55.

Walczuk, Anna. "Text into Text: An Intertextual Reading of Muriel Spark's
Reality and Dreams." *Anglistik* 15.2 (2004): 89–97.

Whyte, Christopher. "Queer Readings, Gay Texts: From Redgauntlet to
The Prime of Miss Jean Brodie." *Resisting Alterities: Wilson Harris
and Other Avatars of Otherness.* Ed. Marco Fazzini. Amsterdam:
Rodopi, 2004. 159–75.

Monographs

Apostolou, Fotini E. *Seduction and Death in Muriel Spark's Fiction*. London: Greenwood, 2001.

Walczuk, Anna. *Irony as a Mode of Perception and Principle of Ordering Reality in the Novels of Muriel Spark*. Kraków: Universitas, 2005.

Ph.D. Dissertations

Becker, Eleanor M. "Image as Reality in Ten Novels by Muriel Spark." Diss. Southern Illinois U, 1999.

Cowan, Susana Martin. "History's Fiction: British Women Realists of the Twentieth Century." Diss. U of Utah, 2001.

Weston, Elizabeth. "Countering Loss through Narrative: Comedy, Death, and Mourning in Evelyn Waugh's *The Loved One*, Muriel Spark's *Memento Mori*, and Graham Swift's *Last Orders*." Diss. U of North Carolina-Chapel Hill, 2004.

CONTRIBUTORS

GERARD CARRUTHERS is the editor of *The Devil to Stage: Five Plays by James Bridie* (2007), co-editor of *Beyond Scotland: New Contexts for Twentieth Century Scottish Literature* (2004), and the author of *Robert Burns* (2006) and *Scottish Literature: A Critical Guide* (2009). He has published essays on twentieth-century Scottish and Irish fiction. He has recently been appointed General Editor of the Oxford University Press edition of *The Collected Works of Robert Burns*.

ALLISON FISHER is finishing her dissertation at Ohio State University, focusing on narrative experimentation in modernist fiction.

JOHN GLAVIN, a professor of English at Georgetown University, has concentrated on issues of adaptation involving page, stage and screen. He has published most recently *After Dickens: Reading, Adaptation & Performance* and *Dickens on Screen*, both from Cambridge University Press. *Death at the Edges*, a memoir of teaching Shakespeare's Italian plays in Italy, is currently under publishers' review, and he has begun work on *Shut Up and Deal: The Films We Need Now*, a book-length study of the relevance of certain iconic American films to the recent economic crisis. He met Muriel Spark in 1987 and has published several articles on her work over the past twenty years.

LISA HARRISON is a final-year postgraduate in the Department of Scottish Literature, currently writing up her PhD thesis on the addiction narratives of Alexander Trocchi and Irvine Welsh. Further research and forthcoming articles examine international and cosmopolitan contexts for contemporary Scottish fiction and writers.

DAVID HERMAN teaches in the English Department at Ohio State University. He has published widely in the areas of narrative theory, modern and postmodern fiction, and storytelling across media. The author, editor, or co-editor of thirteen books and special journal issues focusing on these areas of inquiry, he also serves as editor of the *Frontiers of Narrative* book series and the new journal *Storyworlds*, both published by the University of Nebraska Press.

HOPE HOWELL HODGKINS has published essays on topics ranging from high modern religious rhetorics, to negative theology, to children's literature, in journals including *Rhetorica, Renascence,* and *Studies in Short Fiction.* Her most recent article is "High Modernism for the Lowest: Children's Books by Woolf, Joyce, and Greene" in *Children's Literature Association Quarterly* (Winter 2007). She is working on a book project about the use of style in modern British fiction by women. Hodgkins lives in Greensboro, North Carolina.

JONATHAN KEMP teaches comparative literature, political philosophy, queer theory, and creative writing (fiction/drama) at Birkbeck College, London. His first novel, *London Triptych,* is currently under review for publication.

MARINA MACKAY is an associate professor of English at Washington University in St. Louis. She is the author of *Modernism and World War II* (2007), co-editor with Lyndsey Stonebridge of *British Fiction after Modernism* (2007), and editor of the *Cambridge Companion to the Literature of World War II* (2009). She is currently writing a book about political crisis and the history of the novel.

LEWIS MACLEOD teaches in the Department of English at Trent University. He writes about British, West Indian, and African literature and is currently at work on a series of articles dealing with various notions of violation and transgression in contemporary fiction. His work has appeared in *Modern Fiction Studies, Critique, Mosaic,* and *ARIEL.*

BRAN NICOL is a reader in Modern and Contemporary Literature at the University of Portsmouth in England, where he is also Director of the Centre for Studies in Literature. His publications include *Iris Murdoch: The Retrospective Fiction* (2nd ed., 2004), *The Cambridge Introduction to Postmodern Fiction* (2009), and the edited volume *Postmodernism and the Contemporary Novel* (2002). He is currently working on a study of the figure of the stranger in modern fiction and culture.

ALLAN PERO has published essays on drama, film, and theory. His current research interests revolve around topics like performance and community, theories of love, and technology and theatricality. He is currently working on a book-length project on camp and modernity. He teaches in the Department of English and at the Graduate Centre for the Study of Theory and Criticism at the University of Western Ontario, Canada.

PATRICIA WAUGH is a professor of English at Durham University in England. She specializes in modern fiction and intellectual history and has published numerous articles, monographs, and edited volumes in this area, including *Metafiction: The Theory and Practice of Self-con-*

scious Fiction (1984), Feminine Fictions: Revisiting the Postmodern (1989), Practising Postmodernism and Reading Modernism (1992), The Harvest of the Sixties: English Literature and its Backgrounds, 1960–90 (1995), Revolutions of the Word: Intellectual History and Twentieth Century Literature (1997), and Literary Theory and Criticism: An Oxford Guide (2006). She is currently completing two books: Beyond the Two Cultures: Literature, Science and the Good Society, and The Blackwell History of British Fiction, 1945–Present.

Index

233